Hype and Glory

Hype and Glory

THE DECLINE AND FALL OF THE ENGLAND FOOTBALL TEAM, FROM REVIE TO MCCLAREN

Gavin Newsham

ATLANTIC BOOKS

LONDON

First published in hardback in Great Britain in 2010 by Atlantic Books, an imprint of Grove Atlantic Ltd.

1 2 3 4 5 6 7 8 9

A CIP catalogue record for this book is available from the British Library.

ISBN 978 1 84887 303 2

Printed in Great Britain by the MPG Books Group

Atlantic Books
An imprint of Grove Atlantic Ltd
Ormond House
26–27 Boswell Street
London
WC1N 3JZ

www.atlantic-books.co.uk

For Cissy Mae

Contents

List of Illustrations

1. Alf Ramsey. S&G and Barratts/EMPICS Sport.

2. Joe Mercer. PA Archive/Press Association Images.

3. Ron Greenwood. PA Archive/Press Association Images.

4. Bobby Robson. Peter Robinson/EMPICS Sport.

5. Graham Taylor. Ross Kinnaird/EMPICS Sport.

6. Terry Venables. Neal Simpson/EMPICS Sport.

7. Glenn Hoddle. Chris Turvey/EMPICS Sport.

8. Kevin Keegan. Rui Vieira/PA Archive/Press Association Images.

9. Howard Wilkinson. Mike Egerton/EMPICS Sport.

10. Peter Taylor. Owen Humphreys/PA Archive/Press Association Images.

11. Sven-Göran Eriksson. Steve Mitchell/EMPICS Sport.

12. Steve McClaren. Tom Hevezi/AP/Press Association Images.

13. Fabio Capello. Rex Features.

Prologue

When I was a kid I used to have this recurring nightmare involving a gang of porcelain dolls. It was the kind of dream that was so vivid, so disturbing, that it invariably left me in tears and fearing for my own safety. Indeed, no amount of consoling from my parents could ever help me back to sleep, but then that's probably because no amount of consoling is exactly what my parents offered me.

Faced with sleepless nights and shattered schooldays, I eventually devised my own way of getting back to sleep. It involved lying back down and forcing myself to play back Kevin Keegan's headed goal against Italy in the World Cup qualifier in November 1977 time and time and time again.

Man, that was some goal. A full house at Wembley. Peter Barnes on one wing, Steve Coppell on the other, Dave Watson and Crazy Horse in the centre of defence, Clem between the sticks. As ever, it began with Trevor Brooking. With that languid stride of his, he eased down the right wing like a gentle breeze, before whipping in a cross to the heart of the Italian penalty area.

Enter Kevin Keegan. It mattered not that he was one of the smallest men on the field: King Kev rose like a giant permed salmon and with a deft flick of his head and with his huge hair bouncing around in permanent slo-mo like some shampoo advert, glanced the ball beyond the massive hands of Dino Zoff and into the Italian goal. Whenever that ball hit the net, as it always did, peace returned to my nights.

In the intervening years I have watched countless England games and many, in fact too many, have seemed like living nightmares. Now whenever I go to bed after a dismal draw at home to Norway or another premature penalty shoot-out exit, I just dream of porcelain dolls and the pain goes away . . .

Preface

The email arrived in the inbox. It was brief and to the point:

Dear Gavin Newsham,
I'm sorry but Steve McClaren is not available for an interview.
Regards,
FC Twente

Admittedly, it was a long shot but, on reflection, it's perhaps understandable why Steve McClaren didn't really want to talk about his dark days spent managing the England team. Poor chap. He gave it a go and, like virtually every other coach who had tried (and largely failed) before him, was found wanting. The last thing he probably needed was someone he'd never met shattering the peace and relative anonymity of his new life in the Netherlands.

He wasn't the only one. I had a long and interesting chat with Graham Taylor one afternoon about why he'd rather not talk to me about his time with the national side, and while he politely declined my advances he was nothing but encouraging about the project and unfailingly, well, nice. But then we had been here before. Back in 1994, after Taylor had failed to steer England to the World Cup finals in the United States, I'd been knocked back in an attempt to talk to him on his return to club management with Wolverhampton Wanderers. 'Thanks, but no thanks' came the reply. It was hardly surprising. Like so many other publications, the football magazine I worked for, *90 Minutes*, had given Taylor a torrid time during his years as England boss. We felt we had reason to be aggrieved. If England had qualified for USA 94 we were planning to go out to the States en masse and produce the magazine from there. Instead we stayed behind in South London for the summer.

Still, it's hard to dislike Taylor, not least because whatever happened with England he is nevertheless a thoroughly decent man. Take my interview request. These days, you're lucky to get a reply from their deputy press officer's assistant when you put a request in, let alone a personal phone call from the man himself. For Taylor to pick up the phone and make the effort, even if it was to say no, speaks volumes.

Whether it is post-P45 contractual obligations or merely a desire to refrain from dredging up the harrowing past, England managers, or at least the really unsuccessful ones, are markedly reluctant to discuss their days in the impossible job. They're like Vietnam veterans: weary, battle-scarred, hurting. They have those memories, the trauma, the thousand-yard stare. You can't blame them. When they're strapped in the hot seat, it's a constant assault to their senses, where every utterance, every misplaced word, is seized upon and where every disappointing result is scrutinized, debated and dissected. When the axe falls, as it always does, the wisest way out is to take the severance settlement and disappear, like Reggie Perrin, until such time as a new club comes in with an offer that's too good to turn down. Failing that, at least get your own book deal out of it.

It occurred to me that over the years of my career in journalism I'd met and interviewed most of the England managers in my lifetime, albeit at varying stages in their careers and, for that matter, mine. Indeed, my first ever face-to-face interview was with Glenn Hoddle at a pre-season friendly between Southend United and Chelsea at Roots Hall. Nervously, I stole four minutes in the tunnel with the future England manager and rattled through the questions I'd been rehearsing for the best part of a week. He seemed unimpressed, aloof even. I jumped on the train back to London feeling like Carl Bernstein.

Meeting managers, especially those who have ascended to the England throne, is always fascinating, sometimes irritating and occasionally surreal. Once I was given the opportunity to take part in a training session with Kevin Keegan and his then high-flying Newcastle United side. It was a memorable experience, not for the fact that I met Warren Barton or Keith Gillespie or that I chipped John 'Budgie' Burridge, but because throughout the entire session we didn't do one single moment of defensive work.

On another occasion, I was also given the job of accompanying a competition winner and his friend to an all-expenses-paid night out at Scribes West, the Kensington private members' club owned by Terry Venables. When we arrived we were shown to our table and sat watching the great and the good of the football world (as well as Eric 'Monster' Hall) saunter past. So we sat there, sipping the wine we didn't really like and making awkward small talk, mainly about Howard Wilkinson (I am a Leeds United fan and they were both Sheffield Wednesday supporters). Not surprisingly, that conversation soon petered out, but just as proceedings were reaching the stage where I felt obliged to comment on the wall lights or the cutlery, a pair of double doors behind me opened, some music began and there, microphone in hand, stood Venables, the England coach, singing the Frank Sinatra standard 'Witchcraft', all within a decent right hook of me and my companions.

The look on the young lads' faces was priceless. I told them, jokingly, that this kind of thing happened every night in the bright lights of the capital. Sadly, I think they believed me. Aside from the time I interviewed the late football commentator Brian Moore in the nude – it's a long and mostly dull story – it remains one of the most bizarre moments of my life. Lord alone knows what the two lads from Sheffield made of it.

But of all the England managers, the most approachable, convivial and ultimately fascinating was the late Bobby Robson. On 19 April 1997 I travelled to Spain to interview him ahead of Barcelona's home game against Athletic Bilbao. When I arrived at the Nou Camp, he had just completed a press conference with his words translated by his assistant, the Portuguese coach Jose Mourinho. Lesser men may have struggled in such an environment, not least because he was the man trying to fill the shoes of Barça legend Johan Cruyff. But not Robson. Here, after all, was a man in his element, talking about the game he loved with anybody who cared to listen.

When the Spanish media left that afternoon I approached Robson at the desk at the front of the room and introduced myself. We got talking. Or rather I listened. That morning, Manchester United had beaten Liverpool at Anfield in an early kick-off back in England and the man they called 'Un Señor' (a true gent), who had watched the game on satellite television, wanted to talk about it.

So I pulled up a chair and off he went, deconstructing the game, move by move, play by play, using pens, tape recorders, microphone stands, glasses of water, anything to help him to get his point across. Liverpool's defensive lapses. Manchester United's attacking prowess. The influence of Eric Cantona and the efficacy of David Beckham's dead-ball deliveries. Virtually every significant moment of the game, and most of the insignificant ones, had been duly logged, recalled and analysed. There really was no stopping the man. Fully fifty minutes later, we started the interview.

As for the time I showered next to the ex-FA chief executive Graham Kelly, well, that will have to wait for another day ...

CHAPTER I

A RUN FOR YOUR MONEY

'Don Revie was the cleverest of all of us [England managers].
He walked out before they threw him out.'

Sven-Göran Eriksson, 2003

It had been coming but still it hurt. Nearly eight years after his
and England's finest hour (or rather two hours), Sir Alf Ramsey
was sitting on the train back home to Ipswich with his case in one
hand, and a couple of whisky miniatures in the other. Alongside
him sat his good friend Ted Phillips, cradling two cold cans
of lager. A prolific striker with Ipswich Town, Ted had played
under Ramsey when he was manager at the Suffolk club, but
seven years after retiring from the game he was now working in
London, fitting telephone cables.

As London became Essex and the drinks slipped down, Ted
sensed Ramsey wasn't his usual self, not least because he was
drinking Scotch. Ramsey, though, just shrugged and assured him
that everything was fine. As the train pulled into Colchester
station, Phillips drained his can and grabbed his things. There
waiting for him on the platform, as ever, was his wife Margaret
and as he made his goodbyes, waving to Alf through the window,
Ramsey got up and got another round in.

The following morning, Ted was back at Colchester station,
sprinting to make the 6.45 a.m. to Liverpool Street. Luckily, the
lads in his gang had saved him a seat, and he sat down and opened

his newspaper, turning straight to the back pages. 'RAMSEY SACKED!' screamed the headline. 'I turned to my mate Tony next to me and said, "Bloody hell!" I couldn't believe it,' recalls Phillips. 'He'd just been sacked from the England job and he never said a word. Nothing. But that was Alf. He was a very proud man.'

After eleven years in the job, Ramsey had just been dismissed by the Football Association as the manager of England. Charged with assembling a blueprint to take the English game forward, the FA's new 'Future of Football' Committee had concluded that the future of English football should dispense with the man who had made England the world champions in 1966.

The disastrous, almost farcical game against Poland six months earlier had been the final straw for the Football Association. Needing a win at Wembley to qualify for the World Cup finals in West Germany, Ramsey had sat on the touchline and watched his England team lay siege to the Polish goal, only to be foiled by the man Brian Clough had called a clown, Jan Tomaszewski. That night, England had mustered thirty-nine shots on goal. Poland, meanwhile, managed just two and scored from one. Only Allan Clarke had been able to beat Tomaszewski and that was from the penalty spot.

Knocked out of the World Cup by a man whose name was worth more at Scrabble than he was in the transfer market. It was a sorry, undignified way for the manager to go, but at fifty-three years old and with the FA keen to develop younger, fresher talent, there was nowhere for Ramsey to go.

In keeping with their reputation for forward thinking, but only after the event had long since passed, the FA now found themselves without a manager. The man who had guided his country to the greatest glory of them all had gone, to be replaced by, well, nobody. In its infinite, often misguided wisdom, the FA hadn't seen fit to groom anyone to take over from Alf when he had gone. There was nobody waiting in the wings.

As the search for a new manager began in earnest, the FA's International Committee decided that a caretaker manager should take charge of England in the interim. Committee chairman Dick Wragg had sought permission from the chairman of Coventry City, Derrick Robins, to talk to their manager and the man who had previously led Manchester City during the most successful period in their history, Joe Mercer.

Mercer would restore much-needed pride and fun to the England set-up. Almost immediately, the players seemed more relaxed with the affable and avuncular Mercer taking charge. With a quip and a gag for every occasion, the stand-in coach sent his team out with the minimum of fuss, with his pre-match team talks often no more than 'Go out and show them what you can do,' as the players limbered up.

It was a simple and, as results proved, effective. Under Mercer, some of England's flair players, like Manchester City's Colin Bell, began to emerge from the torpor of the last few months of Ramsey's reign, while new faces like Leicester City's Keith Weller and flamboyant team-mate Frank Worthington would finally get their chance on the international stage. The football was free-flowing and attractive. The response magnificent.

Worthington was one of a growing band of entertainers that at last seemed to be finding favour in the England team. Along with the likes of Stan Bowles of Queens Park Rangers and, later, Chelsea's Alan Hudson, they were mavericks on and off the field. During the game, they would be quick-witted, skittish and cavalier. Off the field, they were heart-throbs and playboys, likeable rascals that were as likely to be holed up in the bookie's or a boozer as they were in training. With talent to spare but lacking the application – Bowles often turned up for games just ten minutes before kick-off – they pleased the crowd but infuriated their managers. For Joe Mercer, who had encountered Bowles's time-keeping as his manager at Manchester City, it was too much and repeated rows would see Bowles lose favour, culminating in his substitution in the 1–0 win over Northern Ireland in 1974, ironically in favour of Frank Worthington.

When his seven-game stint came to an end, Mercer would have just one defeat, to Scotland, on his record. 'Football is a great game. It is all about goals, goalmouth incidents and end-to-end attacking football. There is nothing wrong with the game; plenty wrong with managers, players, directors, legislators and the media,' he would say. 'The object of playing any game is for enjoyment. If you have enjoyed it and done your best you have won no matter what the result.'

The FA, meanwhile, would cast their net wide. Respected names in the game would be sounded out. Adverts would be placed in the national press. Shortlists would be compiled. In time, Jimmy Bloomfield of Leicester City, Gordon Milne of Coventry City and Gordon Jago of QPR would all be interviewed, and while they all impressed in their own way, it was concluded that none really possessed the stature and track record required of an England manager. What the FA needed was a winner. A coach who could put his medals on the table, roll up his sleeves and get on with the job of making England great once more. As the recruitment process stuttered, FA secretary Ted Croker received a call in his office. It was the Leeds United manager Don Revie. He wanted to talk about the England job.

If the candidates to date had lacked the gravitas required to succeed somebody as iconic as Alf Ramsey, Don Revie had it in spades and so what if he hadn't got all his coaching badges, surely two League titles and a glut of other trophies with Leeds was qualification enough. With the best manager in the country now available, a delegation of the FA's top brass – Croker, the chairman of the international committee Dick Wragg, and FA chairman Dr Andrew Stephen – repaired to Leeds to finalize the deal with the man they called 'The Don'.

After lengthy negotiations in which the FA's inspired tactic of conceding to virtually all of Revie's demands, not least his mammoth £25,000 salary (three times what Ramsey had received), proved successful, England had a new manager. 'I am delighted to be given the chance to manage England,' Revie said. 'This must be any manager's dream. I also have a feeling of sadness after thirteen years as manager of Leeds. I have tried to build the club into a family and there must be sadness when anybody leaves a family.

The first result I will be looking for on a Saturday night will always be Leeds United's. Leeds gave me the chance to start my managerial career and we have had our ups and downs, but everybody in the club, the directors, coaching staff and, in particular, the players, have stood by me through thick and thin. I was in contact with the players about leaving them. They all understood and said the England job was a little bit special in their minds. They would have been upset if I had been going to another club.'

While few could doubt the pedigree of Revie's candidature, not everyone was enamoured with his appointment. When Alan Hardaker, the Football League secretary, a man who had never seen eye to eye with Revie, learned of the appointment he told his counterpart at the FA, Ted Croker, that he 'must be off his head'.

Don Revie wasn't in the business of being popular. Under his stewardship, Leeds United had become a formidable force in European football. They had also become one of the most widely detested teams in the game. Tough, rough and ruthless, they were masters of intimidation and their disciplinary record was as bad as their reputation. 'Don Revie used to tell us to go in hard with the first tackle, because the referee would never book you for the first one. We used to call it the freebie,' recalls the defender Norman Hunter. 'I'd go in hard, pick 'em up, say sorry to the ref and sometimes you hardly saw that player again.'

That said, they were also a team of rare talent and application, but because of the style of football (or lack of it), they had found few fans outside of West Yorkshire. Not that Revie cared. His was a team that played for him and for each other. There was an inherent trust between him and his squad. It was his family. Marshalled by the irrepressible Billy Bremner and ably assisted by a roll-call of international stars, like Norman Hunter, Jack Charlton, Allan Clarke, Peter Lorimer and Johnny Giles, the team's success had been built on loyalty and closeness verging on insularity. The team worked together and played together. 'If someone kicks me, he kicks all eleven of us,' said Lorimer.

That togetherness would yield unprecedented success at Elland Road. In thirteen years, Leeds would win two League championships, a Second Division title, an FA Cup, a League Cup and two Inter-Cities Fairs Cup (the predecessor of the UEFA Cup). And yet it could have been so many more. With five second places in the First Division, and another five runners-up spots in cup competitions, Leeds' dominance under Revie could and should have been total.

Faced with the task of succeeding the only manager who had ever won a major trophy with England, Revie's first decision was to invite over eighty current and potential England players to a mass team meeting in Manchester where he outlined his vision for the national team. 'Nobody is really out of the reckoning and there will probably be additions to the squad,' he told them. Interestingly, he also informed the players that while they would still be getting an appearance fee of £100 for playing for England, now there would be a bonus scheme on offer, with £100 bonus for a draw and a £200 incentive for a win.

Keen to impose himself on the job, there would be a raft of new initiatives from the new England coach. He sought to have League fixtures postponed on the Saturday prior to England fixtures. He introduced free drinks and sandwiches for journalists at press conferences. He would oversee a change in the manufacturer of the official England team kit. Out went Umbro and in came Admiral, the company that made the strips for Revie's Leeds United; for the first time, the manufacturer now had to pay the Football Association for the privilege of making the England shirt. They even added a new red-and-blue trim to the white shirt, much to the annoyance of the game's traditionalists. Revie would also have song sheets with lyrics to 'Land of Hope and Glory' handed out before games in a bid to restore some much-needed national pride to England's matches at Wembley.

But not everything Revie did was new or quite so revolutionary. Many of the team-building activities he had employed so successfully at Leeds United would be foisted on the England squad, all in a bid to create the same family atmosphere he had achieved at Elland Road. That meant Friday night carpet bowls or indoor golf, dominoes or bingo. For a team like Leeds that was used to spending almost every day together, it would become second nature. For a disparate assembly like the England squad, who had come from all over the country, it was awkward, uncomfortable and, well, a bit strange. 'He wanted the England team to be his boys, like at Leeds,' said the Southampton forward Mick Channon.

Like many other club managers who had turned to international coaching, the lack of daily contact with his players represented a problem for Don Revie. At Leeds he had been able to create continuity and confidence among his teams. Everyone knew what they had to do and trusted their team-mates to do their job as well. With England, however, it was different. Faced with weeks, sometimes months without seeing his players, Revie would struggle to recreate the team spirit that he had engendered at Leeds.

Initially, though, Revie's England had seemed to respond to the idiosyncratic coach. His first game, a 3–0 win in the European Championship qualifier against Czechoslovakia at Wembley, was notable not for the scoreline, which flattered England, but for the return of two of his old Leeds players, Norman Hunter and Paul Madeley, to the England starting line-up. He would also award full debuts to the impressive young QPR midfielder Gerry Francis and his team-mate Dave Thomas. They would be the first of many, perhaps too many, new faces over the course of Revie's reign.

Revie's honeymoon period would last for the best part of a year. A nine-match unbeaten run had seen England claim some notable wins along the way with a 2–0 against West Germany, a 5–0 European Championship qualifier victory over Cyprus in which the Newcastle United striker Malcolm Macdonald had scored all five goals and, in the Home Internationals, a 5–1 drubbing of Scotland. Though he had captained England to a comprehensive win over the Auld Enemy, Alan Ball, one of the World Cup winning team of 1966, would soon become a victim of the kind of bizarre selection choices that would come to define Revie's era as England coach. By the time the next game, against Switzerland, came round, Ball had not only been deposed as captain but wasn't even in the squad. Moreover, the first he had learned of his omission was when a reporter called his wife asking for his reaction to the news. Ball had become another unwitting victim of the whims of the England manager. Aged just thirty, a World Cup winner, and despite never losing any of his six games as skipper, he never played for England again.

Ball's omission was typical of Revie, a manager for whom reputations meant very little. Already in his short time in charge, he had dropped England's star man, Kevin Keegan, prompting a walkout from the Liverpool striker. He had also discarded Keegan's team-mate Emlyn Hughes, who, at twenty-seven, was at the peak of his career. Not only had Hughes been told that he was not needed for a match against Wales, but as long as Revie was in charge he would not be needed by England again.

It was a style of man management that won him few fans. Unsure and on edge, his players seemed to play every game as though it was their last, doing whatever they could to avoid defeat, rather than strive for a win. It made for dour, defensive football and saw England traipse wearily through the mid-1970s without direction and without success.

Revie's tinkering with his team baffled everyone from journalists to fans, from the FA to the players. Only once in his twenty-nine games in charge of England would Revie field an unchanged side. Contrast that with his time at Leeds, where a settled side provided the very bedrock of his success. The true extent of his indecision would also be reflected in the vast number of newcomers he introduced to the England team. In three years in charge, Revie would award full caps to no fewer than twenty-nine players, and called up fifty-two in total into his squad.

Revie's first defeat as England coach would prove to be a pivotal moment and one that would have grave consequences for him and for England. Despite negotiating a £5,000-a-man bonus for winning the European Championship, a 2–1 defeat to Czechoslovakia in their qualifying game in Bratislava, followed by an uninspired draw in Portugal, scuppered England's chances of reaching the four-team tournament in Yugoslavia.

With England absent from the finals of another major tournament for the third time of asking, major doubts about Revie's suitability for the position emerged, especially when Dr Andrew Stephen was replaced as chairman of the Football Association by his deputy, Sir Harold Thompson. A brilliant chemist, Thompson had made his name as a professor at Oxford University, where he also managed to indulge his interest in amateur football, establishing the famous Pegasus club, a team of mature students drawn from Oxford and Cambridge universities.

While Stephen had seemed relatively content to let Revie get on with the job in hand, Thompson would prove to be his polar opposite. Arrogant and pompous, he would make suggestions to Revie about his team or his tactics and refused to call Revie by his first name, telling the manager, 'When I get to know you better, Revie, I shall you call Don,' to which Revie, uncharacteristically, replied, 'And when I get to know you better, Thompson, I shall call you Sir Harold.' The pair would never make first-name terms.

After the failure to qualify for the European Championship, the World Cup of 1978, to be hosted in Argentina, represented Don Revie's last stab at achieving something with England. Drawn in a group with Finland, Luxembourg and their main rivals Italy, Revie knew that there would be little room for error. While Finland and Luxembourg represented fairly straightforward encounters, the key to qualification would rest on England's ability to beat them and beat them well and, with only one place in the finals in Argentina available to each group winner, the head-to-head with Italy.

As it transpired, it would, effectively, become a qualification campaign resting on just two games for England. In Revie's favour was the fact that their final game was at home to Italy, a team they had beaten in a friendly in New York just two weeks before the World Cup campaign began. Against them, however, was the very real possibility that come that game, the group may have been all but decided.

Predictably, England had few problems in picking up maximum points against Finland, winning 4–1 in Helsinki and 2–1 at Wembley, but their campaign suffered an almost fatal blow in the away fixture against Italy in Rome's Stadio Olimpico in November 1976. Recalling Emlyn Hughes in the centre of defence and QPR's Stan Bowles in attack, Revie also pushed Trevor Cherry and Brian Greenhoff, two players more noted for their defensive roles, into midfield. Despite Revie's overly defensive approach, England were powerless to prevent Italy from cruising to victory with a first-half goal from Fiorentina's Giancarlo Antognoni and an acrobatic diving header from the man they called 'the white feather', Juve's Roberto Bettega, sealing a 2–0 win.

That Christmas, Revie discussed his future with his wife Elsie, concluding that perhaps, after all, the job really wasn't worth the hassle or the heckling, all the grief and no glory. Earlier that year, Revie, publicly disillusioned by the lack of success with the national team, had been contacted by an official from the Football Association of the United Arab Emirates, enquiring if he would be interested in taking over as the manager of their national team. On the table was an offer that would dwarf his current deal with England and set him up financially for the rest of his life. Revie rebuffed the idea, but it wouldn't be long before temptation would get the better of him.

A new year brought little comfort for Revie, as the first team to visit Wembley in 1977, Holland, handed out a beating that not only exposed the lack of progress that England had made under Revie but merely emphasized the gaping chasm that had developed between England and the best that Europe had to offer. With Johan Cruyff in the kind of bewitching form that had made him a three-time winner of the European Footballer of the Year award, the Dutch ran out 2–0 victors when the scoreline could really have been three or four times that number. Yes, Revie could always rely on convincing wins against the likes of Luxembourg, whom England beat 5–0 in their World Cup qualifier six weeks after the

Holland game, but they always seemed to be swimming against the tide whenever quality opposition turned up.

That year's Home Internationals would merely compound Revie's misery, pushing him to the edge of resignation. Despite a lucky 2–1 win in Belfast against Northern Ireland – a game in which Revie made nine changes to his starting line-up – England then lost 1–0 to Wales and 2–1 to Scotland, both times at Wembley and both times to repeated calls for Revie's head. As if defeat to the Auld Enemy wasn't painful enough, England's fans then had to watch Scotland's supporters – the so-called 'Tartan Army' – invade the Wembley pitch and dig up the turf to take back home over the border. Famously, some had even clambered on the goal posts and brought them crashing to the ground. Later, it was revealed that a Glasgow waiter by the name of Alec Torrance was the fan whose weight had finally caused the crossbar to give way. The reason? His platform shoes were so heavy.

That summer, England embarked on a post-season tour of South America, partly to test themselves against the best opposition in the world and partly to warm up for what they still hoped would be their appearance in the World Cup finals the following year. As the squad departed, however, Revie had not gone with them, opting to fly to Helsinki to watch Finland's defeat by Italy, a result which damaged England's chances of reaching the World Cup finals still further. With Les Cocker in charge for the opener against Brazil, Revie had told his team that he would join them in time for the second game against Argentina in Buenos Aires. It made sense. After all, Revie was a manager who prided himself on his preparation and the many dossiers he compiled on opposition teams were the stuff of football folklore.

But only part of the story was true. Yes Revie had watched the game in Helsinki but instead of flying out to join up with England he had made a detour via the Middle East to talk over the job offer from the United Arab Emirates FA that had first been aired the year before. The long flight to Argentina, meanwhile, gave Revie more than enough time to consider his next move.

When he finally joined up with England – his assistant Les Cocker having secured a creditable 1–1 draw with Brazil – Revie immediately convened a meeting with Dick Wragg at which, to the surprise of the international committee chairman, he announced that as he was convinced he was about to be sacked it would be politic for all concerned if the FA paid up the remaining two years of his and Cocker's contracts and they were allowed to leave – a settlement that would cost the FA around £100,000.

Like Wragg, Ted Croker was incredulous when he learned of Revie's proposal. Sir Harold Thompson was apoplectic, and ordered an emergency meeting with the England coach. That Revie was intent on leaving was of no great consequence to most of the FA's powerbrokers, who had long since tired of his awkward manner and his less than impressive results on the field of play. That he wanted paying for the privilege, however, seemed inherently wrong. The final game of the tour, meanwhile, an ill-tempered 1–1 draw with Uruguay, would be the first time in his twenty-nine games in charge that Revie had fielded an unchanged line-up. That it would be his final game in charge of England made it all the more ironic.

Still irritated by the FA's refusal to pay up the remainder of his contract, Revie set about cashing in on his newfound status as former England manager. Selling the exclusive story of his resignation to the *Daily Mail*, he ignored Thompson's invitations to discuss his future and, accompanied by the *Mail* reporter and his close friend Jeff Powell, set off for Dubai to conclude the deal to become the new supremo of football in the UAE. Initial reports suggested that Revie had travelled under an assumed name and wearing Arab dress, but the truth was that, yes, he had changed his name (to that of his son Duncan) but had worn no more cunning disguise than a flat cap and a pair of sunglasses.

Before the pair left, Powell had left two sealed envelopes at his office. One carried the story of Don Revie's resignation, the other details of his new career in the Middle East, the idea being that these were to be hand-delivered to the FA's offices at Lancaster Gate before they closed their doors for the day. Trouble was, they weren't, and the first anybody at the FA heard of Revie's resignation was when they and the rest of the nation picked up their newspapers the following morning and read the *Daily Mail*'s world exclusive. In it, Revie told Powell how the job had brought 'too much heartache' to him and his family, and as everyone seemed to want him to go he was merely 'giving them what they want'.

Two days later, the same paper ran the next of their exclusives, announcing that not only was Revie leaving the England job, but he was leaving the country too, having signed a six-year, tax-free deal worth £340,000 complete with £100,000 signing-on fee, and accommodation, cars and travel expenses.

If the reaction to his resignation had been one of anger, albeit tempered with a little relief, the news that he had abandoned his country for the riches of the Middle East was nothing short of hysterical. Ted Croker felt 'deceived', Brian Clough – who had briefly succeeded Revie as the Leeds manager – called his departure 'despicable', while Bob Stokoe, the former Sunderland boss who had once accused Revie of trying to bribe him and his team, felt that he should be 'castrated' for what he had done.

Against the advice of their solicitors Chethams, the Football Association, led by an incensed Harold Thompson, decided to pursue Revie, charging him on four counts: setting a bad example, acting deceitfully, debasing his official position and damaging the image of football and the FA. It would be a year before Revie finally deigned to attend the FA's disciplinary hearing, primarily because he failed to recognize that the FA still had any authority over him and his career. Besides, he was enjoying himself in the sunshine. 'Sir Harold Thompson, the chairman of the FA, treated me like an employee,' he said. 'These Arab Sheikhs treat me like one of them.'

With Sir Harold Thompson leading proceedings, there would only ever be one verdict: Revie was banned from working in English football for ten years. Inevitably, though, the case would end up in the High Court. Over the course of an eighteen-day hearing in the lead-up to Christmas 1979, Revie's QC, Gilbert

Gray, argued that not only was the FA's ban a restraint of trade, but the nature and composition of the FA disciplinary committee that imposed the sentence was such that Revie would never have been granted a fair hearing. With legal precedent governing Mr Justice Cantley's decision, Revie's ban was duly overturned, although he stopped short of awarding the former England manager all of his costs. That said, it was a decision that didn't sit well with Justice Cantley. 'Mr Revie … presented to the public a sensational and notorious example of disloyalty, breach of duty, discourtesy and selfishness,' he said, summing up. 'His conduct brought English football, at a high level, into disrepute.'

Though Revie felt exonerated by the decision of the High Court, the manner of his departure still rankled with football fans across England. For his part, Revie never really recognized that he had done anything wrong in the manner in which he had left the England job. His only crime, as he saw it, was failing to make England a great team once more. And even that wasn't really his fault …

'The day I took the job,' he told the *Daily Mail*, 'I was excited by the prospect of having the pick of the country. But I'd been spoiled for choice at Leeds and I realized there are no more around like Billy Bremner or Johnny Giles. As soon as it dawned on me that we were short of players who combined skill and commitment I should have forgotten all about trying to play more controlled attractive football and settled for a real bastard of a team.'

CHAPTER 2

THE GENTLE GUNMAN

'Football is a simple game. The hard part is making it look simple.'

Ron Greenwood, England manager, 1978

With Don Revie's suntan coming along nicely in the desert, the FA's international committee once more sprang into inaction in their bid to find a manager who could re-establish England as one of the dominant teams in world football or, failing that, at least make them qualify for a tournament every now and then.

Taking temporary charge of the national side on 17 August 1977 was the general manager of West Ham United, Ron Greenwood. As the coach of the East London side, he had been blessed with a trio of England's World Cup winners in Martin Peters, Geoff Hurst and, of course, the England captain himself, Bobby Moore. With such talent at his disposal, Greenwood had taken the Hammers to their first ever major trophies, winning the FA Cup in 1964 and the European Cup-Winners' Cup the following year.

As the deliberations continued and the fallout from Don Revie's departure seemed set to end in litigation, Greenwood was perceived as a safe pair of hands. An FA man through and through, he had been coach of the England Youth and Under-23 teams, and had long been considered a potential England manager by the FA chairman Sir Harold Thompson. Indeed, he had even been touted as a replacement for Walter Winterbottom, before Alf Ramsey had been given the job in 1963.

As the Revie saga rumbled on, Ron Greenwood was left to pick up the pieces of England's World Cup qualifying campaign. Defeat in Rome had left England needing to win their remaining games while amassing as many goals as possible, given Italy's superior goal difference. After a goalless friendly against Switzerland, Greenwood took his England team to Luxembourg in mid-October, conscious that they had to match or surpass the five-goal win against the minnows in their first meeting at Wembley. While they returned home with both points, the 2–0 victory would leave them needing a comprehensive win over Italy in their final game, or a win and then hope against hope that Luxembourg could go to Rome and take a point away with them.

For a man seen as naturally conservative and occasionally unable to make crucial decisions – he famously alternated between Peter Shilton and Ray Clemence as goalkeeper because he simply couldn't decide who was the best man for the job – Greenwood surprised everyone with his starting line-up for the Italy game at Wembley on 16 November. There were to be debuts for the bustling Everton centre-forward Bob Latchford, the Manchester United winger Steve Coppell and his counterpart from the blue half of the city, Peter Barnes.

Lean, blond and dashing, Barnes would go on to become one of the pin-up boys of Ron Greenwood's England team and now, as a full England international, he was in a position to fully exploit his new high profile. Sometimes, however, he could have benefited from some better advice, not least when it came to the release of his 'Peter Barnes Football Trainer'. Designed to help kids practise their close control, it was, essentially, a piece of string with a lightweight football on one end and a buckle on the other that you then attached to the waistband of your shorts. Though intended to help you master the ancient playground art of keepy-uppy, tragically all it ever did was pull your shorts down.

Gimmicks aside, Barnes and fellow wingman Coppell fitted well into Ron Greenwood's new strategy. England seemed balanced and Kevin Keegan's new role behind the lone front man Latchford clearly foxed the visitors. Within eleven minutes England were ahead. A delightful cross from the trusty right boot of Trevor Brooking was met by the head of Kevin Keegan and his glancing header evaded the giant hands of Dino Zoff to give England the lead. Ten minutes from time, Keegan returned the favour for Brooking, setting up the West Ham midfielder for England's second.

While the 2–0 victory and the performance itself had been a welcome diversion from the Revie affair, the victory celebrations were tempered by the realization that even though England now topped Group 2, they now had to wait for Italy's final game at home to Luxembourg, knowing that all the Italians required to top the group was a 1–0 win. As it was, Italy scored three and England would be absent from the World Cup finals for the second successive tournament. Still, at least they avoided the humiliation that Scotland were to suffer in Argentina, losing to Peru, drawing with Iraq and then, improbably, beating Holland, a team so talented they would get to the final, losing in extra time to the hosts Argentina.

With England out and Don Revie now held personally responsible for their elimination, attention returned to the search for a new permanent manager. The FA began their quest to find Revie's successor by once more placing an advert for the job of England manager in the national press, lest there were anyone in the game who may not have heard that there was a job going at Lancaster Gate. Not surprisingly, they were inundated with replies. Some were even serious, and the applications of coaches like Jack Charlton, the Norwich City manager John Bond, the Southampton boss Lawrie McMenemy, QPR's Dave Sexton and the Jimmys, Bloomfield and Armfield, all warranted consideration. The bookmakers, meanwhile, had made one man the overwhelming favourite to take over – Brian Clough.

As manager of Derby County, Clough had overseen a change in the club's fortunes as dramatic as it was rapid. Assisted by Peter Taylor, Clough had left Hartlepool United to become the new manager at the Baseball Ground in 1967 and within four years had taken Derby from relegation candidates in Division Two to champions of the First Division, beating a pair of genuine football superpowers in Leeds United and Liverpool in a tussle for the title.

In 1975, after a short spell at Brighton and Hove Albion and a controversial six-week reign as Don Revie's successor at Leeds, Clough had joined the team with which he would become synonymous – Nottingham Forest – and set about replicating the success he had enjoyed at Derby County, just fifteen miles away, in Nottingham. And while his first taste of following in Revie's not inconsiderable footprints had ended in catastrophe – he was sacked after just forty-four days – the experience clearly hadn't fazed him and now, as the bookies' and the general public's favourite, all that stood between him and the England job was the Football Association's international committee. Certainly, Clough had support at Lancaster Gate, not least from FA secretary Ted Croker and international committee member Peter Swales. Even the FA chairman, the notoriously impassive Sir Harold Thompson, seemed to warm to Clough.

Readers of a certain age will recall the late Manchester City chairman Swales, if not for the largely unremarkable effect he had on the then Maine Road club, then certainly for one of the most spectacular comb-overs in football since Bobby Charlton called it a day. Swales's hair was a thing of rare wonder. Thick, matted and with a texture that looked not unlike Shredded Wheat, it was a hairstyle made all the more noteworthy by the fact that he had chosen to dye it black, even though he was well into his seventies. For all anyone knows, Swales went to his grave thinking that the world didn't realize he was actually bald.

Like so many other businessmen and non-players, Swales had risen through the ranks of the Football Association without so much as kicking a football, culminating in his appointment as chairman of the international committee. As one of the men responsible for appointing the England manager, Swales was held in high regard by many in the game. Well, kind of. 'Peter Swales wore a wig, a blazer with an England badge on it and high-heeled shoes,' recalls his former manager at Manchester City, Malcolm Allison. 'As a man he really impressed me.'

Despite overwhelming support from the media and the general public, Brian Clough would be overlooked again for the job he craved. 'I was totally comfortable, even though I never like the formal occasion,' Clough said of his interview. 'I didn't really relish sharing the same room with Thompson, now dead and gone. He was a stroppy, know-all bugger who in my view knew nothing about my game.'

Despite a proven track record with Derby County and his new club Nottingham Forest, it had appeared that here was a man who could never fit into the FA's often archaic way of thinking. 'I'm sure the England selectors thought if they took me on and gave me the job, I'd want to run the show,' Clough later reflected. 'They were shrewd because that's exactly what I would have done.' England's loss would be Nottingham Forest's gain. As Ron Greenwood laboured with England, Brian Clough went on to steer the East Midlands club not just to the League championship at the end of that season, but to unprecedented back-to-back European Cup victories.

Later, Peter Swales would concede that Clough had come very close to landing the job. 'He gave by far the best interview of all the candidates – confident, passionate, full of common sense and above all patriotic,' he said. 'If Ron Greenwood hadn't been around, he'd have clinched it.'

On 12 December 1977 the Football Association announced that Ron Greenwood had won the race to become the new England manager. Typically, Greenwood learned of his appointment not by a letter or a telephone call from Harold Thompson or a member of the FA's international committee, but via the radio. Greenwood had been lunching with his wife Lucy in Alfriston, Sussex, when, sitting in his car, the news came over the radio that he had been selected. For his efforts, Brian Clough was awarded the position of joint manger of the England Youth team, alongside his assistant Peter Taylor and the Football Association's Ken Burton. Three men, all in charge of a youth team, one of whom happened to be the most combustible coach in British football. Within a year, though, Clough was gone.

Quite why the FA's international committee saw fit to give the job of national team manager to Ron Greenwood remains a mystery and one which, it could be argued, represents that crucial moment in time when English football had the opportunity to try something new and embrace change but opted instead for more of the same.

It was nothing short of scandalous. Today, of course, we have a foreign coach in Fabio Capello, who is lauded (to the tune of a reported £6 million a year) for his strict disciplinary regime and his no-nonsense approach to the game and man management. England could have had that thirty years earlier. Instead they chose a man who would wear the FA blazer with respect and pride, and not the innate scepticism that, given the organization's track record, it clearly warranted.

But with its fingers still burning from the departure of Don Revie, the last thing the Football Association wanted was someone as opinionated and as resolutely single-minded as Clough. They needed stability. They needed a safe option. And, that, to the detriment of English football, didn't mean Brian Clough.

Not that Ron Greenwood was a bad choice. He was a good man, a good manager. The antithesis of Brian Clough, certainly, but a good man nonetheless. Greenwood was born in 1921 in the village of Worsthorne on the outskirts of the cotton capital of the world, Burnley. Like Don Revie, he had left school at the age of fourteen to pursue his dreams of being a professional footballer, as well as training to be a sign-writer should the football career not work out.

He needn't have worried. With the Greenwoods relocating south to a new home within earshot of the new Empire Stadium at Wembley, Greenwood signed for Chelsea as an amateur, just as the Second World War was beginning. Not even the war could stop the young Greenwood playing football. Even when he was in the RAF in Northern Ireland, he would turn out for Belfast Celtic. Later, when he was posted to Lissett, near Hull, he joined Bradford Park Avenue. When hostilities were over Greenwood resumed his football career in earnest. He played for Brentford and Chelsea, where in 1954–55 he won a League championship medal. His next season was his last, alongside Bobby Robson at Fulham in Division 2. And while he would never win a full England cap, he did play once for the B team.

But coaching was Greenwood's bag. He spent three years as the football coach at Oxford University and was appointed coach to the Middlesex FA, and it was during his time at Oxford that Greenwood first met Professor Harold Thompson, who would become FA chairman in 1976. Greenwood moved to Highbury in 1958 to be one of Arsenal's coaches under the then manager George Swindin, where, despite being the coach of the England Under-23 side, he found himself demoted to the role of reserve team coach. By 1961, though, Greenwood sought a new challenge and took over at Upton Park, succeeding Ted Fenton as the manager of West Ham United. It was a move that would be the making of him and the Hammers.

It would be an encouraging first year for the new England manager, losing just one of his twelve matches at the helm, a friendly away to West Germany in Munich. Famously, Greenwood would also award a first cap to the Nottingham Forest full-back Viv Anderson in the friendly against Czechoslovakia at Wembley in November 1978, making him the first black player to represent England.

Viv Anderson's selection was indicative of a rapidly changing, increasingly global game. Having helped his Liverpool team to a League championship and European Cup double, England's biggest box office draw, Kevin Keegan, had made a £500,000 move to SV Hamburg in the German Bundesliga in the summer of 1977. Soon after, the first crop of foreign players would arrive in the UK. Tottenham Hotspur would secure the services of two of Argentina's World Cup winners, Osvaldo Ardiles and Ricardo Villa, while at Ipswich Town, the England B coach Bobby Robson had signed two Dutch internationals in Arnold Muhren and Franz Thijssen.

Players were spoilt for choice. Lured by lucrative contracts and a change in lifestyle, many, like Bobby Moore, Gordon Banks and Peter Bonetti, opted to cross the Atlantic to play in the burgeoning North American Soccer League (NASL), persuaded that if the league was good enough for Pelé and George Best, for Franz Beckenbauer and Johan Cruyff, it was almost certainly good enough for them.

As the salaries of the top players headed ever upward, so did their transfer values, peaking in February 1979 when the Nottingham Forest manager Brian Clough signed the Birmingham City and England striker Trevor Francis for £1 million, the first time a player had ever moved for a seven-figure sum. At a press conference to announce his landmark move, Francis was asked when he would be making his debut for his new club, a question quickly answered by his new manager. 'When I pick him,' said Clough, typically.

England were starting to develop a more solid look under their new boss but what they had achieved so far was hardly a cause for mass celebration. Indeed, their lack of consistency still gave some cause for concern. In May the reigning world champions Argentina had visited Wembley and paraded a nineteen-year-old box of tricks by the name of Diego Maradona in their line-up. Short, stocky and immensely powerful, Maradona was already being touted as one of the world's hottest properties and it was easy to see why. Brought up in poverty in a shantytown on the outskirts of Buenos Aires, Maradona had made his full debut for his club Argentinos Juniors aged fifteen and his full international debut just six short months later. He had been the player of the tournament in the World Youth Championship in 1979, leading Argentina to victory, and had bagged both the Argentine and the South American Player of the Year awards in the same year. Not that England cared. Two goals by Liverpool's David Johnson and another by the ever-reliable Kevin Keegan gave England a comfortable win in front of 92,000 fans at Wembley Stadium.

Four days later, however, the Home International against Wales at Wrexham's Racecourse Ground had brought England crashing back down to earth. Led by their new manager Mike England, Wales crushed Greenwood's side 4–1, inflicting what was to be the heaviest defeat in his tenure as England manager. That, according to some Welsh supporters, now made Wales the new world champions.

For the sixth staging of the European Football Championship, to take place in Italy in June 1980, UEFA had taken the decision to expand the competition from four teams to eight, with two groups of four all playing each other and the group winners progressing straight to the final. No semi-finals, no second round. It was win or bust.

Without Trevor Francis, sidelined by an injury to his Achilles tendon, England's challenge kicked off against Belgium in Turin, but only after the kind of scenes that would become depressingly familiar during England's participation in major tournaments. After Ray Wilkins's opening goal, Italian police clashed with English hooligans, employing tear gas to restore order and delaying the restart. The 1–1 draw for Greenwood and England would not make the headlines the following day. Instead, the Football Association stood accused of failing to control their supporters and, soon after, UEFA handed down an £8,000 fine for the disturbances.

With two rather than three points for a win, England's defeat against Italy in their second group game gave them scant chance of making the final. Needing a win against Spain in their final game and hoping that Italy could defeat Belgium, England duly fulfilled their side of their bargain, with Trevor Brooking and the FC Cologne striker Tony Woodcock grabbing the goals in a 2–1 win, but watched on as Italy could only muster a goalless draw against some sturdy Belgian defence.

West Germany went on to win a largely forgettable tournament and while England had failed to progress and had their reputation sullied by the idiotic behaviour of some of their followers, at least, after the barren years of the 1970s, they had finally returned to major tournament football.

English football meanwhile continued its rapid and often misguided transformation. On one hand there was the opening of the new national coaching centre at Lilleshall in Shropshire, while on the other there was the sudden emergence of artificial turf. In a bid to alleviate the number of postponements caused by the British winter, and impressed by the growth of the game across the Atlantic in the NASL where it was played largely on synthetic surfaces, the Football League gave their blessing to Queens Park Rangers' request to install a so-called 'plastic pitch' at their Loftus Road ground. Soon, Luton Town, Preston North End and Oldham Athletic would follow suit with Astroturf, but they were anything but popular. Now the ball bounced higher than ever and took an eternity to come down while players backed out of sliding tackles for fear of carpet burns. Inevitably, the pitches were criticized. The Spurs and England midfielder Glenn Hoddle said they turned the game into a 'mockery', while Liverpool's Alan Hansen, quite correctly, argued: 'It's not grass and it never will be.' By 1987, however, the Astroturf would be gone, sent back to the forecourts of petrol stations and butchers' shelves.

Ron Greenwood's preparations for the final four games of England's qualifying campaign for the 1982 World Cup would be hampered by the abandonment in May 1981 of the 1980–81 Home Internationals Championship. While England had drawn with Wales and lost to Scotland, the team was unwilling to travel to Belfast for the game against Northern Ireland because of continuing civil unrest in the province over the IRA hunger strikers in the Maze Prison. It was a situation that had been coming. In recent years, some of Northern Ireland's home games in the competition had been played in Liverpool or Glasgow, purely on the grounds of the safety of those concerned. Now, though, the competition would be abandoned – the first time in its ninety-eight-year history (other than during the World Wars) that it had not been completed.

If anybody had thought that England's reappearance in a major international tournament would be the catalyst for some much-needed change in the fortunes of the national team, they were misguided. Far from building on the relative success of the European Championship campaign, Greenwood's England appeared to be going backwards. Going into the World Cup qualifier in Basle, Switzerland, on 30 May, England had been on a run of five games without a win, the last four of which had failed to yield even a single goal for England. It was, as the papers were only too keen to point out, the worst run in the national team's history.

It would get worse. Although Greenwood was able to call upon the services of Kevin Keegan for his first competitive game in a year, England found itself undone by a Swiss team that revelled in their opposition's insecurity. And while England at least managed a goal this time, thanks to Liverpool's Terry McDermott, two goals in two minutes by the hosts left England pointless. More misery followed. After the final whistle, English fans, some proudly wearing 'Battle of Turin' T-shirts, rioted again, this time causing £60,000 worth of damage to the city centre. Within days, Greenwood would go to his employers and broach the idea of standing down, only to be told to go away and prepare the team for the game against the group leaders Hungary.

Despite his doubts and against the odds, Greenwood somehow managed to mount an entirely unexpected revival against Hungary in Budapest a week later, winning 3–1. It was West Ham's Trevor Brooking, on the occasion of his eleventh wedding anniversary, who dominated proceedings, scoring twice. One of them, a thunderbolt of a strike with his sweet left foot, even saw the ball end up lodged in the stanchion of the goal frame. For Ron Greenwood, however, the result had done little to change his mind. Sickened by the rising tide of violence, tiring of the press and frustrated by his inability to turn the team around, he flew home that night and announced to his senior players that he had taken charge of his last game as England manager. Some not so gentle persuasion followed and by the time the plane touched down at Luton airport, Greenwood had relented and agreed to defer his retirement from the game until after the 1982 World Cup finals in Spain.

If he had felt frustrated by the response of his players and the seemingly futile quest for consistency, the result that followed in Oslo against Norway would also have had the England manager tearing out what was left of his hair. Though Bryan Robson had opened the scoring for England, two goals for the Norwegians before half-time were enough to consign England to defeat, their first ever by Norway, against whom they had never scored less than four goals before. Much like the match at Wembley in 1953 when Billy Wright and England had been humbled by Ferenc Puskas and Hungary, the Magnificent Magyars, it marked another turning point in the history of English football, a day when the rest of the world realized that England were not merely beatable but there for the taking.

Famously, the Norwegian commentator Bjorge Lillelien then laid waste not just to the English football team, but to the nation itself. Switching between English and Norwegian, he launched into one of the most partisan pieces of commentary ever broadcast.

> We are the best in the world! We have beaten England! England, birthplace of giants … Lord Nelson, Lord Beaverbrook, Sir Winston Churchill, Sir Anthony Eden, Clement Attlee, Henry Cooper, Lady Diana, *vi har slått dem alle sammen, vi har slått dem alle sammen* [we have beaten them all, we have beaten them all]. Maggie Thatcher, can you hear me? Maggie Thatcher … your boys took a hell of a beating! Your boys took a hell of a beating!

It wasn't just the team that would take a beating. The following day, the press went for the manager in a way that was above and beyond anything he had suffered before. Suddenly, allowing himself to be talked out of retirement seemed like the single worst idea Ron Greenwood had ever entertained.

*

Luck, as Field Marshal Montgomery might have said, was in Ron Greenwood's rucksack. With all the evidence suggesting that England were destined to miss out on their third World Cup finals in succession, a string of strange, almost freakish results conspired to give England a chance of qualifying. Romania lost at home to Switzerland, and then, in their return fixture a month later, could only manage a draw. It left England needing to beat Hungary in their final group game at Wembley to qualify for Spain.

For once, England took the chance that had presented itself. A single goal from Paul Mariner was enough to give Greenwood's men the victory and though they had lost three of their eight qualifying games and suffered some of the most humiliating defeats in the nation's football history, England had reached the World Cup finals.

Buoyed by their qualification, England finally found some form. They beat Holland at Wembley and won all three games in the 1981–2 Home Internationals to take the title. There was also some extra-curricular activity to attend to.

As it was the first time in twelve agonizing years that England had qualified for the World Cup finals, this also represented the first opportunity for the England squad to record their own World Cup single. Written and produced by former Smokie members Chris Norman and Peter Spencer, 'This Time (We'll Get It Right)' was another of those songs that talked the talk but only ever succeeded in making the England team look rather stupid once they had been eliminated from the tournament. Set to a melody of synthesized pan pipes and what seemed to be an oompah band lurking menacingly in the background, it was an undeniably catchy ditty and it went on to reach number 7 in the charts, just ahead of 'We Have A Dream' by the Scotland World Cup squad. And this being the age of the team themselves being forced to sing the official song, and not some lightweight pop stars on the make, it was down to Keegan, Brooking and the boys to confront the horror of the *Top of the Pops* studio.

For professional footballers, used to mud, sweat and battle-fields of pitches, this was alien territory. Put them in front of

100,000 people at Wembley and they were at home. Stick them in front of 200 awkward dancers in a television studio in West London, though, and they went to pieces. The Ipswich striker Paul Mariner, as hardy a Mancunian as you could ever meet, recalls that day. 'It was one of those things you don't really want to do but you've got very little choice in,' he says. 'But it was good to see how the show and the music business worked and, of course, to see Legs & Co.'

But, according to Mariner, there was a secret in keeping out of the spotlight, even if you were on live television in front of millions of viewers. 'If you look back at the tapes I was right at the back. Phil Thompson had taken me to one side and said, "If you're clever you'll get on the back row and nobody will see you." So that's what I did. Well, that and push Kevin Keegan right to the front because he was the smallest. It was bullying – but in the nicest possible way.'

Today, of course, it's hard to imagine any of the current England squad shuffling into a TV studio to sing a song they didn't really care about. Aside from the logistical problem of getting all of the players in the same place at the same time, you would have to assume that unless there was some incentive, some brand extension, then it simply wouldn't be worth their while. But back in 1982, it was pretty much mandatory, regardless of how talented a vocalist you were.

Greenwood's squad for Spain, meanwhile, would contain few surprises. Indeed, perhaps the biggest shock was that he had finally settled the ongoing debate between Peter Shilton and Ray Clemence, opting for the Nottingham Forest man as his number one. And though doubts persisted about the fitness of two of England's stalwarts, Kevin Keegan and Trevor Brooking, both were included in Greenwood's final twenty-two-man squad.

Going into the finals, Mariner had been in impressive form, scoring in each of his last four games for England. But his had been a recovery from an Achilles injury that had verged on the miraculous. When the Ipswich striker had ripped his tendon in January 1982 his dream of playing in a World Cup finals had seemed all but over. It was only the intervention of the surgeons and physiotherapists at Cambridge University that made his dream a reality. 'I really thought I was on the shit list,' he says now. But buoyed by the support of Ron Greenwood, Mariner made a complete recovery. 'He [Greenwood] was a remarkable manager. He was softly softly but still had that air of authority about him. You always knew exactly what you had to do,' he adds.

While confidence in the squad was higher than it had been in months, the tension around the England hotel near Bilbao was palpable. With emotions running high over the Falklands conflict – there were many Argentinian sympathizers in Spain – and concerns about the concomitant threat of the Basque separatist group ETA, a heavy police presence surrounded the grounds right around the clock. For Ron Greenwood, though, this was what he had agreed to stay on for. The first manager to actually qualify for a World Cup since Walter Winterbottom took England to Chile in 1962, he could look forward to a group that contained Czechoslovakia, Kuwait and, in their first game, France.

England would get off to an improbably good start against the much-fancied French, scoring after just twenty-seven seconds. A Steve Coppell throw-in deep in the French half was flicked on by Terry Butcher and there at the back post was Bryan Robson who hooked the ball in, past Jean-Luc Ettori in the French goal. As the fastest ever goal in the history of the World Cup, Robson would receive an inscribed gold watch to mark his achievement. The only problem was that the strap was too big, but after having a couple of links taken out of the bracelet, it fitted perfectly. What became of the missing links? 'He offered to give them to me as a reward for the throw-in,' says Steve Coppell. 'I politely declined.'

In the stifling heat of Bilbao's Estadio San Mamés – the temperature reached 100°F – England seemed entirely unfazed by the reputation of the French. 'France were a great team – one of the favourites – and they had some big players too: Platini, Giresse, Tigana,' recalls Paul Mariner. 'But we were organized and disciplined and we stuck to our gameplan of pressurizing them when we got a chance. Then we got off to a flyer with Robbo's goal and we didn't look back.'

Though France equalized with a goal by Gerard Soler, England still seemed at ease, and when Robson restored their advantage with a header on sixty-seven minutes there was only going to be one winner. With eight minutes to go, it was Paul Mariner, his socks rolled down, who would seal England's first win in the World Cup finals since Allan Clarke's goal beat Czechoslovakia in Guadalajara on 11 June 1970. This was the fifth game in succession in which Mariner had scored for his country, and his sixth goal in seven games, equalling a record set by Jimmy Greaves.

Having beaten the French, England progressed comfortably to the second phase. Against Czechoslovakia, they led 1–0 thanks to a goal from Trevor Francis. When Jozef Barmos put through his own net to double England's lead, the game was all but over. Desperate to maintain his run, Paul Mariner would even try and claim the goal. 'These days they might have given it to me but not back then,' he shrugs. A final group win against Kuwait saw England top their group

Worryingly for Ron Greenwood, the crocked duo of Kevin Keegan and Trevor Brooking were showing little sign of progress, although Brooking had a specialist fly out to give him an injection in his groin. Keegan, meanwhile, was desperate to recover. Having already undergone an epidural in Bilbao to no great effect, he had gone to his manager and suggested a possible remedy for his ongoing back problems. He wanted to go and see his specialist, Jurgen Rehwinkel, in Hamburg. Under the cover of darkness, Keegan borrowed an old Seat 500 from a member of the hotel staff and drove the 250 miles to Madrid airport where he took a flight to Hamburg. Four days later, Keegan was back, and his back was back to somewhere near its best.

Winning their group had done England few favours in their bid to win the tournament. Now, as a reward for emerging from their group with an almost faultless record, they found themselves in a group with West Germany and the hosts Spain. The game against West Germany would end goalless, even though the Germans looked vulnerable, while Ron Greenwood would once again leave Kevin Keegan and Trevor Brooking on the substitutes bench for the all-important game against Spain.

Greenwood's gamble would backfire. With the match scoreless and England needing to win, the England manager brought Keegan and Brooking on with just eighteen minutes to go. Within minutes, Keegan had missed an open goal and Brooking too had gone close, his shot saved by the Spanish goalkeeper Luis Arconada. It was too little and, for Ron Greenwood, too late. 'Leaving us on the bench was Ron Greenwood's biggest mistake,' Keegan said later. 'We were his two best players, we were very influential in the way England played and I do not believe any other country in the world would have made that decision, even if the team had done all right without us.'

Having conceded only one goal and remained unbeaten after five games, England found themselves out of the tournament. It seemed unjust, plain wrong even, but by virtue of the fact that West Germany had beaten Spain 2–1 in their game, England were out. For the next World Cup FIFA would change the format so that after the initial group stages, the competition would revert to a straight knockout. Not that that was any consolation for Greenwood and England. Now Ron's twenty-two were heading home and this time, more than any other time, Greenwood was definitely calling it a day.

CHAPTER 3

KIND HEARTS
AND CORONETS

'Quiet years, the England years ...'
Bobby Robson, England manager 1982–1990

To say that Bobby Robson loved the game of football is plain wrong. The man adored it. Over the course of forty-one years in football management, he proved himself time and time again one of the finest, most intuitive coaches in the professional game. At Ipswich Town, PSV Eindhoven, Sporting Lisbon, Porto, Barcelona and Newcastle United he either won trophies or revitalized a club in dire need of salvation. Even when he was sacked at Lisbon, he left with the club at the top of the table, the first time they had occupied that position in fifteen years. All of which must have made his failure to win a major tournament with England all the more irksome.

Bobby Robson had arrived at Lancaster Gate as the new England manager on 7 July 1982. Following terrific success with the unfashionable Suffolk club Ipswich Town, which he guided to glory in the FA Cup and the UEFA Cup, and having beaten the public's favourite Brian Clough to the job, he had succeeded Ron Greenwood on his departure after the World Cup finals, and in doing so, become the second Ipswich manager in nineteen years (after Sir Alf Ramsey) to take the top job in English football.

And what a job. Four years after Robson stepped down, Terry Venables would become the England coach. Nothing more, nothing less. One man paid, specifically, to coach the team – England. In the days of Bobby Robson, the role of England manager, however, would be all-encompassing. Not only would Robson have to manage the senior squad but he was also required to oversee the Under-15, Under-17, Under-19 and Under-21 teams and be the head of all coaching for English football. What's more, with no scouting network available to him, Robson would also have to drive himself around the country most evenings to watch games and keep tabs on his players. Then there was the paperwork, the media commitments and the expectation of an entire nation hanging over you, day in, day out. For this, Robson would be paid £65,000 – or about seven thousand pounds less than he received as manager of little Ipswich Town.

Working alongside him would be the FA's Director of Coaching, Charles Hughes. Part coach, part football scientist, Hughes had been at the Football Association since 1964 and was the man who had invented what he believed was a winning formula for the game: the 'position of maximum opportunity', or POMO to give it its abbreviated and no more sensible name. In his years studying the game and as the successful coach of the England amateur game, Hughes had deduced that some 90 per cent of goals were the result of moves that involved five or less passes and that three-quarters of all goals came from crosses. In short, POMO and direct, no-nonsense football were the key to success. 'Why fanny around with twelve passes when they're not going to get you a goal anyway?' he would say to Robson.

Only in England and in the dusty rooms of the Football Association could such a one-dimensional strategy ever gain credence. To take a game as expressive and as spontaneous as football and reduce it to a system of probabilities and percentages is nothing short of insane. If the sole aim of the game is to get the ball and get rid of it, preferably with a high ball straight into the opposition half or penalty area, what chance would there ever be that players would learn the discipline of patience or feel comfortable with the ball at their feet?

Born in Sacriston, County Durham, Robson had forged a successful playing career, although not for his beloved Newcastle United as he had dreamed of. Lured away from his job as an apprentice electrician at the National Coal Board by Fulham manager and fellow Geordie Bill Dodgin in May 1950, he had moved to the capital to establish himself in the First Division. An inside-forward, Robson proved to be a competent, reliable performer for the Cottagers, scoring 68 goals in 152 appearances. He was equally prolific at his next club, West Bromwich Albion. Inevitably, his was a name that would soon figure in the plans of England manager Walter Winterbottom, making his full international debut against France in November 1957, scoring twice in a comprehensive 4–0 victory. He would go on to win twenty caps in total.

Just as he had played a key role in encouraging Ron Greenwood to go into football coaching and management, Winterbottom would again be the man to persuade Bobby Robson to try his hand at these skills after finishing as a player. In 1959, a year after Robson had played in the World Cup finals in Sweden, the England manager suggested that Robson had the makings of a good coach, and encouraged him to try one of the FA's coaching courses at the national coaching centre that he had helped establish at Lilleshall. In time, Robson would describe Winterbottom as 'a prophet'.

As a grounding in the art of coaching, Winterbottom's support and the training he received at Lilleshall would stand Robson in good stead, although his first managerial appointment suggested that maybe he wasn't cut out for coaching. In January 1968 Robson took over at his old club, Fulham, with the team languishing in the First Division having taken just sixteen points from twenty-four games. Though he acquired the services of a bustling young full-back from non-league Tonbridge Angels by the name of Malcolm Macdonald for just £1,000, turning him into a striker who would go on to represent England, Robson was unable to prevent Fulham being relegated. When he was sacked soon after, he only learned of his fate from an *Evening Standard* placard on Putney High Street that read 'Robson Sacked!'

Then came Ipswich Town and a job that would transform the fortunes not just of the provincial side but of Bobby Robson as well. Several times during his thirteen years at Portman Road, Robson could have left for bigger clubs, including Barcelona, for significantly more money. It was only when Ron Greenwood vacated the England job after the World Cup in Spain in 1982 that Robson finally found a job that was simply too hard to resist, even if it did entail a pay cut.

Robson's first game in charge of the national side would be a European Championship qualifier against Denmark in Copenhagen on 22 September. Without the luxury of a friendly or two to find his feet, it would have been entirely natural for Robson to keep faith with the bulk of the team from the World Cup finals. By and large, that is exactly what he did, although he did leave out his old captain at Ipswich, Mick Mills, and bring back his former charge Russell Osman to replace Liverpool's Phil Thompson at the heart of the defence. He also drew a line in the sand in the tiresome 'Peter Shilton or Ray Clemence' debate, making it clear that Shilton would be his first choice-goalkeeper and not Clemence.

There was one major decision that Robson made, however, that showed not only that he was his own man, but also that he had much to learn in the world of PR. Omitting Kevin Keegan from his first squad, Robson had opted to let the world – and Keegan – know through the media and hadn't even phoned to tell him of his decision. Though Keegan was now thirty-one and perhaps not in his prime he still had much to offer in the game, but Robson, the new broom, felt his performance at the World Cup finals, and his recent injury woes, meant he was never going to be the same player he once was.

Keegan was livid, not least because on taking over, Robson had said that Keegan was still part of his plans. The pair had even met a few weeks earlier when Robson had attended Keegan's first game for his new club, Newcastle United, and told him that he would see him in a few weeks' time, a reference to the squad get-together prior to the Denmark game. When the news finally broke, Keegan learned about it in the same way that every other person in the country did – in the papers. 'A phone call would have left the door open,' reflected Keegan later. 'Instead he slammed it in my face.'

From being the captain of England to not even being considered for a place in the squad, it had been a sad end to an international career stretching back a decade and sixty-three games. Still fuming from the treatment he had received, Kevin Keegan duly announced his retirement from international football and carried on doing for Newcastle United what he once did for England. In his next game for the Magpies – Bobby Robson's beloved Magpies! – Keegan scored four times in a 5–1 victory over Rotherham.

The game against a dangerous Denmark side would mark a new chapter for England. Though they emerged with a point, the result could have gone either way. With England lucky to be leading 2–1, thanks to two goals from Trevor Francis, just one of many English players who had ventured abroad, lured by immeasurably better salaries, it had looked as though Robson's England would, somehow, return home with a win and two points to start their qualifying campaign. But with a minute left on the clock, Jesper Olsen, a player who would go on to star for Manchester United a couple of years later, danced round Bryan Robson, Terry Butcher and Russell Osman to level.

Publicly, Bobby Robson declared his debut to be a relative success. Not everybody agreed. Despite Denmark having more than enough chances to win the game comfortably and demonstrating precisely why they were one of the fastest improving nations in European football, this was a game that fans and media alike still expected, even demanded, that England would win.

For Bobby Robson, it was the first taste of what was expected of an England manager and his first taste of what would happen if he failed to deliver. Results, it seemed, were everything, closely followed by a performance that showed guts, guile and pride. For many, Robson's new look England had shown precious little of those qualities in the game in Copenhagen. Moreover, the failure to get a result would also cost England dear in their quest to reach the European Championship finals in France.

Two other games would scupper England's chances. The first, a goalless draw against Greece at Wembley in March 1983 (a team they had beaten easily, 3–0, in the away fixture five months earlier) would be a dropped point that would cost them dearly come the final group reckoning. The second, a home defeat by a single goal in the return game to Denmark in September 1983, thanks to a converted penalty by the industrious Barcelona striker Allan Simonsen, would see the Danes go through at England's expense.

It was a desperately close call for England. Despite scoring twenty-three goals in their twelve qualifying games – they had beaten Luxembourg 9–0 at home and 4–0 away – the failure to beat Greece at home in a game they should and could have won had let in Denmark to top Group 3. With just eight teams participating in the finals – the competition would not be expanded to sixteen teams until Euro 96 in England – it meant England's second place and their vastly superior goal difference counted for nought.

With no major tournament to occupy them in 1984, Robson's England had no option but to concentrate on the final playing of the Home International Championship, appropriately on its centenary. The impact of Northern Ireland's 'Troubles' (which led to the abandonment of the 1980–81 competition) and the high-profile hooliganism that had blighted some of the encounters, gradually eroded public enthusiasm for the Championship. Moreover, with the improvement of international teams the world over, the perception of the event was that it had become little more than a quaint anachronism, one that the players, under pressure from more and more matches each season, could have done without and one that gave the national sides little help or experience in playing the kind of teams and tactics they would encounter in the European Championship or World Cup.

Indeed, the format of the event had become so protracted that it was difficult for supporters to muster the excitement or the passion that they could during the high-octane, nerve-racking few weeks of a major tournament. The final Home International Championship was a case in point. With the international calendar increasingly congested, the six games that made up the competition would take more than five months to play. The first game, Northern Ireland's 2–0 win over Scotland, opened proceedings on 13 December 1983 and the last, a 1–1 draw between Scotland and England that handed the Irish the title, took place after the domestic season had finished on 25 May 1984. It was less a football tournament and more of an endurance test.

The sense that England were merely treading water was certainly prevalent in 1984. Though Bobby Robson had yet to take England into a major tournament, dreary displays against the likes of France in Paris, where they were undone by the brilliance of Michel Platini in a 2–0 defeat, and at Wembley where they lost 2–0 to the USSR just a week after the Home International draw against Scotland, had seen his position already come under scrutiny.

But it would be after England's penultimate game in the Home Internationals against Wales in Wrexham on 5 May that the fans and the press began to turn on Robson. Inspired by a headed debut goal by the young Manchester United striker Mark Hughes, the Welsh outplayed England, and the *Sun*, that most reliable of agitators, issued badges to its equally disillusioned readers soon after with the slogan 'Robson Out, Clough In'.

Bobby Robson was unimpressed. 'I am caught up in a tabloid circulation war, and they are saying and doing outrageous things just to sell newspapers off my back,' he said, as though the papers had never resorted to such tactics before. 'All the football reporters I talk to tell me it is not they who are putting the boot in, but their editors. It is disgraceful.'

But if proof were needed that Robson was one of the luckier men to occupy the position of England manager, it would come just eight days after the brickbats and catcalls at the USSR game.

With the *Sun* campaign now in full flow, England headed to South America for a three-match tour, their first fixture being a date with the best team in the world in their own stadium, the cavernous Maracanã.

It had all the hallmarks of a hiding: England, down and dispirited; Brazil, great, gifted and at home. If Robson was daunted by the prospect of facing one of the most formidable attacking units in world football, it didn't show. With eighteen of his first-choice players unavailable, either through injury or fatigue – the tour came at the end of another long season – Robson would field a side where the majority of the team were not yet into double figures in terms of international caps. It was also a line-up noticeable for its attacking options, not least the introduction of two wingers, Stoke City's Mark Chamberlain and Watford's John Barnes.

With just 56,126 people in the stadium – famously, it had held a world record crowd of over 199,000 for the 1950 World Cup final – England settled quickly. Shortly before the interval, Barnes received the ball on the left wing, chesting down Mark Hateley's pass and setting off on a run towards the Brazilian penalty area. With the ball seemingly stuck to his boot, the twenty-year-old cut a swathe through the opposition defence, beating man after man after man and then, just as the Brazilian keeper Roberto Costa dived to take the ball off his feet, Barnes dragged the ball around him and simply guided it into the unguarded goal. It was a goal of rare beauty, made all the more memorable by the fact that it came, incredibly, from the feet of an Englishman. Balance, pace, poise, elegance, it was simply magnificent.

For Barnes it would be a career-defining goal, even if he doesn't remember much about it.

> I always liken it to an out-of-body experience. I look at it on TV now and I can't remember doing any of it. When you score from a free-kick or a penalty you build an image in your head of what you're going to do with it, which corner of the net you want to put it in, but with a goal like that you never

get the chance. You just react instinctively to the changing situation. You've got the ball and you react to what comes towards you.

None of it was planned, it was just instinct and reaction, and I didn't know exactly what I was doing. The only thing I slightly remember is wanting to shoot when I got to the edge of the area and Tony Woodcock runs across me and gets in my way so I had to try to dribble again. That was half-way through the run and it was only because of him that I had to beat a couple more defenders and take it round the keeper.

Another goal midway through the second half by Mark Hateley, starting an England match for the first time, would give England a magical, entirely unforeseen victory and suddenly, in ninety memorable minutes, the *Sun* was left with a stockpile of badges they needed to get rid of.

It was the little moments like the Barnes goal, and the piecemeal improvement in the team's form, that kept Robson's head above water in the mid-1980s. It mattered not that England had gone on to lose against Uruguay or draw with Chile; the fact that they had beaten a team of Brazil's stature, and in such convincing fashion, had not just bought Robson time but rendered any notion that he might soon be leaving entirely redundant.

But English joy would soon turn to despair. The following year, there would be two incidents that would render all talk of titles and trophies utterly pointless. Two events that would mark 1985 down as the darkest year in English football's long history.

On 11 May the game between Bradford City and Lincoln City at Valley Parade was halted when a fire broke out underneath the ageing wooden main stand. Within four minutes the flames had engulfed the roof and despite the best efforts of the stewards and the emergency services to evacaute the stand, fifty-six people died, with another 256 injured. What had started out as a day designed to celebrate Bradford winning the Third Division title – they had presented the trophy to Bradford skipper Peter Jackson before the game – had ended in tragedy.

Worse was to follow. Just eighteen days later, thousands of Liverpool supporters had travelled to Brussels to watch their team contest the European Cup final against Italy's Juventus at Belgium's crumbling national stadium, Heysel, but poor crowd segregation and inadequate fencing, coupled with drunkenness and stupidity, would lead to disaster.

An hour before kick-off, a group of Liverpool hooligans had charged the nearby Juventus supporters, situated on the other side of a temporary fence. As they breached the fence, the Italians ran for the exits and while many of them died having been trampled underfoot, many more also lost their lives when a wall collapsed as they tried to make their escape.

In total, thirty-nine people died that night, all but one of them Italian, and some 400 others suffered injury. In scenes more reminiscent of a battlefield, with the dead and dying lying all around, a game of football was the last thing on anyone's mind, showpiece event or not. Quite why the decision was taken then to play the game was nothing short of baffling. The result, a 1–0 win for Juventus, was of utter insignificance. The same could also have been said of England's friendly against Italy in Mexico City, which went ahead as planned just a week later.

Two days after the disaster, the Football Association, under immense pressure from the public, the media and Parliament, announced that English clubs would not be permitted to take part in European competition for the 1985–86 season. But that would not be the end of the matter. The decision arrived soon after one from the Belgian government banning all English football clubs from their country indefinitely, as well as Liverpool FC's decision to withdraw from the following season's UEFA Cup.

The Conservative Prime Minister Margaret Thatcher, who had summoned the FA chairman Sir Bert Millichip and the FA secretary Ted Croker back from the Mexican leg of England's tour of America to attend a meeting at Number 10, gave her backing to the self-imposed ban. 'We have to get the game cleaned up from this hooliganism at home and then perhaps we shall be able to go overseas again,' she said. It was a view reinforced by Croker. 'It is now up to English football to put its house in order,' he said.

If the promptness of the FA's action had been designed, in part, to head off any more stringent action from the game's governing body in Europe, UEFA, it had failed. Two days later UEFA president Jacques Georges passed sentence on English football, banning the country's clubs indefinitely from their competitions. The European ban would not just halt the spread of hooliganism across the continent but it would also have severe repercussions for the domestic game, and not just for the teams who were due to play in Europe in the following season, namely Everton, Manchester United, Liverpool, Norwich City, Tottenham Hotspur and Southampton. Attendances would fall, star players would migrate, and interest in the game would wane. For a nation with such a proud and successful record in European competition in the preceding decade – English clubs had won seven European Cups, three UEFA Cups and one Cup-Winners' Cup – it was an outcome, both professionally and financially, they could ill afford. The only saving grace from the whole sorry, sickening episode was that the England team were still allowed to travel overseas.

After the ill-advised and unnecessary tour of Mexico and North America at the end of the domestic season, England resumed their qualification for the 1986 World Cup finals with a home fixture against Romania. Tragically, the night before, during Scotland's 1–1 draw with Wales at Ninian Park, the Scotland manager Jock Stein, the man who had led Celtic to the European Cup in 1967, suffered a heart attack on the touchline and died. While England's result – a 1–1 draw – was less than ideal, it made little difference to their inevitable qualification and their place in the finals was assured with two games to spare when Northern Ireland beat Romania in Bucharest, giving England top spot in their group.

In early 1983 FIFA had withdrawn the offer it had made to Colombia to stage the tournament some nine years earlier, amid growing concerns over the financial stability of the country as well as the safety of the teams and supporters, given the pernicious and pervasive influence of the country's drug cartels. Three nations would bid to replace Colombia – Canada, the United States and the 1970 host country, Mexico. For the United States it was a must-win pitch, not least because their much-vaunted North American Soccer League (NASL) was rapidly losing support after the thrills, spills, bells and whistles of the Pelé and New York Cosmos-inspired era in the mid to late 1970s.

Yet bizarrely, incredibly, the tournament would be awarded to Mexico for the second time in just sixteen years, despite ongoing concerns that, with its high altitude and often searing heat, it was one of the least suitable places on earth to play the game. Not that FIFA seemed to care. For them, the 1970 spectacle dominated by the incomparable Brazilians was one of the most successful tournaments ever staged, and though they were keen to see the game develop in the biggest market of them all – the United States – when it came to the American bid, presented by no less a world figure than Henry Kissinger, the FIFA president João Havelange simply wasn't taken by the idea.

With the tournament now being held in the punishing heat of Central America, England's prospects of challenging for the title of world champions receded, not least because no European team had ever won the event outside of their own continent. Keen to impress on the biggest stage of all, however, Bobby Robson had nevertheless assembled a squad that was built around the experience and drive of the captain Bryan Robson in the middle, the towering presence of Terry Butcher at the back and the safe hands of Peter Shilton in goal. Factor in a nucleus of players from the dominant Everton side of the time – Peter Reid, Gary M. Stevens and Trevor Steven – and some promising attacking talent in the shape of the Geordie duo Chris Waddle and Peter Beardsley, and though just seven of the squad had appeared at the previous World Cup in 1982 this was a unit that still had the potential to go far in the tournament, especially with the goals of the First Division's leading scorer, Everton's Gary Lineker, in attack.

Shortly before the tournament began, the squad left for Colorado Springs, USA, for some altitude training ahead of the rigours of playing in the rarefied air of Mexico. The Football Association even paid to fly the wives and girlfriends of the players out to the States too. Nothing, it seemed, was too much for the England squad.

It was on the trip that the England squad bonded in the most unexpected of manners. 'There was a big drinking culture in and around football and we had some players in the squad who could drink,' explains Tottenham's Gary Stevens. 'but we all decided that that was it, we're not drinking while we're still in the tournament ... I don't think I have ever been with a squad that was so dedicated and so focused.'

While the facilities at the US Air Force's Broadmoor Center were exceptional and the training itself precisely what the squad needed ahead of the competition, England's build-up would be rocked by an injury to the captain Bryan Robson, who fell in a warm-up game against Mexico in Los Angeles and dislocated his shoulder. The captain had originally sustained the problem back in March of that year, but had decided against surgery as it may have jeopardized his participation in the World Cup finals. Now, however, it looked like he was going to be out anyway.

But for Bobby Robson, there was another headache looming, albeit one he had created for himself. Known throughout football for his inability to get names right – the midfielder Graham Rix was known as Brian, for instance – he had selected three players with names so similar that it could only end in disaster, as Stevens reveals. 'There was myself, the other Gary Stevens and there was Trevor Steven,' he recalls. 'You can only imagine the problems Bobby had.'

The problem would resurface again later during the trip. Arriving for breakfast one morning, the captain Bryan Robson was greeted by his manager. 'Morning, Bobby,' he said.

'You're Bobby,' replied the captain. 'I'm Bryan.'

England's base for the tournament would be the north-eastern city of Monterrey, near the Sierra Madre mountain range.

Winners of their last eleven games, the team was in a confident mood and having been drawn in the same group as Portugal, Morocco and Poland, they were the bookmakers' favourites to go through. Often, in the group stages of major tournaments, there is a group with so much talent, so many mouth-watering encounters, that's it's quickly labelled the 'Group of Death'. Not this one. Indeed, the local press were describing it as the 'Group of Sleeping'.

But what did the bookies know? After a disastrous opener against the Portuguese all that would change. Beaten 1–0 by a Carlos Manuel tap-in fifteen minutes from time, they had clearly struggled to adapt to the stifling heat in Club Monterrey's Estadio Tecnologico, a stadium described by the England keeper Peter Shilton as being like a 'bad Third Division ground'.

The following day, Robson took his England team away from the press and the pressure of the hotel – the BBC and the ITV teams were staying there too – to visit a monastery and conduct a debrief as to what had happened in the opener against Portugal. As the team relaxed and thoughts turned to the game against Morocco in just three days' time, they even had a few beers.

But if the Portugal game had jeopardized England's chances of a trouble-free route into the last sixteen, the match against Morocco would merely compound matters. England, unchanged from the first game, laboured once more against another team they were expected to beat. Approaching half-time and with no score, the England captain Bryan Robson had raced into the Moroccan penalty area only to be held back. The result, sadly, wasn't a penalty, but a recurrence of the dislocated shoulder that he had sustained in the warm-up game in Los Angeles. Leaving the field in tears, Robson handed his captain's armband to his former Manchester United colleague Ray Wilkins, but the man they called 'Butch' would only wear it for a few minutes. Taking issue with an offside decision, the AC Milan midfielder picked up the ball and hurled it in the direction of the referee, Gabriel Gonzalez. Unfortunately, for Wilkins and England, it found its target.

For Wilkins, it was a moment of madness, a fleeting, foolhardy act of petulance that would make him the first England player in history to be dismissed in a World Cup final tournament. As he left the field, with England's World Cup campaign in tatters and an immediate two-match ban to mull over, Wilkins handed the armband on once more, this time to the goalkeeper Peter Shilton. It was another first. Never before had three players captained England in the same game.

With just one point to show from two games, and the last match being against the seeded team in the group, Poland, it seemed as though England's World Cup adventure was destined to end in disaster as opposed to glorious triumph. At the team's isolated hotel outside of Monterrey, meanwhile, England's players were beginning to feel the pressure, not merely from the press but from the supporters back home too. 'It was tough,' explains the Queens Park Rangers central defender Terry Fenwick. 'After the first two games we were getting loads of shit so we just tried to shut ourselves away from it all. Well, that and not read any of the newspapers.'

The final group game against Poland would be pivotal. If England continued in the same depressing form as they had shown in the games against Portugal and Morocco, they would be home before the postcards. And Bobby Robson would be looking for a new job.

A team meeting was convened. There, Robson went over the first two games, drawing what positives he could from the matches. When he had had his say, he threw it open to the floor. Terry Fenwick was one of the most vociferous critics. 'I just felt that our tactics at the beginning of the tournament were all wrong,' explains Fenwick. 'It was too English. We were trying to close everyone down, chasing everything, and in that heat and altitude you can't do that for ninety minutes. So me and Peter Reid chirped up ... We just felt that we needed to sit back more, keep the ball and counterattack. We needed to conserve energy. And Bobby listened, he really did.'

With Bryan Robson going home and Ray Wilkins suspended, Bobby Robson duly opted to scrap the 4-3-3 system employed to such unspectacular effect against Portugal and Morocco and revert to a more familiar 4-4-2, this despite the squad having done little or no work together on playing that way. It wasn't the only change. Out too went the striker Mark Hateley and the winger Chris Waddle and in came Peter Beardsley upfront with Peter Reid, Trevor Steven and Steve Hodge manning the midfield alongside Glenn Hoddle.

It was win or bust for Robson and England. Any concerns he may have had for his team, or his job, however, disappeared within thirty-five minutes of the kick-off, and this despite being forced to listen to Simple Minds' 'Alive and Kicking' before they went out. Gary Lineker, ably assisted by Peter Beardsley and Glenn Hoddle, carved open the Polish defence to such an extent that by half-time Lineker had a hat-trick to his name and England had one foot in the next round. Meanwhile, in the stands of Monterrey's Estadio Universitario, the same fans that had abused the team as they left the field after the Portugal and Morocco matches were performing a conga.

For Lineker, it would be the catalyst to propel him into international football superstardom. 'It changed my life,' he recalls. 'Before I was just trying to make my way in international football, and after that game I went on to win the Golden Boot [for the top scorer in the tournament] and got a move to Barcelona on the back of it.'

With a place in the second round and a game against Paraguay guaranteed, England too would grow in confidence after the Poland victory. Despite the best efforts of the Paraguayans to antagonize the English team – Terry Butcher recalls they spat at him and tried to elbow him in the face – England would produce another convincing performance. Once more, they finished the game strongly and once more it was two goals from Gary Lineker, with the other from Newcastle United's Peter Beardsley, that saw Bobby Robson's team through to a quarter-final showdown with

Argentina and their talisman, the man universally regarded as the greatest player in the world, Diego Maradona.

Everyone knew about Maradona. An Argentinian full international at the age of just sixteen, he had enjoyed a remarkable rise to football stardom with Boca Juniors, Barcelona in Spain, and, after a then world record £6.9 million transfer in 1984, at Italian Serie A side Napoli. Short in height but huge in stature, he was a dashing, darting dynamo of a player, capable of almost single-handedly defeating teams in one momentary flash of virtuosity. Playing behind the strikers, Maradona had a free role to go wherever he pleased, although usually that meant straight to the very heart of the opposition's defence. Strong and solid, he was virtually impossible to shake off the ball, and when he had a chance to score, he rarely missed.

England, like every other team that had been confronted by him, needed a battle plan to cope with the threat Diego Maradona undoubtedly posed. With ongoing doubts about Peter Reid's fitness, Bobby Robson and his assistant Don Howe took the Tottenham utility player Gary Stevens to one side and asked him whether he had ever played a man-marking role, the idea being that he would tail Maradona for the game, denying him the space and the freedom to play his normal, usually destructive game. Eventually, though, Robson plumped for the PFA Player of the Year, Peter Reid. 'There were a lot of discussions and doubts about how we as a team were going to deal with Maradona,' explains Stevens. 'In hindsight, I think there was probably too much focus, too much emphasis on him.'

Or, as it transpired, not enough. Almost four years to the day after the Falklands war had ended in bloody defeat for General Galtieri's military junta, and twenty years since their infamous clash in the World Cup at Wembley, Argentina lined up against England with fire in their hearts and revenge at the forefront of their minds.

Throughout the build-up to the game, Bobby Robson had been at pains to point out to the media that any questions referring to the Falklands War would be given short shrift. To further reinforce the message, the FA chairman Sir Bert Millichip even ventured into the England dressing room shortly before the match and, at a time when the team needed to focus on the World Cup quarter-final, he instead embarked on a lecture about the importance of international relations and how the players should refrain from mentioning the conflict. 'If Brian Clough had been the manager,' reflects Terry Fenwick, 'he would have told him to fuck off.'

It would be a nervy, unadventurous first half at the Estadio Azteca, Mexico City, with few chances for either side. England, despite the noon heat, seemed to be coping not just with Maradona but with the conditions as well and as the teams went in at the interval, there was nothing between them.

Six minutes into the second half, though, it was Argentina who made the breakthrough, albeit in the most controversial fashion imaginable. As the South Americans pressed deep into the England half, Steve Hodge, the left-sided midfielder, attempted a clearance but succeeded only in miscueing the ball back towards Peter Shilton in the England goal. As the ball looped up temptingly and Shilton came to punch it clear, Diego Maradona, just 5ft 6ins tall, leapt with him and, realizing he had no chance of getting his head to the ball, simply guided it into the net with his left hand instead. Expecting the referee's whistle to blow and a free-kick to be awarded, the England players turned around, only to find that the Tunisian referee, Ali Bennaceur, had failed to spot the infringement and the 'goal', much to the bewilderment of the England team, was given.

England's central defender Terry Fenwick was the closest outfield player to the incident. 'I could have challenged for it but I left it for Peter Shilton because I thought there was no way Maradona could beat him to it,' he recalls. 'It was disbelief really. The first thing I did was look at the referee and he was just looking at the linesman, and as he started back-pedalling he was still looking at his linesman waiting for one of them to make the call. Truth is, they bottled it.'

The feeling in the England dugout, meanwhile, was one of equal incredulity. 'The reaction on the bench was something's gone wrong,' says Gary Stevens. 'There was no way he could head that ball or outjump Peter Shilton's fist. We were probably eighty or ninety yards away in the dugouts so I couldn't put my hand on my heart and say that I knew he handled the ball but then when you see the reaction of Peter Shilton, Terry Fenwick and the players on the pitch, chasing after the referee and running over to the linesman and indicating that he'd handballed it, I knew he had … Let's just say there were a few choice words used.'

As the England players pursued Ali Bennaceur like fox on a hunt, and Diego Maradona ran to the corner flag, summoning his team-mates over to him to celebrate with him, it was fast becoming clear that England had been the unwitting victim of a massive injustice. Try as they might, though, the goal would stand. 'I started remonstrating with him but then he went for his cards and as I'd already been booked in the game [for fouling Maradona] and didn't want to be sent off, I left it,' adds Fenwick.

But if Maradona's first goal had been the kind of sucker punch to have English fans reaching for the revolver (and Scottish fans crying with laughter), then his second just four minutes later was nothing short of miraculous. Picking up the ball inside his own half, he spun past a bewildered Peter Reid and left what seemed to be the rest of the England team for dead. On and on he went, weaving his way past Hoddle, past Fenwick, past Sansom, past Butcher. Even at the end of such a long and winding run, Maradona could have been forgiven for shooting at the earliest opportunity. Instead, he advanced on goal and as Shilton rushed from his line to thwart him, he still had the imagination (and the energy) to drag the ball round him with his left foot before steering it home.

'People often say why didn't someone just bring him down but Terry Fenwick, who was my room-mate at the World Cup, had already been booked so he would have been sent off,' points out Gary Stevens. '[But] I can't help thinking what might have been if I'd been man-marking Maradona.'

Fenwick, meanwhile, maintains that there was nothing any of the players could have done. 'Would I have done anything differently? Maybe I should have pushed him across but he went through on the inside and the rest is history,' he says with a shrug. '[But] for years after the World Cup, all I seemed to hear was how it was Terry Fenwick's fault and that I should have taken him out when I had the chance. Slowly, a few more of the England players from that day have started accepting their share of the responsibility. I'm glad to get that monkey off my back, I can tell you.'

Gallantly, England would mount a comeback, with John Barnes and Chris Waddle coming on for Trevor Steven and Peter Reid. With nine minutes remaining, Gary Lineker pulled a goal back, his sixth of the tournament, getting on the end of a perfect cross from Barnes. Moments later, Barnes did it again, sending in another tantalizing centre from the left wing that required only the merest touch from Lineker to bring England level. Miraculously, though, the ball stayed out and England, undone partly by deception, partly by genius, were out. 'Take the two goals away and Argentina barely had another chance,' insists Terry Fenwick. 'By the end we were really on top. John Barnes had made one goal for Gary Lineker and when he did it again we thought we'd equalized. You know, if Gary Lineker had been a bit braver, you know, a little bit of blood and guts, we would have equalized and from then on there's only one winner.'

At the final whistle, the Argentinian team celebrated as though they had won the tournament itself and while they would have to wait just seven more days before they could claim their second World Cup, beating West Germany 3–2 in a thrilling final (with Maradona being named the Player of the Tournament), the English players were heading home. On the pitch, one of the men left for dead by Maradona during his second goal, Aston Villa's Steve Hodge, approached the diminutive genius and, as England's left-back that day, Kenny Sansom, reveals, exchanged shirts. 'We said "What do you want his shirt for? He's a cheat," and started having a go at him,' he explains, before adding, 'now it's worth

£250k, so we all wish we'd got it!' In the days that followed England's controversial exit from the World Cup, Maradona's insistence that he had done nothing wrong irked not only the English squad but the entire English nation, while his belief that the goal was 'a little with the head of Maradona and a little with the hand of God' would also inflame the situation. Bobby Robson wasn't convinced, preferring to credit the goal to 'the hand of a rascal' rather than that of the Almighty. In 2002 Maradona's goal – his second one – was voted the Greatest Goal in the History of the World Cup, by a poll on the FIFA website. Whatever you felt about his first 'goal', it was impossible to disagree. Even Gary Lineker, who had watched the goal from the other end of the Estadio Azteca pitch, reflected that it was 'probably the one and only time in my whole career I felt like applauding the opposition scoring a goal'.

It was another deeply disappointing exit for England, not because they had failed to perform (as they had in 1982) but because they had been cheated out of the tournament by almost laughable incompetence. Some England players, like Terry Butcher, still bear the mental scars from that day. In November 2008 he revealed to *The Times* that he and his England team-mates debated whether or not they should get Maradona and 'fill him in' when he was celebrating in the doping room after the game. And when he was asked about Steve Hodge and the shirt that he swapped with Maradona that day, he declared, 'That shirt is the last thing I wanted. I would not even clean my car with it.'

Others, like Butcher's central defensive partner that day, Terry Fenwick, are prepared to let bygones be bygones. 'I think he was, without doubt, the world's best player over two decades, but like so many players of his type, he had his problems too. I can never agree with the Hand of God goal, because it's just not in my nature, but I do appreciate what he achieved in the game. The man's been through a lot and he deserves a chance now.'

England returned home, via Miami, as heroes, as they often do, albeit ones that had failed once more to live up to the expectations of their nation. Whatever spin you put on their exit – misfortune, the unbearable conditions, Peter Shilton's peculiar inability to outjump a man some six inches smaller than him, etc. – it would now be four long years before they could try yet again to scale the heights of Moore and Charlton, Hurst and Peters.

Given the nature of the team's exit from the finals and the collective sense of injustice that fans and players alike felt, Sir Bert Millichip and the Football Association decided not to seek to replace Bobby Robson on his return. For Robson, the pressure was now off. Given time by the FA and a break by a tabloid press who now had a new target, Diego Maradona, firmly in their sights, he could look forward to building on the relative success of the World Cup, and set about creating a team that could mount a serious challenge at the European Championship in West Germany.

But success, of course, was relative. A valiant defeat at the hands, quite literally, of the world's greatest player was nothing to be ashamed of, but would other footballing superpowers, say Germany or Italy or Brazil, celebrate such mediocrity? It was a certain sign that while England's management and players could talk the talk with the best of them, they still had some way to go before they could walk the walk as well.

England's progress would be maintained throughout the qualification for the 1988 European Championship. Confident, untroubled and unbeaten, it would prove to be one of England's less fraught campaigns. Indeed, the only point they would drop would be in the away fixture against Turkey. Six months later, as if to emphasize that the result was little more than a blip, Turkey were beaten 8–0 at Wembley, with a hat-trick for Gary Lineker, a brace for John Barnes, and goals for Bryan Robson, Peter Beardsley and Neil Webb.

Come the European Championship finals in West Germany, Robson made only a handful of changes to the squad that had run Argentina so close in Mexico City. Limited to a total of twenty players, rather than the twenty-two he enjoyed at the World Cup two years earlier, the England manager chose to bolster his defence, especially as Terry Butcher was back in Britain still recovering from a broken leg sustained playing for his club, Glasgow Rangers. Three central defenders came in: Everton's Dave Watson, Mark Wright of Derby County and Arsenal's twenty-one-year-old stopper Tony Adams. There was a place for Chelsea's Australian-born left-back Tony Dorigo and even the midfield recruits, Liverpool's Steve McMahon and Nottingham Forest's Neil Webb, were players ideally suited to breaking up the opposition play.

Strength in depth at the back, and in Lineker, Waddle, Beardsley and Barnes – Bobby Robson called them 'the best front four in Europe' – up front, suggested England had a great chance at a tournament in which they had traditionally failed to impress.

Ahead of them were group games against the Republic of Ireland, now managed by England's World Cup-winning centre-half Jack Charlton, the Netherlands and the Soviet Union. For the Irish, it would be the first ever appearance in the finals of a major tournament and it was largely down to the revolution that Charlton had enacted since he took over from Eoin Hand in 1986. Realizing that there was a dearth of talent available to him in the Emerald Isle, Charlton had crossed the Irish Sea and started recruiting British players, especially those unlikely to get into their national teams. All they needed was an Irish grandparent and, according to FIFA rules, so long as they hadn't played representative football for another country, they were free to wear the shamrock with pride. And how they came. There was the Barnsley-born centre-half Mick McCarthy and the Welsh-born midfielder Kevin Sheedy, there was the Brummie striker David Kelly and the most Liverpudlian man on Merseyside, John Aldridge.

With an Englishman at the helm, and a team packed with adopted Irishmen, Charlton had created a unit that was the most English team in international football, not because of the personnel he had employed, but because of the manner in which they played the game. Tough and direct, they were one of the most accomplished exponents of the long-ball game and, imbued with an indomitable team spirit, they were resolute and difficult to break down. And so what if they weren't the most attractive team in world football to watch? Nobody cared, least of all the thousands of loyal fans clad in emerald-green that followed them across the globe.

Inevitably, it would be one of Charlton's 'foreign' recruits, Liverpool's Glaswegian midfielder Ray Houghton, who would make the difference against England at Stuttgart's Neckarstadion. Just six minutes into the game, Houghton had taken advantage of some shoddy defending by the English defence and looped a header over and beyond Peter Shilton into the English net.

It was a testament to the resolve of Charlton's team of triers that they held on for the rest of the game to record their first victory in a major tournament on their very first appearance, and this despite England having eighteen chances in comparison to just four for the Irish. That it was against England, well, that just made it all the sweeter.

Six days after the Ireland game, England would be going home, bottom of their group and without a point. They deserved no more. A 3–1 defeat by tournament favourites Holland had seen as almost perfect a display of the art of striking as one could imagine, by the young AC Milan forward Marco van Basten. Three times he scored against England, and three times he turned the English defence inside out. Later, in the final of the tournament against the Soviet Union, he would score a volley that defied belief and most of the principles of physics too, as Holland deservedly went on to win the title.

For Peter Shilton, winning his one hundredth cap for England, it was a game to forget. Yes, he made some critical saves, but standing behind a defensive line being ripped asunder by the potent Dutch strikeforce of Ruud Gullit and van Basten, he was unable to keep them at bay. The game over, Shilton's misery would later be compounded when he learned he had been dropped for the final group game against Russia in favour of his long-time understudy, the Glasgow Rangers keeper Chris Woods. 'Devastated' and 'totally nonplussed' was how he would describe his reaction to being dropped, even though the game, as far as England was concerned, meant nothing. Having lost their opening two matches, England were already out of the competition. They were playing for pride, something that had been conspicuous by its absence in the tournament to date.

The change made little difference. Three days later against the USSR, England capitulated yet again. In his fifty-third and what turned out to be his final appearance for his country, Glenn Hoddle had a game to forget, surrendering possession in midfield and allowing the Soviet Union to score on the break, but then so did the rest of the England team, especially Gary Lineker, who, it later transpired, had been suffering from hepatitis for the duration of the championship. Going down 3–1 again, it signalled the depressing end of a wretched event for Robson's England.

It was particularly galling for the captain Bryan Robson. Plagued by injury in his last tournament appearance, he had come into the competition in the best shape in years, only for the team to implode. 'We knew we had underachieved,' he said, 'and I was particularly hacked off because I never went through a tournament fitter than I was in Germany.'

Again, though, England's tournament would be overshadowed by more much-publicized outbreaks of rioting. Wherever they went – Cologne, Stuttgart, Frankfurt, Düsseldorf – hundreds of English fans, many wearing T-shirts emblazoned with the slogan 'Invasion of Germany 1988', seemed intent on destruction and violence, clashing with right-wing German fans and the police. The arrests ran into the hundreds, the damage into millions. Moreover, just as there was some suggestion that UEFA would consider lifting their ban on English clubs in Europe, now, with yet more images of drunken football fans rampaging through otherwise peaceful foreign towns being broadcast across the world, the idea that English football could soon rejoin the European football fold seemed further away than ever.

In his autobiography, *Robbo*, the England skipper Bryan Robson also revealed that the fighting in Germany in 1988 didn't just start on the streets and end with water cannons. With the competition over for England, a group of the players had made their way to the hotel bar to drown their sorrows and drink to forget what had, in truth, been an abject performance. As the players conducted their own inquest into what went wrong in West Germany, Peter Shilton, still seething at being dropped for the final game and angry that the outfield players had produced their worst showing in living memory, began taunting Bryan Robson, questioning the validity of his 'Captain Marvel' nickname and accusing him of being a 'bottler'. It was too much for Robson, who had grown tired of Shilton's propensity to pass the buck when things went wrong and he lashed out, punching the veteran keeper as he sat on a bar-stool. Undignified and juvenile, it was the culmination of a rotten week for England. As two of the most senior players in the squad came to blows in some anonymous hotel bar, it seemed impossible that this England team could ever regroup in time to make a decent fist of the World Cup qualifying campaign that was to begin in under four months' time.

The nature of England's exit at the European Championship and the depressing re-emergence of their hooligan tendency had all but erased the positive steps the team had taken two years earlier in Mexico. Now, more than ever, the press seemed determined to force a change in the England management. The headlines were merciless, unforgiving and deeply personal.

Two years earlier they had a prospering cheat to harangue; now the focus had returned to Bobby Robson. 'Win and you are a hero. Lose and you are a prat – and that was one of the more polite descriptions of me,' Robson told the *Daily Mirror*'s Bob Harris in 1996. 'It became even worse after we lost all three games at the European Championship in Germany in 1988 … Newspaper campaigns, stories about your private life, your own fans abusing you at Wembley. It was all very vitriolic and not the sort of thing any club manager has to face, no matter how badly his team are doing nor how much the fans want him out. But it still didn't stop me travelling on the Tube from Liverpool Street to Lancaster Gate!'

Ever the Englishman, though, Robson had already spoken with Bert Millichip after the European Championship and had offered to resign, but his employers had sent him on his way, instructing him to prepare the England team for the World Cup finals. 'I thought my time was up,' Robson wrote in his autobiography, *Farewell But Not Goodbye*. 'I thought that by offering myself at the guillotine I was giving them the chance to let me go, but they were as solid as teak … Had they said yes, I would have walked out of Lancaster Gate feeling I had fulfilled my duty to the country.'

If the cheerless display in the European Championship had suggested that England were a team out of sorts and out of the World Cup reckoning, the months immediately after the tournament did little to hint at anything approaching a recovery. While new faces in the team, such as Nottingham Forest's stylish defender Des Walker and the uncompromising left-back Stuart Pearce, were welcome, there had been a discernible lack of interest in their games. For the friendly against Denmark at Wembley on 14 September just 3,000 tickets were sold in advance. Eventually, over 25,000 fans would watch England's 1–0 win but it was still a worrying sign that, after the shambles in Germany, the appetite for Bobby Robson's England wasn't just on the wane but verging on complete apathy.

If there was one man who had the energy and enthusiasm to help mount a revival in the fortunes of the national team, it was the player who came on for his debut appearance against Denmark as an eighty-fifth-minute substitute – Paul Gascoigne. Signed by Tottenham Hotspur from his hometown club Newcastle United that summer for a British record transfer fee of £2.3 million, Gascoigne – Gazza to his friends, and, for that matter, the rest of the world – had emerged as one of the most exciting young talents in the English game and had been voted the PFA Young Player of the Year for the 1987–88 season. Gifted on one hand, juvenile on the other, he was a bristling, bustling dynamo, with an eye for goal and a penchant for practical jokes. And Mars Bars. Prophetically, his team-mate at Newcastle, John Bailey, described Gascoigne as 'a loony with a fast mouth', adding that, 'he's either going to be one of the greats or finish up at forty bitter about wasting such talent.'

England's torpor, though, would continue. Without Gascoigne and his sumptuous array of skills for the opening World Cup qualifier at Wembley against Sweden on 19 October, England were shapeless, unconvincing and bereft of imagination and while they would salvage a point with a goalless draw, the knives were already out for Bobby Robson. At the press conference after the game, Robson seemed taken aback to the point where he managed to forget the result and the name of the opposition. 'It wasn't my fault we lost,' he insisted, adding that, 'We made all the running against a hard-working Denmark side.'

A month later, England were lured to the Middle East on the promise of a bumper payday and a trip on Concorde to play a pointless friendly against Saudi Arabia in Riyadh. It would be a contest where only a second-half Tony Adams goal saved them from the most humiliating defeat of Robson's tenure. Cue one almighty press backlash. 'England Mustafa new boss,' screamed the *Sun*, next to a photograph of Robson with a fez on his head. 'In The Name Of Allah, GO!' said the *Daily Mirror*. While the match was, perhaps, the nadir for Robson, the reviews now seemed to be even more personal, even more angry, presumably because, for once, the journalists were not permitted to share the flight with the England party.

It would be a long, cold winter for Bobby Robson. But even when his team returned to action, some three months after the Saudi Arabia debacle, the knives were not only still out, but they had been sharpened. At the friendly against Greece in Athens, the *Mirror*'s football correspondent Nigel Clarke got off the plane and announced to the television cameras that he was 'here to fry Bobby Robson'. Faced with a tabloid press more intent than ever on removing him from office, Robson kept his head down and England escaped with 2–1 victory.

The win against Greece would mark a turning point of sorts for Robson and England, and the team would embark on an impressive fourteen-game unbeaten run. Learning to ignore the bugles and the beagles of the media, Robson had refocused on England's attempts to qualify for Italia 90 and achieved his aim without being beaten and without conceding a single goal. It was typical England. Just as you felt that you had the right and the inclination to abandon them, they came roaring back, and with a gutsy display here and a few goals there, they get you right back onside again.

That run, of course, would be interrupted by the most shocking disaster in the history of British football. At the FA Cup semi-final between Liverpool and Nottingham Forest at Hillsborough on 15 April 1989, thousands of Liverpool fans had congregated at the Leppings Lane end of the ground ahead of the game. With kick-off fast approaching and a bottleneck developing at the turnstiles, the South Yorkshire police opted to open a set of gates to ease the crowding and ensure that the fans got in. Inside the ground, however, the two central pens were already dangerously overcrowded and when the fresh influx of people tried to enter, many fans found themselves crushed, with those at the front penned in by the same fences that had been erected to keep supporters off the pitch.

In total, ninety-six people would die, with another 766 injured. In an age when trouble at football grounds invariably meant hooliganism, the Hillsborough Disaster was totally, tragically different. In time, on the recommendation of the report of the official inquiry chaired by Lord Taylor, perimeter fencing and standing terraces would become a thing of the past and plush, new and entirely soulless all-seater stadiums would be introduced across Britain. But on that April Saturday, English football changed for ever.

On 9 December 1989 the Football Association headed en masse to Rome for the draw for the following summer's World Cup finals. Joining England at the tournament would be three teams making their debut in the competition: Costa Rica, Jack Charlton's Republic of Ireland and the United Arab Emirates. Also invited to the twenty-four-team party would be the United States, back in the event for the first time since they famously beat England in Belo Horizonte, Brazil, back in 1950.

After a stirring performance from the tenor Luciano Pavarotti, a performer who would become synonymous with the tournament, the draw began. What seemed like several days later, Bobby Robson eventually learned the names of the other teams in Group F – the Republic of Ireland, Holland and Egypt. It was a tough draw for Robson. Ireland under Jack Charlton had become one of England's bogey teams over recent years, while the Dutch were never going to be anything other than a stern test. In Egypt, meanwhile, reaction to what was an almost impossible task for them was muted. The *Egyptian Gazette*, for instance, chose to profile the England manager ahead of their clash the following summer. 'Eighteen years as a profession player in Framham and West Bromwitch Albion,' it read. 'A manager for Ibswich … and England's managing job after the World Cup finals in Spain when Mr Wood Green retired.'

England's fourteen-game unbeaten run would finally come to an end against Uruguay in a friendly at Wembley just three weeks before their first match in the finals against the Republic of Ireland in Cagliari, but while Robson's team had grown in confidence and restored some pride to the national game, not everybody at the Football Association was convinced that Bobby Robson was the man to take England forward once the World Cup finals had ended.

Before the event kicked off, Robson had been summoned by Sir Bert Millichip and the FA's international committee and told that, despite qualifying for the World Cup in an almost faultless fashion, they would not be renewing his contract once England's interest in Italia 90 was over.

Robson was stunned. After all the years of abuse from journalists and supporters, from ex-players and managers, his time was finally up. Faced with impending unemployment, and with the

Football Association's blessing, Robson explored his options, eventually settling on an offer from the Dutch club PSV Eindhoven.

Initially, both Robson and the FA had agreed to announce his departure after the World Cup. The press, however, got their stories wrong. Many papers labelled Robson a traitor for leaving his country on the verge of the biggest tournament of them all, when the truth was that his departure was not of his choosing. Later, Robson would sue the now defunct *Today* newspaper for their accusations, settling out of court.

Infuriated and disappointed, Robson would lead England into the World Cup with, as he said, a 'stigma attached to my reputation'.

He needn't have worried. In a little over a month, that reputation would be unimpeachable.

Qualifying for the World Cup finals was one arduous task that the England team had had little trouble negotiating. Actually getting to Italy, though, would prove to be more problematic. As the team prepared to fly out to their base on the island of Sardinia – FIFA had placed the English there to keep the numbskull division of their fans out of reach and out of trouble – Paul Gascoigne discovered that he had left his passport back in Newcastle, prompting a frantic and ultimately successful bid to have it delivered to him in London.

Life was never simple when Paul Gascoigne was around. Funny, yes, but not simple. The life and soul of the party, of any party, he was a hyperactive bundle of nerves, a man incapable of behaving himself and seemingly immune to fatigue. Bobby Robson would famously describe him as 'daft as a brush', although the truth was that brushes had better table manners.

When Gascoigne was around, you were never far from a joke or a jape, some mishap or mayhem. In the build-up to the World Cup in 1990, he was at his most mischievous. When the organizers of Italia 90's TV coverage had the splendid idea of augmenting every team's line-up with a headshot of each player mouthing his own name, Gascoigne subverted the process by, instead, mouthing 'Fucking Wanker'. The BBC had to use it all the way through the tournament.

Then, just seventy-two hours before their first match, Gascoigne, the skipper Bryan Robson, Steve Bull, Terry Butcher, Steve McMahon, John Barnes and the Chrises, Waddle and Woods, decided to repair to a local bar in the village of Pula for one final drink and some good-natured arm-wrestling with the locals. Returning to the hotel, the group went to Gascoigne's room and, as Bryan Robson would later describe it, began 'larking about'. The high jinks continued until Robson tried to tip Gascoigne off his bed, only succeeding in catching his own big toe on the corner of the bed and ripping his entire toenail off. With the blood pouring from his toe, Robson desperately tried to stem the flow by sticking his foot in the bidet, but to no avail. When Chris Waddle saw the carnage, he summoned the England physios.

When Bobby Robson found out about his captain's injury and that the players had been drinking, he was furious, not least because Robson would now require an injection to get him through the first game against Ireland. As for Gascoigne, he told his manager that Robson had merely been washing his feet in the bidet when he had slipped. In other words, it was nothing other than a freak accident. Unimpressed, Bobby Robson would warn Gascoigne as to his future conduct, although he might as well have been talking to the wall. A couple of days later, Gascoigne was seen diving into the hotel swimming pool, naked but for some strategically placed toilet paper.

Thanks to the tireless efforts of Paul Gascoigne, the mood in the England camp at their Is Molas complex was exceptionally good and the players passed the downtime playing cards, reading or watching films. Bryan Robson, for instance, would set a new record, managing five movies in one day. By the time the game against the Republic of Ireland arrived, England were rested and ready. Against them were the same familiar players that they played against week in week out in the English First Division: Staunton, Moran, McGrath, Houghton, Sheedy. There would be no surprises from the Irish. Under instructions to launch ball after ball into Peter Shilton's penalty area, they played the game the way they always had under Jack Charlton – fast, frenetic and uncompromisingly direct.

England would make the perfect start, with Gary Lineker opening the scoring after just eight minutes. But with the game seemingly heading England's way, second-half substitute Steve McMahon lost possession, allowing the ball to fall for Kevin Sheedy whose famous left foot wasted no time in exacting the ultimate punishment. To the neutral, a draw seemed to be a fair result from a match that was tense and hard-fought.

Again, however, the reaction to the outcome of what was always going to be an awkward encounter was bewilderingly hysterical; the *Sun* even demanded the withdrawal of the team from the competition under the headline 'Bring 'em Home'.

You had to laugh. Or perhaps despair. Only in England, and only with a tabloid press as venomous and vindictive as ours, would a draw in the first of three games in one of the toughest groups in the competition justify the immediate removal of the team. Still, at least England weren't Scotland. On the same day they had lost their first game to the minnows Costa Rica.

While the media's reaction to England's less than startling opener was undoubtedly over the top, it was true that they had underperformed against the Irish. Too many times they could not find an answer to the stifling tactics of Charlton's gang. Bogged down in a midfield battle with little or no end product, it was clear that a change would be needed against the talented Dutch in their next game.

In 1988 at the European Championship, Holland and their strike duo of Ruud Gullit and Marco van Basten had memorably carved England's flat back four to pieces, embarrassing the central defenders Tony Adams and Mark Wright time and time again. Fearing the same outcome, England decided on a bold new strategy. Myriad rumours still circulate about who was responsible for the change in formation. Some stories have it that a group of senior players approached Robson and demanded the switch;

Bobby Robson always insisted that was emphatically not the case. 'It's a ludicrous concept,' he said. 'The manager who allows his players to determine the shape or composition of his team is dead in the water.'

For their next game, England would now play a sweeper system with Mark Wright in the libero role, supported by Terry Butcher and Des Walker. Stuart Pearce and Paul Parker, meanwhile, would act as wing-backs, with a licence to attack.

The shift in emphasis would prove the making of the England team. Freed from the constraints of their traditional and predictable 4-4-2, they coped effortlessly with the threat of the Dutch and but for two disallowed goals, one from Lineker and one from Pearce, they could and should have run out comfortable winners. Gascoigne too was in his element. Tirelessly probing the Dutch defence with his clever passes and darting runs, he even had time to ruffle Ruud Gullit's dreadlocks and ask Marco van Basten just how much he was earning these days.

While it was another draw, it was nevertheless a performance that augured well for the remainder of the tournament. The only negative from the game was the second-half withdrawal of the luckless captain Bryan Robson with an Achilles tendon injury that put him out of the World Cup and on a flight back to Britain.

England's place in the last sixteen would be assured with a 1–0 win over Egypt just five days later, a glancing Mark Wright header securing the points and ensuring England topped their group. Next up were the Belgians, a side who had come through a tough group containing Spain, Uruguay and South Korea. In the days leading up to the match, the England keeper Peter Shilton had told Bobby Robson that when England's tournament was finally over, so too would be his international career. Now over forty, Shilton had made his England debut back at the beginning of the 1970s and two decades and four World Cups for England later, his body and mind were telling him to call it a day.

If Shilton thought he could slip quietly into retirement with a golden handshake and a carriage clock, he was wrong. There was much, much more football to play, starting with Belgium. For a country so small, Belgium had an unhealthy and dangerous number of world-class players in their ranks, like Frankie van der Elst, Enzo Scifo, Eric Gerets and the imposing striker Jan Ceulemans. Once more, however, it would be Paul Gascoigne, ably assisted by Bryan Robson's stand-in David Platt, who would see England through. Goalless at ninety minutes, the game was apparently destined for penalties. That is until the last few moments of extra-time. Winning a free-kick midway in the Belgian half, Gascoigne floated a tempting chip into the opposition area and watched as David Platt, with his back to goal, swivelled round and hooked the sweetest of volleys past Michel Preud'homme in the Belgian goal. With no time for their opponents to respond, England now found themselves in the quarter-finals for a game against the tournament's surprise package – there's always one – Cameroon.

By now, there was no stopping Paul Gascoigne. Giddy with excitement and enlivened by the rave reviews he was garnering for his performances to date, he was a man on a mission, not just to help guide England to a second World Cup victory but also to enjoy himself, even if team rules and the management frowned upon that kind of thing. It was as though he had cast himself as the Cooler King of the England set-up and no matter how you tried to curtail his extracurricular activities, he would always find a way to break free.

On the eve of the quarter-final, for instance, Gascoigne, Waddle, Barnes and Bull snuck out of their new hotel in Bologna in a bid to find refreshment. Mission accomplished, they returned to the hotel to find Bobby Robson waiting at the front door. Spotting him from a distance, Gascoigne whizzed around the outside of the hotel, found a side door and pretended to be asleep when Robson came calling at his room soon after.

If the England camp appeared to be like some secondary school trip overseas, that's because it was. Long spells of inactivity – they weren't allowed to play golf or tennis because of the exertion involved – were only ever punctuated by the occasional movie or video game or, inevitably, Paul Gascoigne attempting a triple pike with tuck into the hotel pool. Curfews meant nothing. Punishments were futile. But what if Gascoigne hadn't been there with his never-ending antics and his ceaseless pursuit of fun? What then?

For all the grief and worry he caused him, Bobby Robson knew that without Gazza, England lacked that crucial spark, that invention, which could take them further in the competition. As the tournament progressed and England grew stronger and more confident, so Gascoigne blossomed. Where he had begun the World Cup as a player still unproven at the highest level, he had matured – correction, developed – into one of the most creative, inventive players in the modern game. This, it appeared, was Gazza's stage.

He was no less energetic in the quarter-final against Cameroon. Featuring the ageless talents of Roger Milla, a man who had won the world over with a distinctive goal celebration that involved running to the corner flag and, well, dancing with it, Cameroon were a strong, athletic side and, as the reigning world champions Argentina would doubtless testify after they had lost to them in the opening game of Italia 90, could play a bit too.

Despite the England team's scout, the Leeds United manager Howard Wilkinson, reporting that a game against the Africans was as a good as a bye to the next round, England, like Argentina, found Cameroon to be tough and uncompromising. At ninety minutes the game was poised at 2–2. England having taken the lead from a textbook downward header from the increasingly influential David Platt, Cameroon had levelled on the hour mark, Gascoigne having conceded a penalty converted by Kunde, before taking the lead just minutes later through the substitute Ekeke. With just seven minutes left on the clock, England were facing one of the most sensational exits in World Cup history.

It wasn't to be. A Gary Lineker penalty – England's first since Bryan Robson's against Israel in February 1986 – was awarded when he was brought down by Kunde, and duly dispatched. For the second successive game, England headed into extra-time. As it had against the Belgians, the first period of extra-time came and went, and, if anything, it was the Africans that looked the more likely winners. Mark Wright was suffering from a gash to the head, Des Walker was limping, Peter Beardsley anonymous. Then, on cue, Paul Gascoigne produced a pass from within his own half that ripped open the Cameroon defence and set his Tottenham Hotspur team-mate Gary Lineker through on goal. As the England striker advanced, he took the ball round the Cameroon goalkeeper Thomas N'Kono, but as he did so, N'Kono's momentum took his legs away. From just two penalties in eight years, England now had their second in less than half an hour.

For England's first penalty that night Gary Lineker had opted for placement rather than power, tucking the ball to N'Kono's left as the keeper went the other way. But now, with tired legs and shredded nerves, there was no room for subtlety. Instead, Lineker simply smashed the ball low and true down the middle of the goal as N'Kono, guessing a repeat performance, dived to his left. England, the Three Lions, had squeezed past the so-called 'Indomitable Lions' of Cameroon and become the first England team in history to reach a World Cup semi-final on foreign soil.

For the Queens Park Rangers full-back Paul Parker, it's an achievement that will never lose its lustre. Alongside Paul Gascoigne, his performance at Italia 90 would prove to be one of the most accomplished. Originally picked for the squad as cover for Glasgow Rangers' Gary Stevens, he had missed the first game against Ireland but had been selected ahead of Stevens for England's second game against the Netherlands. From then on, he was ever present for England in the competition. 'You know, there aren't many players in this country who can say they've played in a World Cup semi-final overseas and I'm extremely proud to be one of them,' he reflects. 'I look upon it as a bronze medal and every year that goes by without England winning a major tournament it just gets bigger and bigger.'

Bobby Robson, meanwhile, paid tribute to the opposition and the 'outstanding game' they had played, although he must have known that his team had come within a whisker of elimination.

He was right. The game had been the match of the World Cup finals to date, but luck had been on Robson's side that night in Naples. Ahead of him now, however, was a semi-final against West Germany, and he – and England – would need more than good fortune to see them through to the final.

That night, England's celebrations would be muted, a sure sign that they knew they had ridden their luck against Cameroon to emerge with their chance of winning the World Cup still intact. The following day, Terry Butcher was relaxing by the hotel pool, reading, when he was interrupted by Bobby Robson. The England manager sat down, informed the centre-half of his plans for the semi-final against West Germany and asked what he thought of them. Butcher thought long and hard, and gave his considered opinion. When he looked up Robson was asleep on his sun-lounger. He laughed. If the players felt exhausted from consecutive games that had gone into extra-time, here was conclusive proof that the manager too was beginning to feel the strain.

Robson wasn't alone. As each round was safely negotiated, the idea that the Football Association had already removed a manager who may have been on the verge of winning the World Cup became an increasingly awkward situation to handle. Meanwhile, Robson's new employers at PSV Eindhoven must surely have felt they had pulled off the coup of the century. Something, somewhere, had to give.

Ahead of England, almost inevitably, was the team that always seemed to come between them and glory, West Germany. Coached by the man who had lost at Wembley in 1966 but then triumphed in León in the World Cup quarter-final in 1970, Franz Beckenbauer, they were the complete footballing machine, and in their captain Lothar Matthäus possessed a midfield player as good as any in the world, capable of dictating games single-handedly and scoring spectacular long-range goals to boot. Upfront, meanwhile, they had Rudi Völler and Jürgen Klinsmann, one of the most dynamic strike partnerships in the game.

Faced with the challenge of nullifying the threat that Matthäus certainly posed, Paul Gascoigne assured his manager that he was up to the job and set about preparing for England's biggest game in almost a quarter of a century in the only way he knew how. The night before the semi-final, with the rest of the England team tucked up in bed, dreaming of World Cup glory, Gascoigne, yet again, sneaked out of his room and began playing tennis with some American tourists on the hotel's floodlit courts. When he heard Bobby Robson prowling the hotel grounds, looking for him, he dropped his racket and sprinted back to his room, pretending to be asleep when the manager finally came calling.

On the evening of the match, Turin's Stadio delle Alpi, home to both Juventus and Torino, was awash with Union flags and Crosses of St George. By now, England were a settled side. David Platt had more than filled the void left by Bryan Robson's premature departure, Chris Waddle was becoming increasingly influential and the much-debated defensive system of employing three centre-halves was becoming second nature.

The first half began with England in command. From the off, Gascoigne seemed intent on imposing himself on the game. In the opening minute, he had a volley saved by Illgner in the German goal and later he would even nutmeg the man Bobby Robson had tasked him with marking, Lothar Matthäus. With the bulk of possession, England would enjoy chance after chance and when the half-time whistle sounded they could count themselves unlucky not to be leading.

It would be Germany, though, that would make the breakthrough fifteen minutes into the second half. When Stuart Pearce was penalized for a foul on the Cologne midfielder Thomas Hässler on the edge of the penalty area, up stepped the left-back Andreas Brehme to take the free-kick. As he did so, Paul Parker broke from the defensive wall to try and charge it down but succeeded only in deflecting the ball high into the air to loop over the head of the frantically back-pedalling Peter Shilton into the England goal.

England continued to press but to no avail. Off came Terry Butcher, on came Trevor Steven, and the team reverted to 4-4-2 one more. It was a tactical switch by Bobby Robson that would pay dividends. With ten minutes to play, and with England's luck on the verge of running out, they finally got their reward. A through ball from the outstanding Paul Parker dropped perfectly for Gary Lineker inside the German penalty area. Controlling it with his knee, he switched the ball to his left foot and hit a low cross shot through the sea of German defenders and into the corner of Bodo Illgner's net. At last, a deserved equalizer and the sense of relief in the England camp was palpable.

In the Stadio delle Alpi the England fans erupted, while back home in the UK a record television audience of 30 million laughed, cried and embraced. Surely, now there could only be one winner.

The final whistle blew, and another game, England's third in a row, had gone into extra time. Robson walked on to the pitch to rally his troops, while the physios Fred Street and Norman Medhurst handed out massages to the fatigued and the flagging. If England had harboured any doubts about their right to be in the semi-finals against a football nation as powerful as Germany, it hadn't shown. Ahead of them was thirty more minutes of football, thirty minutes that could end in triumph or despair.

As the first half of extra-time drew to an end, Gascoigne was still full of running. He careered around the pitch, winning tackles, setting up chances and asking questions of the German defence. But when he lost possession on the halfway line, he threw himself into a challenge on Germany's Thomas Berthold, but rather than win the ball back, he simply clattered the defender and watched as he collapsed dramatically in a heap on the turf as if he had been felled by lightning.

Though he held his hands up and apologized immediately, Gascoigne knew he was in trouble. Having already been booked in the tournament, a second caution would mean an automatic one-match ban for the next game – the World Cup final. When the Brazilian referee Jose Ramiz Wright reached for his pocket and pulled out a yellow card, it was too much for Gascoigne.

With one poorly timed tackle, Paul Gascoigne's dreams had been shattered. Now, if England were to win the game and progress to the final, they would have to contest it without the most creative, most intuitive player in their squad. For Gascoigne the reality hit home almost immediately. Tears welled in his eyes and his lip started trembling. Sensing he had lost the plot, Gary Lineker consoled his young team-mate, but realizing there was little more he could do, he turned to Bobby Robson on the England bench and, pointing to his eyes, asked his manager to 'have a word with him'. Nearly two decades later, Lineker is still inundated with fans mimicking his gesture from that day. 'I get asked about it as much as which flavoured crisps I like,' he says, through gritted teeth.

The second half of extra-time ended. England had come perilously close to winning. David Platt had had a goal disallowed for offside. Chris Waddle had hit the inside of the post and watched on as Gary Lineker failed by millimetres to connect with the rebound. But to no avail. With the scores tied at 1–1, the place in the World Cup final would be decided on penalties.

Penalties. Harsh and arbitrary. Dramatic and nerve-racking. Commentators often say that it's no way to settle a game of football, but if there is a fairer way to decide matters, it has either yet to be invented or it simply can't match the shoot-out for unbearable drama.

For England, and their goalkeeper Peter Shilton, it would be their first ever tournament experience of a penalty shoot-out. Robson selected his five takers, overlooking Gascoigne in favour of David Platt, as the young midfielder was, by now, in no fit state to take one. They were, in order, Gary Lineker, Peter Beardsley, David Platt, Stuart Pearce and, finally, Chris Waddle. It was a strong, confident line-up, all proven goalscorers or, in the case of Stuart Pearce, a regular penalty taker for his club, Nottingham Forest.

Before extra-time had finished, Robson had even toyed with the idea of bringing on his stand-in goalkeeper, Chelsea's Dave Beasant, for Peter Shilton purely for the spot-kicks. Since rising to fame in the Wimbledon side that upset Liverpool in the 1988 FA Cup final – a game in which he famously saved a penalty from John Aldridge – Beasant had earned a reputation as one of the better penalty savers in the game. In the end Robson decided against it, keeping faith with Shilton instead.

The brutal truth was that it had been one, maybe even two major tournaments too many for Peter Shilton and tonight, of all nights, was the one when that would become painfully apparent. Not once did he even look like he was going to save a German penalty, but then they were expertly taken. Even in 1986, when he barely got off the ground in his infamous and unsuccessful aerial duel with Diego Maradona, it could have been argued that he was already over the hill. Yes, goalkeepers tend to have a longer shelf life than outfield players, but when you can't outjump a man who is six inches shorter than you, that surely represents a problem.

One by one the German penalties whistled past the England number one, all without the ageing keeper getting anywhere near them. And England, for the first three kicks at least, matched them. Up strode Stuart Pearce, his shorts hiked up in a statement of aggressive intent. Huge of heart (and thigh), Pearce was as passionate an England player as had ever crossed the white line. A rock in the defence, he had given his all in England's pursuit of glory but his penalty, though hard and low, was straight down the middle and was saved by the legs of the German goalkeeper Illgner.

As Shilton watched Olaf Thon's fourth penalty for Germany sting the corner of his net once more, it was down to the Olympique Marseille winger Chris Waddle to keep England in the World Cup. Opting for power, Waddle, now shorn of his trademark mullet haircut, blasted the ball, but it went high over the crossbar, before bouncing off the athletics track and into the grateful hands of a child in the stands.

Down and now out, England had been beaten by the narrowest and most heartbreaking of margins. As the German players ran to congratulate Illgner (not that he had actually had anything whatsoever to do with Waddle's miss), Bobby Robson sat on the bench in his England blazer and tie, and bowed his head, his international swansong shattered. With a consoling pat on the back from the England physio Norman Medhurst, Robson pulled himself together and set off for the pitch to speak to his players, stopping to accept the commiserations of the German coach Franz Beckenbauer.

After the game the England team boarded their bus, a case of beer hidden under the seats. Next to them was the German bus. Within minutes, the England team were all singing. There was a rendition of 'Blaydon Races' in honour of the Geordie trio Gascoigne, Beardsley and Waddle, followed by 'Knees Up Mother Brown' for the players from the south of the country. To the casual passer-by it was difficult to tell who had actually won the match.

It had been a remarkable, improbably exciting tournament for England. Bobby Robson, a manager who had seemed to spend most of his tenure fending off calls for his resignation, had so nearly confounded everyone (even himself in all likelihood) in almost taking England to the World Cup final. It was a performance, as he would later write to Sir Bert Millichip, that had 'restored our credibility and pride in world football'.

Nearly two decades on from what might have been, the players involved that night are now almost as famous as their counterparts from 1966. Some even more so. Paul Gascoigne would become one of the greatest midfield players England had ever had. Gary Lineker would forge a successful career in broadcasting (and potato crisps), and Stuart Pearce and Chris Waddle would bag themselves a Pizza Hut advert. Paul Parker, meanwhile, is still dining out – quite literally – on the heady days of Italia 90. 'It's incredible that twenty years on and everyone still talks about it,' he says. 'Even the other day, a young kid came up to me when I was having a meal in a restaurant. He said he was watching a DVD of the World Cup in 1990 and that his dad had pointed me out and told him that me and Paul Gascoigne were England's best players in the tournament.

'It's good for me and my ego, I guess, but in another way it's disappointing because it means that we still haven't eclipsed that achievement. We've had so many false dawns and that's got to change. Mind you, if it doesn't I'm still happy to dine out on it for a bit longer.'

For Gary Lineker, it was another painful reminder of how close England had come yet again, as if he needed reminding. 'I didn't think we were that great a side in '86, but in '90 we were one step off the World Cup final,' he reflects, 'a couple of penalties away from being probably the favourites to win the final against Argentina.'

That night, England, both the team and the nation, drank their way through their sorrows. In Turin the violinist and Aston Villa fanatic Nigel Kennedy turned up at the England hotel and entertained the squad, while Bobby Robson was thanked by the players – by being thrown in the swimming pool head first and fully clothed.

Having lost the third-place play-off to the hosts Italy 2–1 and seen their German conquerors go on to win the World Cup, England returned to the UK drinking champagne all the way home and arriving at Luton airport to be greeted by an estimated 100,000 well-wishers. For the squad and Bobby Robson it was a chance to reflect on what they had achieved at Italia 90 and offer their thanks to the some of the supporters who had cheered them on. For Paul Gascoigne, meanwhile, it was the perfect opportunity to don some comedy breasts. Some things, it seemed, never changed.

Robert William Robson, meanwhile, would walk away from England as the most successful England manager since Sir Alf Ramsey. His record in qualification for major tournaments – just one defeat in four campaigns and twenty-eight matches – was exceptional, although the nagging sense that he wasn't quite capable of making that one small step, that giant leap, to a final must still have grated. But as he said in his autobiography, Robson didn't leave the job 'embittered, mistrustful or traumatized'. And so what if England hadn't won the World Cup again; the game, our national game, had turned a corner.

CHAPTER 4

THE CRUEL SEA

'I used to quite like turnips but now Rita refuses to serve them.'

Graham Taylor, England manager 1990–1994

Graham Taylor was a kid with designs on the big time. Born in Worksop, Nottinghamshire, and raised in Scunthorpe, Lincolnshire, he was the son of a sports journalist and, certainly, he could play a bit. As a talented wing-half, he had represented England Grammar Schools and England Under-15s and had signed a professional contract with Grimsby Town in 1962, aged seventeen, later making his debut for the first team on the occasion of his eighteenth birthday.

Throughout his formative years in the professional game, Taylor had shown a passion for learning the art of coaching. Confident and mature beyond his years, he had already secured the FA's full coaching badge by the age of twenty-one – the youngest ever to do so – so when his next club, Fourth Division Lincoln City, offered him the position of player-manager in November 1972, Taylor, cocksure as ever, grabbed the £45-a-week opportunity with both hands.

It was a prudent move. Soon after, Taylor's playing career would be ended prematurely by a serious hip injury. Despite a dreadful start – his team failed to win in their first twelve games under him – Taylor gradually moulded Lincoln into his team, a quick, direct and brutally effective attacking outfit. By 1975–76, City were the runaway winners of the Fourth Division, collecting a record 74 points (under the old system of two rather than three points for a win) and scoring 111 goals along the way.

Barely into his thirties, Taylor had already been earmarked by club chairmen across the country as the most promising young coach in the game. Indeed, several clubs would come calling, most notably First Division West Bromwich Albion, but Taylor stayed at Sincil Bank until the summer of 1977 when, surprisingly, he dropped back into the basement division to take the reins at Watford.

That summer, Taylor had taken a phone call from the then England coach Don Revie who told him, somewhat mysteriously, that he had suggested Taylor to a new club chairman who had just entered the game. When Taylor learned it was the world famous singer and lifelong Hornets fan Elton John who had just taken over at Fourth Division Watford his heart sank. 'I thought: "Rock star in charge of a Fourth Division club. This is crazy!"'

Stagnant and unfashionable, Watford were a club going nowhere until they had been bought by John. But with someone as charismatic, enthusiastic and media friendly as John footing the bill, what the club really needed now was someone to match his ambition and talent on the playing side. A meeting at the singer's Windsor mansion was convened. John told Taylor he wanted to take Watford into Europe. Taylor told him it would cost him a million. John didn't care. The two clicked and a deal was done. 'We had an agreement that if he didn't tell me which team to pick, I wouldn't tell him which songs to sing.'

While any venture with a man as cavalier as Elton John would, inevitably, be conducted at breakneck speed, what happened next was, even by the Rocket Man's excessive standards, nothing short of a whirlwind. Within six years, the chairman's Taylor-made team would be runners-up to Liverpool in the 1982–83 First Division title race and the 1984 FA Cup final at Wembley, and playing in Europe in the UEFA Cup. They would also win the FA Youth Cup in 1982. It was a breathtaking, irrepressible surge through the ranks of English football, based on the kind of direct play that delighted Watford fans but appalled the game's purists.

But how it worked. For all his critics, Taylor had a knack of wringing the maximum out of limited resources and unearthing players who could fit seamlessly into his system. And while many observers lambasted his style of play for its over-reliance on long balls and perceived lack of imagination, Taylor nevertheless helped make undeniably skilful players like Luther Blissett and John Barnes the players they became and the household names they remain to this day.

In the case of Barnes, particularly, it was proof that Taylor's preferred method of trawling local leagues rather than dipping into the expense of the transfer market for new players could pay huge dividends. Taylor had heard about a gifted boy who had been playing for Sudbury Court in Brent, north-west London, and having watched him play for the Middlesex League side invited him to Vicarage Road for a trial. Then, in a reserve game against Leyton Orient, Barnes dazzled everyone with his almost balletic grace on the ball and his ability to glide past an opponent with ludicrous ease. When Barnes then hit the crossbar with a shot from a yard inside his own half, Taylor had seen enough and in the summer of 1981 John Barnes became a Watford player. The records show that Sudbury were paid an undisclosed fee for Barnes. Not so, says Graham Taylor. 'We offered Sudbury a set of kit and John signed for us.'

With Taylor's Watford confounding their critics and mounting a genuine challenge to the hegemony of the bigger clubs like Liverpool and Arsenal, it was inevitable that the Football Association would soon come calling and at the beginning of October 1982, just one week after Watford had annihilated Sunderland 8–0 at Vicarage Road (they could easily have scored thirteen), Taylor was offered the chance to coach the England youth team on a part-time basis.

While his time in charge of Watford had seen the club progress far beyond anything the most optimistic supporter could have imagined, Taylor nevertheless sensed by 1987 that he had perhaps taken his team as far as he could. And so, after ten extraordinarily successful years at the club, and despite the fact that he had signed a new six-year deal in 1984, he tendered his resignation and accepted an offer to manage Second Division Aston Villa.

If Watford were the little club made great by Taylor, Villa were an altogether tougher proposition. Seven times winners of the First Division title, FA Cup winners on seven occasions, three times winners of the League Cup and, most memorably, the European club champions just five years earlier, they had slipped into the Second Division, a drop that had cost Billy McNeill his job.

Charged with working his magic once more, Taylor now faced a challenge on an entirely different level to that at Watford where he had everything to gain and pretty much nothing to lose. There was no real expectation that the little Hertfordshire club would be successful, let alone barge through the leagues with scant regard for reputations or record books; this was something to be treas-ured, not expected. The situation was the polar opposite at Villa Park, not least because Villa were still one of the biggest clubs in British football. Moreover, Taylor would be working under 'Deadly' Doug Ellis, one of the most demanding, impatient chairmen in the entire Football League.

That Graham Taylor was prepared to take on the challenge was testament to his confidence in his coaching ability. He didn't disappoint. In his first season, Taylor took Villa straight back up to the First Division, declaring the achievement to be the greatest of his career. 'I'm thrilled,' he said. 'This is the top of the pile for me, seeing this great old club back where it belongs.'

Despite a less than auspicious first season back in the top flight – Villa finished just one point and one place ahead of the relegation zone – Taylor's new recruits, such as the Republic of Ireland defender Paul McGrath and the free-scoring midfielder David Platt, made terrific strides the following year, finishing a com-fortable second behind the runaway winners Liverpool.

With his managerial star in the ascendant, Taylor's name rose inexorably to the top of the list, ahead of Howard Kendall of

Everton and the lesser-fancied Oldham Atheltic boss Joe Royle, to replace Bobby Robson as England manager. (Remarkably, the name of Terry Venables wasn't even on the shortlist. His turn would come four years later.) Where once he had been just one of many managers in the frame, now having proved his mettle at a 'big club', Taylor had become the overwhelming, outstanding favourite to take charge.

In April 1990 he was approached by the Football Association, without the knowledge of his chairman at Villa, Doug Ellis. In the business world, it's called 'headhunting'. In modern football parlance, it's called 'tapping up'. Whatever you called it, back then it was merely part and parcel of the management recruitment process. Yes, there would be unhappy chairmen and aggrieved supporters but nothing that a few quid in compensation couldn't remedy.

At the beginning of June, with Bobby Robson's World Cup squad already in Italy, Graham Taylor was offered the job of England manager, a position he readily accepted, even though it would be six weeks until a compensation package with Aston Villa could be finalized.

At his first press conference at Lancaster Gate, Taylor was bright and beaming, a man who had finally realized his lifelong ambition of leading his country. He spoke at length, perhaps too long, about how he could build on the success, or at least relative success, of the Robson era and take the team that crucial step further.

Here was a coach at home on the training field, a manager who enjoyed the day-to-day interaction with his players and the challenge of fostering a team spirit and bond that transcended tactics and formations. Taylor knew how to talk a good game too, even if the style of some his teams in the more recent years of his managerial career suggested that there was much more to football than mere entertainment. It was immediately apparent that Taylor was a man at ease with the media. Hardly surprising really, given he was the son of a sports reporter and had himself flirted with the idea of following in his father's footsteps. That he was comfortable with the circus that followed the England team was significant. That he knew how to play the game was crucial.

Positive, cocksure even, and with a knowing glint in his eye that suggested everything was going to be all right, he was the kind of coach who imbued confidence in the fans, a manager who could see past the ever-inflating egos of the new breed of football superstars. And while his address that day was pockmarked with the kind of unique Taylorisms that would come to be an increasingly predictable characteristic of his tenure, it nevertheless set the tone for the new era of England. 'It is my intention to be the most track-suited manager England have ever had,' he said. 'I'll be bringing in different people to have a smell of international football. Some will take to it like ducks to water, others will have problems. But there is bags of talent and experience out there and I will be trying to create a structure for the future.'

Taylor's backroom team would be a mixture of relative youth and proven experience. On the one hand, he enlisted the help of the former Southampton manager Lawrie McMenemy as his assistant and as coach of the Under-21 team. On the other, he called in Phil Neal, the vastly experienced former Liverpool defender then in charge of Bolton Wanderers. Both, unlike Taylor, had won major trophies – McMenemy as manager of the unfancied Southampton side that shocked Manchester United to win the 1976 FA Cup, and Neal as a full-back in the great Liverpool team that won just about every honour in the modern game in the 1970s and early 1980s. In McMenemy, Taylor had his own version of Bertie Mee, an old head on hand to offer advice as and when required. In Neal, he had a young manager, tirelessly enthusiastic and eager to prove his worth in the world of coaching. On the face of it, it seemed like a solid set-up.

For his first game, Taylor faced a friendly against Hungary at Wembley on 12 September 1990 and his starting line-up included the spine of the team that had come so close in Italy: Stuart Pearce and Des Walker, Paul Gascoigne and David Platt, Chris Waddle and Gary Lineker (who had been made captain in Bryan Robson's absence). But it also included a few surprises, with Arsenal's Lee

Dixon coming in at right-back and the prolific Wolves striker Steve Bull receiving a starting berth alongside Lineker, much to Peter Beardsley's surprise.

This, of course, was also the long-awaited opportunity of the goalkeeper Chris Woods to emerge from the shadow of England's record-breaking and recently retired goalkeeper Peter Shilton and claim the number 1 shirt for himself. It had been more than five years since Woods had made his international debut under Bobby Robson on the tour of Mexico and the USA, and with Shilton keeping him out of the side (as he had when the two were team-mates at Nottingham Forest) he had been limited to appearances mainly as a substitute or in friendly games. 'There's no denying that it was really frustrating to get called up then wait so long to play,' he explains. 'But I was already used to the feeling. I was behind Peter at Nottingham Forest too. I was good friends with him both on and off the pitch, and if you have to be second to somebody, then you couldn't pick a better keeper.

'Peter was such a big influence on me that it didn't feel so bad missing out. I wouldn't have liked it if I'd been behind someone else, I'm sure, but Peter helped me a lot with my game in training.'

Fortunately, Woods would begin his England career proper with a clean sheet and a 1–0 win against the Hungarians, courtesy of a Gary Lineker goal on the stroke of half-time, setting Taylor's England up nicely for their first competitive game under the new regime, a European Championship qualifier against Poland. A month later, England began their qualifying campaign with a comfortable 2–0 win over the nation that had ruined England's World Cup chances at the same ground seventeen years earlier. Taylor's team, Taylor's England, were off and running.

Just three games into his reign, though, Taylor made the first real gamble of his tenure when, for the European Championship qualifier away to the Republic of Ireland in Dublin, he decided to drop the man who had just become a national hero, Paul Gascoigne. It was a decision, much like Bobby Robson's to omit Kevin Keegan from his first game in charge of England, that was as much a statement of authority as it was a tactical judgement.

Since he had returned home from Italia 90 a household name, Gascoigne's life had changed irrevocably. Faced with an insatiable public appetite for all things Gazza, the Spurs midfielder transformed into a one-man money-making machine. Lucrative national newspaper columns, supermarket openings, kiss and tells; there was even a number 2 hit single, the appalling 'Fog On The Tyne', that he had reworked with Lindisfarne, the Newcastle folk band that had originally recorded the song back in 1971. When he appeared on Terry Wogan's BBC chat show, the host introduced him as 'literally the most famous and probably the most popular person in Britain today'. As the demands on his time grew, though, Gascoigne found it increasingly difficult to cope, often criticizing the tabloid press for not taking him seriously as a man or a footballer. It was as though they couldn't see past the comedy breasts and the novelty records.

In a few short but seismic weeks, Gascoigne had become one of those rare footballers, like George Best or Pelé, that cross the line from mere professional athlete into bona fide, A-list celebrity. The only man busier than Gascoigne was his agent and lawyer Mel Stein.

None of which seemed to matter to Graham Taylor. Gascoigne was just like any of his other players and if he didn't fit the bill, then he had to stand aside. Taylor's omission of Gascoigne was controversial enough in itself, but replacing him with the Aston Villa veteran Gordon Cowans, a man who hadn't played for England for half a decade, seemed inexplicable. Taylor's reasoning, though, seemed sound. This, he figured, was going to be one of those ugly games; a roll-up-your-sleeves, up-and-at-'em battle against a team renowned for their direct approach to playing, conducted on a poor pitch in even worse conditions. The choice facing Graham Taylor was stark. Get it right and England's chance of qualification (and his reputation) might be enhanced. Get it wrong and he ran the risk of alienating his most gifted player and, for that matter, the entire nation.

It was the first time a fully fit Gascoigne had ever been left out of an England squad and the nation's new golden boy was seething.

'I was devastated,' he would say in his autobiography, *Gazza*. 'Graham never really explained to me why ... All he said to me was that I wasn't in the right state to play, which really pissed me off.'

The game over – England secured an acceptable 1–1 draw thanks to a goal by Taylor's former Aston Villa charge David Platt – the coach sought to explain his selection. 'I picked a midfield which I thought would cope better with the onslaught we knew we would face,' he said. Cowans, meanwhile, never played for England again.

While most England managers are blessed with what journalists euphemistically term a 'honeymoon period' (i.e. the time it takes the reporters to take the boxing gloves off), Taylor had had few qualms in taking a decision that was not just courageous but potentially career-threatening. Nobody could deny the man had the courage of his convictions.

By the time England played their next game – a home friendly against the surprise package of Italia 90, Cameroon – Gascoigne would be back in the team and the furore over his omission in Dublin had largely subsided, not least because Taylor's England remained unbeaten. Joining him for the game at Wembley would be the prolific Crystal Palace striker Ian Wright. Aged twenty-seven, Wright had only joined the professional game just before his twenty-second birthday, when he had turned his back on a career as a plasterer to sign for Steve Coppell at Selhurst Park. Now he was about to make his international debut at the home of football and plastering's loss was Graham Taylor's gain.

With Cameroon's typically physical game undone by a couple of goals from Gary Lineker – his thirty-eighth and thirty-ninth for his country – England resumed their European Championship campaign with morale high and the nation expectant. Their form, however, was still far from impressive. In the 1–1 draw with Jack Charlton's Republic of Ireland at Wembley, Taylor's team had been drawn into the kind of ugly, unattractive long-ball battle that the sell-out Wembley crowd patently hadn't come to see. Then a little over a month later, England laboured again in the qualifier against Turkey at Izmir's Ataturk Stadium, somehow emerging with a 1–0 victory, when the Turks clearly deserved at least a point from the game.

While results were going in Taylor's favour, there was still a glaring lack of real ingenuity in his side. It would be a problem compounded by a serious injury to his one true creative talent, Paul Gascoigne. With a £5.5 million move to the Italian club Lazio agreed, Gascoigne had been determined to leave Tottenham with a trophy and, through some virtuoso performances, had almost single-handedly steered Spurs to the 1991 FA Cup final against Nottingham Forest. Just minutes into the game, though, a hyped-up Gascoigne challenged the Forest full-back Gary Charles with a dangerous knee-high tackle. It was the kind of wanton, reckless challenge that can end careers, only this time it was Gascoigne's career that would hang in the balance. Diagnosed with ruptured cruciate ligaments, Gascoigne would miss the whole of the following season and his move to Lazio would be put on hold.

Gascoigne's injury aside, luck was still very much with Graham Taylor. That summer, England successfully negotiated six friendly games (including four on a tour of Australia, New Zealand and Malaysia), winning five and drawing one, during which Gary Lineker took his international goals tally to forty-five, just four away from Bobby Charlton's record total. It also saw a clutch of new players tested at international level. Some, like Leeds United's David Batty, would become part of the England reckoning for years to come. Others, like the Oldham Athletic defender Earl Barrett, would not.

It was only on their return that Taylor's luck would finally desert him. In September 1991, almost a year to the day since his first game in charge, Taylor's unbeaten twelve-game start to his tenure as England coach finally came to an end when Bertie Vogts brought his reunified Germany side to Wembley and left 1–0 winners, thanks to a goal from the Lazio striker Karl-Heinz Riedle.

The loss to Germany had done little to hamper England's progress in the European Championship and qualification would be secured with a 1–0 win at home to Turkey and a 1–1 draw away in Poland. That England had qualified without losing a game was undeniably impressive, especially given the tricky nature of some of the ties they had had to play. Indeed, in reaching the finals in Sweden, Graham Taylor had become the first England manager in history to qualify for a tournament at his very first attempt.

Clearly, England had become a team that was resolute and difficult to break down. That said, they were, at times, dreary to watch and their lack of goals in reaching the final stages was perturbing. In their six games they had scored just seven times, despite having the usually prolific Gary Lineker spearheading the attack.

As England's warm-up games for Euro 92 came and went, so Lineker edged ever nearer to Bobby Charlton's record of forty-nine goals for England. In the penultimate friendly at home against Brazil in May, and what was Linker's last ever game at Wembley, he would have an opportunity to equal Charlton's tally from the penalty spot, but his shot was too cute, too clever, and was easily saved by Carlos in the Brazilian goal.

Not only was it a dreadfully poor penalty but it was entirely at odds with the way Lineker played the game. Never was he a fancy dan or a showboater. His remit was clear. Get in the six-yard box and get on the end of the crosses. Now contrast that Brazil penalty with, say, the pair he took against Cameroon in Italia 90. Then, he hit the ball as hard as his tired frame would allow, scoring both of his efforts. Simple, efficient, ruthless. Now, with Bobby Charlton's record just one kick away from him, he had tried to be far too subtle with his spot-kick and was left looking more than a little embarrassed. The only consolation, perhaps, was that Lineker, who had announced that Euro 92 was to be his international swansong, still had a minimum of four games in which to draw level with or even eclipse Charlton.

All of which made Taylor's final squad for the 1992 European Championship all the more perplexing. Faced with the finest opposition the continent had to offer and in charge of a team that was desperate for some attacking options, Taylor stunned most observers with a squad that was as unpredictable as it was concerning.

Certainly, he had been particularly unfortunate with injuries, especially in his defence. Indeed, even the replacements for the injured first choices were pulling out and Liverpool's Rob Jones, Rangers' Gary Stevens and Arsenal's Lee Dixon all fell by the wayside in the right-back berth. Out too was Dixon's Highbury team-mate Tony Adams, overlooked after his problems on the field and some high-profile ones off it, not least a drink-driving offence that saw him serve eight weeks of a three-month prison sentence at Chelmsford open prison.

But it was his selections for attack that suggested Graham Taylor was perfectly content to try and bore his way to victory in Sweden. Deprived of the creative nous of Paul Gascoigne and his long-term ally John Barnes, who had ruptured his Achilles tendon in the final warm-up game away in Finland, Taylor had, bafflingly, omitted many of the players that appeared to be ideal replacements, if not first-choice starters in their own right. There was no place for Peter Beardsley, a player who had forged a reliable and intuitive partnership with Lineker. There was no place for Chris Waddle, who, just thirty-one and one of the stellar names of the French Championnat with Olympique Marseille, had played his last game for his national team. And there was no place for Arsenal's Ian Wright, the striker who had just finished the season as the First Division's highest scorer, with twenty-nine goals.

Instead, Taylor opted to give just three places in his squad to strikers, with Lineker joined by Wright's Arsenal colleague Alan Smith and the young Southampton centre-forward Alan Shearer. The son of a sheet-metal worker, Shearer was, like Peter Beardsley before him, another product of the famous Wallsend Boys Club in the north-east of England. After rejections from Manchester City, West Bromwich Albion and the club he supported, Newcastle United, he had been taken on by

Southampton. On his full debut against Arsenal at The Dell in April 1988, aged just 17 years and 240 days, Shearer had scored a hat-trick in a 4–2 win, making him the youngest scorer of a hat-trick in the First Division. It also beat a record held by Jimmy Greaves for thirty years.

When international recognition came his way, Shearer excelled. In Dave Sexton's England Under-21 side he plundered a record thirteen goals in his eleven appearances, and his promotion to the full squad, especially with Gary Lineker's career coming to an end, had always been viewed as a matter of when and not if. When he had finally made his debut for Taylor in the friendly against France in February 1992 he didn't disappoint. A well-taken goal on the turn in the first-half suggested that here was a striker with the potential to fill the boots of Gary Lineker after his retirement.

The day after the France game, it was announced that a new competition, the Premier League, had been formed. Sanctioned by the Football Association as the new FA Premier League but with commercial independence from both the FA and the Football League, it was a breakaway league formed by the twenty-two clubs that were then in the First Division and was designed to take advantage of some of the increasingly lucrative television rights deals that were on the table, most notably from the satellite television broadcaster BSkyB. By 27 May, all twenty-two top-flight clubs would resign their membership of the Football League and a new commercially driven era in English football had begun.

Talented though Lineker, Smith and Shearer were, the lack of any other options in attack was another massive gamble. From being the manager behind the teams that had rampaged their way through the lower divisions scoring goals at will, Taylor had grown more conservative as the years had passed, and while he had been unable to pick the players he really wanted for his squad, his replacements suggested – as always with England managers under pressure – that if he couldn't guarantee a victory then his only option was to ensure they didn't lose. Why else would he have instructed his players to take the kick-off and then find touch with the ball as far into the opposition half as possible? At times it was like rugby union, only with less finesse.

England had been drawn in the same group as the hosts Sweden, perennial rivals France, and Denmark. (The Danes had been given a place in the finals at the last moment at the expense of Yugoslavia who, despite topping their qualifying group, had been prevented from participating because of the ongoing conflict in their country.) From the outset, England's lack of attacking and creative options was painfully exposed. Both of their opening games against Denmark and France would finish goalless, leaving them requiring a win against the hosts Sweden to progress.

Come the game, England would make an ideal start, taking the lead after just four minutes through David Platt and holding on to their advantage until the interval. Six minutes after the break, though, the Swedes would pull level through Jan Eriksson, leaving England to chase the game for the goal they needed. With a little less than half an hour to go, Taylor signalled for Arsenal's Alan Smith to warm up. If the Gascoigne decision in the early days of his England reign had baffled many, what he was about to do would prove to be one of the defining moments of his time in charge of the national team.

With forty-eight goals in seventy-nine international games, a Golden Boot from the World Cup in 1986 and the level of major-tournament experience that Taylor needed now more than ever, Gary Lineker, the team's captain and talisman, seemed the least likely player on the pitch to be taken off in what could be his final game in the white shirt of England. But, as he had shown with Gascoigne in just his third game in charge, Taylor was in no mood to bow to sentiment.

That Lineker patently wasn't getting any service was largely irrelevant, as was his astonishing goalscoring record for his country. Taylor wanted a change, and, just as Alf Ramsay had chosen to take off Bobby Charlton in what turned out to be his 106th and final game against West Germany in the quarter-finals of the 1970 World Cup, off came England's second-highest goal-scorer, his face a picture of barely concealed rage. In his place came Arsenal's Alan Smith, a striker with just twelve caps and two goals to his credit and a player who was an unlikely figure to spearhead any kind of England revival. For the record, Gary Lineker would stick to his decision to retire after the championship and would never play for England again. Nor, for that matter, would Alan Smith.

'He [Taylor] thought Lineker was a busted flush going into Euro 92 and there was a young striker in the squad called Alan Shearer but Taylor didn't want to be the man who shot Liberty Valance – he just didn't want to leave him out,' explains the former *Today* journalist Rob Shepherd. 'And then it comes down to the decisive game against Sweden and he takes him off. Now, in all honesty, if you're desperate [for a goal that would keep you in the tournament], do you take Gary Lineker off and put Alan Smith on or do you put Alan Smith on with Gary Lineker and take someone else off? Shearer didn't come on. It was one of those moments where [Taylor] just seemed to have lost it.'

With just eight minutes to go, England fell behind to a wonderfully crafted goal by Thomas Brolin, aided and abetted by his striker partner Martin Dahlin. There would be no way back, especially without the creativity of the sidelined Gascoigne and the goal-getting knack of Gary Lineker on the bench. England were out of the European Championship and Taylor, who had suffered only his second defeat in twenty-four matches in charge of the national team, was out of favour.

For Lineker, it was a frustrating finale to his international career and his quest to eclipse Bobby Charlton's goalscoring record for England would fall one agonizing goal short. How he must have regretted that penalty against Brazil at Wembley. Seventeen years on, Lineker, to his credit, bears no malice to the man who called time on his international career. 'Managers make their decisions at the time for the reasons that they think are right and in a strange sort of way he made a martyr out of me really,' he explains. 'But I see Graham lots of times now and we get on fine.

I never felt [bitter towards him] at any stage. I don't think it was the right thing to do as I always believed that I could get us a goal when we needed one but I'm not one to bear grudges.'

Taylor too regards his 'big decision' at Euro 92 as part and parcel of the game. 'Our relationship is all right now, although it did suffer,' he told the *Guardian* in July 2006. 'I [had] made Gary Lineker captain, so when I became the villain for substituting him at Euro 92, I felt poorly treated. I know that he wanted to break the England record for international goals against Sweden, in our final match, [but] all I saw was a player wearing number 10 who wasn't in the game.'

'Villain' was an understatement. Back home, the press unleashed a torrent of abuse that made their treatment of Bobby Robson look like just a quiet word in his ear. Chief tormentor, as always, was the *Sun* which, under the famous 'Swedes 2 Turnips 1' headline demanded Taylor resign with immediate effect, and then superimposed a picture of the England manager's face on an image of a turnip. 'That headline was the work of a sub-editor called Alan Sleeman, and not Brian Alexander [then editor of the *Sun*] who was down the pub at the time and who's lived off that thinking he came up with the greatest headline of all time,' says Shepherd.

As the son of a journalist and a man who once considered a career in newspapers, Taylor could see the tempest coming but the story, and in particular the imagery, was a step too far. 'That did upset my parents,' he said.

Thirty-eight 'fucks'. Three 'cunts'. Two 'shits' and a single 'wanker'. It may have sounded like the title of Barry Fry's autobiography, and how the Football Association would have wished it was, but no. This was the official, FA-sanctioned fly-on-the-wall documentary covering Graham Taylor's England and their qualifying campaign for the 1994 World Cup in America.

As a TV programme, *Graham Taylor: An Impossible Job*, was bewilderingly compelling and was not so much a warts-and-all exposé of the England manager's position but an hour-long career suicide note. As a lesson in swearing, it was indeed exemplary. As a case study for film students, it was required viewing. As a PR exercise, for Graham Taylor, England and the FA, it was catastrophic.

Taylor and the FA had been approached by the documentary maker Ken McGill to participate in a programme they were planning to make for the Channel 4 series *Cutting Edge*, the concept being that the camera crew would follow England on the final stretch of their qualifying campaign for USA 94. 'The idea came from us sitting in a pub getting drunk and talking about the worst jobs we could think of,' explains McGill. 'One of the ones that came up at the end was the England manager's job. We thought that's a pain-in-the-arse job, let's put it on the list. So we contacted the England manager, pitched it and eventually found out that Graham Taylor was really interested in it. He spoke to the FA, they said "can't see why not" and it was really that simple. Before we knew it we had an agreement.'

The early exchanges in England's qualifying group passed off without incident, much to Ken McGill's disappointment. Sure, the home draw with Norway had been below par, but three consecutive wins against Turkey (4–0), San Marino (6–0) and Turkey away (0–2) had put England in a commanding position in Group 2. England's campaign was going well which meant, in turn, that McGill's film was not. 'The initial shooting we did with Graham was fairly dull and nothing juicy was happening,' recalls McGill. 'So we said if you really want to continue we've got to get Graham to wear a radio mic in training and at matches and if he trusts us enough we can have a powerful documentary.' Little did McGill know but the next few games would provide him with the kind of footage that a team of Hollywood's finest scriptwriters couldn't conjure up.

It was no accident that England's impressive start to the World Cup qualifying campaign had coincided with the long-awaited return of Paul Gascoigne. His return would also help the director Ken McGill. Having made a documentary about Gascoigne's rehabilitation from his knee injury, McGill already had an 'in' with the squad and soon found the players warming to him and his crew. 'The players were great with us,' he says. 'Gazza was a great help. We've got a scene which didn't go in the film where the players are training and the boss has got the radio mic on and the subject [of conversation] gets on to me and they all start taking the piss out of the Scotsman in their midst. That's the kind of humour you have to expect when you're around a football team. High hilarity.'

The domestic season in England had ended with the inaugural Premier League championship going to Manchester United. After a twenty-six-year drought, to land the top-flight title, Alex Ferguson's side, led by the battle-scarred centre-back Steve Bruce, had dominated the season from its start to its predictable finish and their winning margin – ten points – merely reinforced their superiority over the rest of the field. When they received the new trophy at Old Trafford on 3 May, Bruce held one handle and let the former England skipper and United stalwart Bryan Robson take the other.

The season over, Taylor and England reconvened for two crucial World Cup qualifiers away from home, first against Poland in Chorzow and then four days later in Oslo for the return game against the group leaders Norway. Against the Poles, England were once more at their fortunate worst. A goal down with just six minutes to go, it was Ian Wright who snatched an undeserved equalizer – his first international goal – and spared England's blushes.

If the game in Poland had seen England fortunate to emerge with a point – Taylor described his team as 'headless chickens' – the Norway match would see them get their just deserts. Ahead of the game, however, Paul Gascoigne was in the mood for mischief and while he was back from his career-threatening injury his brush with premature retirement had done little to dampen his enthusiasm for tomfoolery. After training, Gascoigne had been asked by a local TV crew if he had a message for the people of Norway. 'Yes,' he replied. 'Fuck off Norway.' Ever the diplomat, it was left to England's assistant manager Lawrie McMenemy to step in with a public apology. 'You'll have to excuse Gazza,' he said. 'He's got a very small vocabulary.'

Choosing one of the most important England games since Italia 90 to experiment, Taylor fielded a three-man defence behind a four-man midfield and a three-man attack. Not surprisingly, the team seemed utterly clueless, unlike the home side.

Images of a bewildered Nigel Clough being summoned into action from the substitutes' bench and not knowing where to go or what to do, or Taylor screaming so fiercely at Les Ferdinand from the touchline that his voice gave way, would be just minor scenes in a performance that ran the gamut of theatrical genres. From comedy ('Do I not like that!') to farce and, ultimately, tragedy, it was a display that plumbed new depths. Chief victim, surprisingly, would be Phil Neal. Throughout the game, Taylor's head coach was seen sitting on the England bench, often repeating Taylor's asides verbatim ('This is a real test') and appearing to be little more than a parrot, albeit one sat next to his boss rather than on his shoulder. 'I felt awful, especially for guys like Phil Neal,' admits Ken McGill. 'He's got a wife, he's got kids and he got terrible stick after that. He couldn't go into a football ground after that without being ridiculed and I feel terrible about that.'

Gross misrepresentation of his character or unfavourable editing? Neal would forever after be known not merely as a 'yes-man' but as a yes-man to one of the most unpopular English managers of all time. 'The mistake I made was that although I had editorial rights with Chrysalis to actually make the programme, when they sold the programme to Channel 4 I had no say on how it or I was presented,' Taylor later told the *Guardian* in Neal's defence.

Ken McGill sees it differently. 'I made this film with Graham and I had an agreement with him that I would run it by him. Now strictly speaking you shouldn't do that but when you make a film like that you need the person on your side. There was a first cut of the film that we went through together and, to be fair to him, he wasn't that concerned about how he was portrayed because he had agreed to do it. But he would look at parts and say, "Could we tone that down because it makes a particular person look bad?"

'There was one Les Ferdinand moment when they [the players] were in the dining room and they're all sat round this big table. We were there with our big boom mic over the table with the long black sponge bit on it when Gazza looks up and shouts "Look! It's Les Ferdinand's cock!" When Graham saw that he just looked at me and said, "I don't think so. He's got a wife."'

A goal either side of half-time would do for Taylor's men and once more, just as they had in 1981, England had suffered another 'hell of a beating' at the hands of the Norwegians. The *Sun*'s headline, as England returned home with just one point to show from their two games and with their hopes of qualification for the World Cup in the balance, pretty much summed up their performances. It read 'Norse Manure'.

That summer, Taylor's popularity, or wholesale lack of it, had plummeted still further and he knew it. Indeed, he would even joke that he received letters from Diana, Princess of Wales, thanking him for helping to get her out of the headlines. A three-game, four-team tournament in the United States, the US Cup, certainly hadn't helped matters. Designed as a mini-rehearsal for the World Cup finals the following year, it saw Taylor's team humbled 2–0 by the host nation; even Taylor called it 'a national disgrace'. Though the team salvaged a modicum of pride with a 1–1 draw against Brazil and a narrow 2–1 defeat to Germany, they had nevertheless finished last in the competition and returned home with their morale anything but boosted.

Yet the dissatisfaction now went far beyond the realms of the press and ever-growing numbers of disillusioned England supporters. At the Christchurch by-election on 29 July, for example, independent candidate Peter Newman stood for the Sack Graham Taylor Party and came in seventh in a fourteen-strong field, polling 80 votes, some 20 votes ahead of the Save the National Health Service Party and a massive 62 votes ahead of the Alfred The Chicken Party. 'My one and only policy,' raged Newman, 'is to hold a referendum on the England managership.'

With the tide not so much turning as turned, qualification for the World Cup finals was an absolute necessity, now more than ever. Ahead of Taylor and England lay three concluding World Cup qualifying games, at home to Poland and away to Holland and, finally, against lowly San Marino in Bologna. Win all three and they would be through to USA 94.

Come September, and it seemed, quite unexpectedly, that the recent woes of Taylor and England were behind them. In the return game against Poland, England looked a different side. Ostensibly, of course, they were. With five changes to the starting line-up that had failed in Oslo, they were back to a more familiar 4-4-2 formation. Importantly, Paul Gascoigne, in a rare outing for Taylor, also put in one of his better performances since the highs of Italia 90, scoring a goal in a 3–0 win that, for once, didn't flatter England. Morale boosted, confidence restored and hopes high, the team flew out to Rotterdam for the crunch game against Dick Advocaat's Holland.

With Norway topping the group and already assured of their place at the World Cup finals, it was now a straight shoot-out between England and Holland for the second qualifying spot in the group. Before the game, Taylor appeared outwardly confident of getting the right result, insisting that 'We are going to win.' But his jocular demeanour at his press conferences was suspicious, suggesting that far from being certain of the result, Taylor knew that he was one more poor result away from unemployment. His exchange with Rob Shepherd, the football correspondent for the *Today* newspaper, for example, in front of the massed ranks of the football media, certainly sought to deflect any unease about the match. When Shepherd voiced his concerns about the way the team would approach the game and suggested that it had all the hallmarks of the strategy Taylor had adopted so ruinously in Oslo, Taylor let rip.

'What's the problem? What's the matter with everybody?' he asked. 'Listen Rob, I cannot have faces like yours round about me. I'll tell you now. If you was one of my players with a face like that I'd fucking kick you out. You wouldn't have a chance.

Get yourself up, man. Put a smile on your face. We're here for business. Come on … the whole nation rests on whether Rob Shepherd is happy or not.'

Today, Shepherd can see the funny side. 'After the flop of Euro 92, I think he saw this as a eulogy to his managerial expertise and I think some of the stuff he does is affected, almost over-dramatic. There's certainly an element of theatre about it. I don't think there was any malice in it – I certainly didn't take it badly. He was just playing to the gallery. There was a great shot of Paul Ince and Paul Merson in the wings and when he was going for me they whispered something. You know exactly what would have happened after that. They would have gone back upstairs and told the rest of the team that Taylor had lost it.'

The following day – match day – Ken McGill and his crew learned that they had not been accredited by the Dutch FA for a match crucial to their whole project. Even some intervention by the English FA had failed to yield any result. With just an hour before the team left their hotel for the stadium, McGill was at his wits' end and resorted to knocking on Graham Taylor's hotel room door. 'I said, "Graham, I am in the shit here," and explained the situation and he just said, "Bollocks to that," and sent Fred Street off to get some tracksuits and kitbags and bring them back to the room. So then you have the scene of a Scottish director, Scottish cameraman and an Irish sound recordist putting on England tracksuits and putting all the cameras and sound mixers in these kit bags. So we got on the bus with the team and went to the ground and as we got off the bus, the team went one way to the dressing room and we spotted our chance and went the other on to the pitch. We even had to show Graham how to put his radio mic on and then hope for the best that when he came out we could actually hear something. Amazingly, it worked.'

Certainly, Taylor's team for the game was hardly the kind of line-up to imbue confidence; even the players weren't convinced the manager had got it right. With Gascoigne sidelined by injury yet again, Taylor opted for the leggy Sheffield Wednesday midfielder Carlton Palmer to replace him. It would be Palmer's nineteenth and final cap for England. 'I'm a huge fan of Graham Taylor, but there was a problem in Rotterdam: square pegs in round holes. I was man of the match at Wembley [in the 2–2 draw against Holland] playing centre midfield, but Incey [Paul Ince] kicked up a fuss about playing there. If Graham had said, "Ince is better [in the centre], you're on the bench," I could have lived with that. But then he played me on the right,' said Palmer later.

Irrespective of formations or tactics, however, the game in Rotterdam would be a match that England could never win, not with a referee as inept as Germany's Karl Josef Assenmacher dictating proceedings. Famously, the game would turn on some appalling decisions. With the game goalless and with England ahead on chances created, David Platt was put through by a long ball from Andy Sinton but as he bore down on goal he was hauled down by the arm of the Dutch captain Ronald Koeman on the edge of the penalty area. Under the new FIFA law on professional fouls, it was an instant red-card offence. Moreover, at first sight, it appeared like a penalty. Finally, it seemed, Graham Taylor's luck was about to change.

But no. Not only did Koeman escape with a yellow card – he later admitted that he should have been dismissed – but England's hopes of a penalty kick were dashed as well. When the resultant free-kick was taken it was charged down by a Dutch defender almost as soon as Tony Dorigo had taken it. Instead of ordering a retake for encroachment, Assenmacher allowed play to continue. Moments later, Holland were awarded a free-kick of their own just outside the England penalty box for Paul Ince's foul on Jan Wouters. This time, though, when Paul Parker charged it down, Assenmacher decided that it should be retaken, and then also booked Paul Ince for protesting.

What happened next, though, would have Taylor reaching for the revolver. When the kick was retaken, up stepped the man who should have been back in the dressing room, Ronald Koeman, and flicked a delicate chip up, over the defensive wall and into the top corner, past the despairing dive of David Seaman. 'I was on the right side of the goal to defend the free-kick,' recalled David

Seaman in his autobiography, *Safe Hands*. 'If he had scored in my side of the goal, it would definitely have been down to me but as he chipped it up and over the wall to the other side, with no defenders on the line, there really wasn't much I could do about it.'

For the documentary maker Ken McGill, sat on the sidelines with his tracksuited crew, there were mixed emotions as the game went Holland's way. 'As it all unfolded, the director in me said this is great, but the man in me thought, poor Graham,' he recalls. 'Everything was going against him. Everything. He told me that just the week before he had been to a FIFA meeting where the new rule on professional fouls was introduced and then it goes and happens and Koeman doesn't get sent off.'

Six minutes later, Inter Milan's Dennis Bergkamp compounded England's misery with a second goal and as England unravelled, the game slipped away. Time and time again, Taylor's men found themselves on the wrong end of some increasingly inexplicable decisions. Gary Pallister, for instance, took a nasty blow to the mouth, courtesy of one of the De Boer twins, leaving him with a split tongue.

Taylor's behaviour, meanwhile, grew ever more absurd. Pacing his technical area, he berated the fourth official, Markus Merk, for the woefully inadequate officiating of his colleagues. Indeed, Taylor's line to Merk that night – 'I was just saying to your colleague that the referee's got me the sack. Thank him ever so much for that' – may have become yet another in his long line of unwanted catchphrases, but it was entirely accurate. 'The fourth official, Markus Merk, was excellent to me,' reflected Taylor in 2006. 'He could have sent me off. He knew that the referee had made a major mistake. He kept saying: "I know Mr Taylor, I know Mr Taylor, please sit down." All these years later I still feel the team was cheated.' For the record, Karl Josef Assenmacher never officiated at an international match again.

At the final whistle, the game was all but up for England. Though simple mathematics may have suggested otherwise, they were out of the 1994 World Cup finals, the first time they had failed to qualify for the event since 1978. Ahead of Taylor and

England lay a final qualifier away to the part-timers of San Marino on 17 November, to be played in Bologna, Italy. While it was a game they were expected to win comfortably, they now had to do so by seven clear goals and then hope against hope that Poland could beat the Dutch in their final game to stand any chance of progressing through to the finals.

That night, England fans, so long the scourge of continental Europe, once more went on the rampage, in full view of officials from the World Cup organizers from the USA, who had made the trip across the Atlantic to see how best to handle security arrangements with some of the football world's more problematic hooligans. As the trouble finally subsided that evening, and with almost 1,000 English fans detained during the build-up and after the match, the only consolation for the World Cup officials was that England was one less team that they would have to deal with come the summer.

Anyone sat at home in front of the television that November night in 1993 will not easily forget the farcical first eight seconds of that game against San Marino. John Motson's commentary has certainly accrued a ghoulish fascination in the intervening years.

> The stage is set for England's last and decisive match in this World Cup qualifying group. England in red, San Marino in blue. England needing to win by a seven-goal margin and hope that Poland can do them a favour in Poznan against Holland. I'm sure you're aware now of what's at stake … and Bacciocchi, number 9, picks the ball up straight away and San Marino launch the first attack … And a mistake by Stuart Pearce and San Marino have scored! I don't believe this!

The BBC's John Motson wasn't the only observer left dumbstruck by what had happened straight from the kick-off at Bologna's Stadio Renato Dall'Ara. On the London radio station Capital Gold, for instance, their commentary went as follows:

> Welcome to Bologna on Capital Gold for England versus
> San Marino with Tennent's Pilsner, brewed with Czechoslo-
> vakian yeast for that extra Pilsner taste ... and England are
> one down.

With the goal recorded at just 8.3 seconds, Davide Gualtieri's stabbed strike for San Marino was the fastest in the history of the World Cup, and while England would return with seven goals of their own, including four for Arsenal's Ian Wright, the result would be immaterial, at least in terms of England's qualification for USA 94.

So it was that England's final qualifying game in their ill-fated 1994 World Cup campaign would also be Graham Taylor's final game in charge of the national team. Despite a 7–1 victory against the part-time players of a team some 112 places below them in FIFA's world rankings, Taylor was out of luck and finally out of time. Within twenty-four hours of the game in Bologna, he had met the FA chief executive Graham Kelly and offered to resign, a decision that was formally announced on 23 November, just six days after the San Marino game. Later, Taylor told the media that he was anything but a broken man and that he would 'be back'. Later, he would even say, 'If I could do any job it would be the manager of England again. If the FA asked me tomorrow I would go back. Any man, woman, football manager with ambition should want to do it ... You have to take it. Your country needs you. You have to have a go. Even if it does not work out – and it did not work out for me – it is still the greatest job in the world.'

Taylor's decision to quit saved the Football Association the trouble of dismissing their head coach as well as the expense of paying up the remaining eight months of his contract. Even now, though, with Taylor gone and the search for a new England coach under way, the *Sun*, with its mission duly accomplished, still wouldn't let it lie, reporting Taylor's departure with a front page consisting of their tried and trusted 'Graham Turnip' image and the headline 'That's Your Allotment'.

For Graham Kelly now was not the time for recrimination but for a wider, much-needed debate as to how English football could recover from this latest setback. 'I'm desperately disappointed, as all England supporters are,' he said. 'If anything positive comes out of all this, it's the realization that the [English] game needs to be shaken up. There are people who must look at themselves and ask if they've done enough to help England's cause. We've got to get a new system in place. But we must make sure we don't throw the baby out with the bath water. Experience at the international level is a hard-won, precious commodity. We and Graham Taylor have been very unlucky, and I feel very sorry for him.'

Amid the anger, disappointment and resignation(s), there was one man who seemed delighted at the turn of events. When asked, the chairman of the 1994 World Cup committee Alan Rothenberg remarked that there were three countries in the world whose presence at the finals would have created logistical problems for the organizers, adding, 'so we're very pleased they won't be coming – Iraq, Iran and England'.

England's failure to make it to the finals capped a miserable qualifying campaign for all the British nations. Scotland had failed to make it through a group including Italy, Switzerland and Portugal; Northern Ireland performed admirably in Group 3 but lost out to Spain and their neighbours the Republic of Ireland, while Wales lost to Romania in their final game when a win would have taken them through to their first finals since their only other appearance, in Sweden in 1958.

As ever, there was a raft of ideas and proposals suggested as to how to remedy the malaise in British football but, for the most part, there was ridicule and buck-passing. England's World Cup hero of 1966, Bobby Charlton, knew exactly where the blame lay. 'We seem to accept mediocrity with regard to our children playing the game. They don't get the right technical coaching at an early age. Many countries playing against us are inferior in terms of commitment, but control the ball better than our players. The World Cup without any British teams, it's outrageous. And we shouldn't let it happen again.'

The Welsh manager Terry Yorath, meanwhile, attributed the problems in the British game to the seemingly ceaseless pursuit of money. 'The problem we have is a Thatcherite Premier League. It is breeding greed, and eventually you get found out. I'm afraid we've been found out. They had a chance to reduce the number of teams in the League and decided not to. The rich just got rich and the poor poorer. The League should have been reduced. The players should be playing less [League] games to give international sides a chance to qualify.'

Not surprisingly, even Sepp Blatter, the verbose general secretary of football's governing body FIFA, weighed in with his thoughts on the demise of the England team, not that anybody really cared. 'English football,' he suggested, 'is thirty years out of date. The players can hardly stop a high ball without having it bounce four metres from their feet.'

Game over. Hounded, lampooned and vilified, Taylor had borne the brunt of England's failure to make any kind of impact on the European Championship and the unthinkable notion that England had failed to qualify for the 1994 World Cup finals. Indeed, Taylor's treatment by the media was nothing short of abysmal. Never before had the national team manager had to endure the kind of vicious, deeply personal abuse that Taylor received. Sure, Greenwood and Robson had their critics, but somehow the invective directed at Taylor went way beyond anything that had happened before.

In many respects, it was Taylor's tragic tenure and its calamitous unravelling that marked a sea change in the way the media, or, more specifically, the tabloid press, treated the England coach. Now, if you're fortunate (or unfortunate) enough to be in charge of the national team, you are only ever one upset or poor performance away from a hammering, only one result away from going out in a blaze of root vegetables.

Moreover, it has changed, demonstrably, the way the supporters respond and react to the England team, especially at their home games. Now, if England come in goalless at half-time against a supposed minnow of international football, the team are invariably booed off the pitch at Wembley. Without reason, rationale or any kind of empirical evidence, England is still expected, by fans and media alike, to be the best in the world at football. England is not Germany or Italy, yet alone Brazil, and 1966 aside they have no international record to speak of. They are what they are: a good second-tier international football team capable of beating anybody given a good referee, a fully fit team and a fair wind.

Graham Taylor, of course, had none of these. With the fans' fury feeding the tabloids and the newspapers, in return, egging the fans on, he was in a no-win situation. Indeed, if anything, his employers at the Football Association were probably the least of his worries. That he chose to resign and not wait for the sack and the accompanying pay-off as other managers have done since spoke volumes for the man. He knew he had failed. He knew he had let the nation down and, what's more, he didn't need a rampant tabloid press reminding him of his failure in its own unique way.

In his defence, Taylor, more so than Bobby Robson, suffered significantly with the hangover from the European club ban, imposed in the wake of the Heysel tragedy of 1985. His crop of players, with a few notable exceptions like Gary Lineker, were all largely untested in European competition, the net result being that when they were exposed to higher-class continental opposition with different approaches to the game, they, and their manager, struggled to adapt.

Certainly, Taylor tinkered with his squad selections, calling up seventy-eight players and playing fifty-nine of those in his time at the helm, but he also lacked that vital twelfth man that the very best managers can always call upon – luck. Crucially, though, he lacked the services of the most gifted English player of his generation, Paul Gascoigne. In his thirty-eight games in charge of the national side, Taylor had been able to call on Gascoigne in just ten. Not only did Gascoigne miss the trip to the 1992 European Championship in Sweden through injury, but a broken leg sustained when he was at Serie A side Lazio meant that he was unavailable for most of the doomed 1994 World Cup qualifying campaign either.

While Taylor's decision to drop Gascoigne in just his third game in charge would, arguably, prove to be of little material consequence, it was the first sign of an eccentricity that would later manifest itself in a number of peculiar decisions (playing Andy Gray in Poland in 1991, Andy Sinton and David Batty at right-back and Alan Smith replacing Gary Lineker at Euro 92, Gary Pallister at left-back in Norway in 1993, and so on). But with a few notable exceptions, there was undoubtedly a paucity of genuine creative talent within the English game. Without Gascoigne for almost three-quarters of his games, Taylor had little else to work with. Grafters, stoppers and tough tacklers he had in abundance (and there's no denying he used them) but whenever England needed some flair, some imagination, there were precious few players Taylor could call upon. Which, in short, is why England ended up with a midfield packed out with likes of Carlton Palmer and Andy Sinton.

There's no denying that Taylor was one of the most successful club managers in English football history and his record with Watford is beyond reproach. But while running a football club on a day-to-day basis, where relationships could be nurtured, problems ironed out, and decisions made without recourse to committee meetings, suited Taylor perfectly, the sporadic, flee-ting nature of coaching an international team seemed difficult for him to adapt to. Give him time and continuity with the players and there was no doubting what he could achieve. Give him a few days here and there, sandwiched between the players' hectic club schedules and some of their inflated egos, however, and it became a task too far.

The truth was that Graham Taylor was a good man, earnest to a fault and undeniably passionate about what he did. Always he conducted himself impeccably, always finding time for an auto-graph or a photo with a wide-eyed fan and answering all of his critics with respect and a refreshing measure of humour. There was no cynicism, scepticism or bitterness. Not even a suggestion of a libel suit when he patently had just cause to mount one. Just a decent man who has emerged from what turned into an unpleasant and unsavoury experience with his dignity – and his sanity – intact.

He also managed something that the tabloid press singularly fail to do and that is to maintain some kind of perspective. 'The thing is that I always took my job very seriously but you can't take yourself *that* seriously. It's ridiculous to do that,' he told the *Guardian* in 2004. 'When I look at the Premiership now, it's full of people who take themselves far too seriously and who can't laugh at themselves.'

It's a valid point. After *The Impossible Job* documentary was broadcast, Taylor received a postbag of some 1,500 letters delivered to his house. All but three were positive and in support of him. Yet those three letters would not be filed in the bin. Instead, Taylor took time out to call each of the authors, beginning each call with 'Hello I'm Graham Taylor, I believe you've got a bit of a problem.' Cue the sound of jaws hitting floor on the other end of the line.

It's typical of the man. Years later, on the Radio Five Live sports punditry show *Fighting Talk* in 2006, Taylor was asked to 'defend the indefensible', his topic being why he should succeed Sven-Göran Eriksson and become the new England manager. 'I've failed once and I can fail again,' he insisted, before concluding that 'There is only one person who can take England back to greatness and that is me.'

CHAPTER 5

MY LEARNED FRIEND

'A lot of people seem to think I'm just a slippery Cockney boy with a few jokes.'

Terry Venables, England coach 1994–1996

Two days after Graham Taylor's resignation, the phone rang at Jimmy Armfield's desk at the Manchester office of the *Daily Express* newspaper. It was Graham Kelly, chief executive of the Football Association. Tasked with finding suitable candidates to take over from Graham Taylor, Kelly had decided that he needed someone with the requisite experience and standing in the game to help find their new coach, not least because the FA's international committee (which comprised Kelly himself, FA chairman Bert Millichip, Liverpool chairman Noel White and Oldham Athletic chairman Ian Stott) included not a single football professional in its ranks.

In fifty-eight-year-old Jimmy Armfield, Kelly had found a man (and a fellow Blackpool fan to boot) who fitted the bill perfectly. With over 600 games at right-back for his only club, Blackpool, he had played forty-three times for England, captaining them on fifteen occasions, and had been a member of the 1966 World Cup-winning squad, winning £248 15s. for his part in England's finest football triumph. Later, as a manager, Armfield had steered Bolton Wanderers to promotion from the Third Division and then succeeded Brian Clough as manager of Leeds

United, guiding them to the 1975 European Cup final where they lost 2–0 to Bayern Munich in a match noted for poor refereeing and even poorer behaviour by the aggrieved Leeds United fans.

Meeting for tea at Old Trafford, Kelly outlined the role he had in mind. Armfield, surprised and delighted by the approach, was taken with the idea. Having been promised an annual salary of more than the £18,000 he received at the *Daily Express*, he returned home that evening to mull over the offer. He didn't take long to reach his decision. Soon after, he travelled to Lancaster Gate for a meeting with Graham Kelly and Bert Millichip and with his appointment approved, Jimmy Armfield began the search for the man who could revive the English national team and lead them into the 1996 European Championship, the finals of which were to take place in England. 'Looking back,' said Armfield, 'I was probably searching for Clark Kent.'

With Superman unavailable, though, Armfield had to find a coach with a proven track record, not just in the domestic game but, crucially, in the European arena as well. If anything had been learned from the Taylor era, it was that English football had become predictable, pedestrian and one-dimensional with an over-reliance on perspiration rather than inspiration. And while England had laboured with their conservative long-ball game, the rest of the footballing world had caught up and bypassed them.

Moreover, now the Football Association had to find a coach who could also handle the weight of national expectation that would come with being the only man since Sir Alf Ramsey to lead England into a major tournament on home soil. And while that would bring new pressures all of its own, conversely it meant that the manager would not have to endure the problems and pitfalls of a qualification campaign, as the host nation received a place in the finals as of right. That, mercifully, meant no disasters in Dublin or nightmares in Norway. Instead, it meant that ahead of the new England manager lay two and half long years of friendly games in which to tweak his team, tinker with tactics and experiment as much he liked, safe in the knowledge that the only thing that really mattered was how the team was progressing and developing on their way to Euro 96.

With the idea of a foreign coach (or even a Scottish one) anathema to the Football Association, Armfield began polling the opinions of respected club coaches like Manchester United's Alex Ferguson and Arsenal's George Graham, as well as former England managers such as Bobby Robson and, intriguingly, Graham Taylor, to help him in his task.

With a handful of names under consideration, Armfield turned his attention to sounding out the men in the frame. Twice he met Gerry Francis, the QPR boss. He also interviewed the former England captain Bryan Robson who, although yet to go into management, was still regarded as a potential England coach by some at the FA. Methodically, he discarded other managers on his list. Some, like Glenn Hoddle at Chelsea, Billy Bonds at West Ham United and Peter Reid at Manchester City, had done well with their clubs but were still relatively new to management and too much of a gamble to entrust with the most important job of all. Others, like the Howards, Wilkinson of Leeds United and Kendall of Everton, were also overlooked, while the Newcastle United manager and former England captain Kevin Keegan had ruled himself out of the running.

But as the names came and went and Armfield's shortlist got shorter, one name continued to leap out from the page – Terry Venables. Here was a coach who was the very antithesis of Graham Taylor. While Taylor was that nice man from the north, Venables was the Cockney wide-boy made good. Taylor liked to lump it long. Venables wanted to get the ball down and pass his way through the opposition. Taylor's favourite night in was with his feet up catching up on *Coronation Street*. Venables owned his own nightclub. If it was flair and entertainment that the Football Association pined for, then Terry Venables seemed the ideal man, both on and off the pitch.

While few could question the calibre of Venables's candidacy, the FA's international committee had severe reservations about giving the job to a man who hadn't even made the shortlist when the search was on for Bobby Robson's successor, much to Venables's displeasure. As in 1990, the question marks were not over Venables's ability as a coach – he had, after all, won more major trophies than Graham Taylor – but over his business interests – his baggage, if you like – off the field.

The primary concern was an ongoing dispute with the Tottenham chairman Alan Sugar. Having managed the north London side since 1987 with varying degrees of success, Venables had mounted an unsuccessful £20 million takeover bid for the club with the property developer Larry Gillick in March 1991, but when one of their Arab backers had pulled out, the bid collapsed. With Tottenham's debt threatening the club's very existence, it was then left to the founder of the electronics giant Amstrad, Alan Sugar, and the newspaper magnate Robert Maxwell to fight it out for control, a battle which Sugar would win in June, just a month after Spurs had lifted the FA Cup for a then record eighth time.

When Sugar appointed his fellow East Ender Venables as the club's new chief executive, it had seemed to be the dream ticket for Tottenham. Business acumen matched with football nous in a meeting of Cockney minds. But then it all turned sour. When Venables hired his own financial adviser, Eddie Ashby, for the club, Sugar was irritated, not least by the fact that Ashby had been declared bankrupt, had been banned from company directorships and had some forty-three failed businesses on his CV. When he asked Venables to let Ashby go, though, Venables refused. So Sugar, being Sugar, sacked Venables as well, and the two went their separate ways on 14 May 1993, prompting legal action from Venables and yet more hand-rubbing from London's lawyers. Later, when Sugar saw the backlash from the Tottenham fans he said, 'I felt as though I killed Bambi.'

Apart from getting on with Alan Sugar, there was virtually nothing Terry Venables couldn't do. A born entrepreneur, his father had called him 'Terry' after seeing an advert for Terry's All Gold chocolates and the young Venables had even turned himself into a limited company at the age of just seventeen. But football was the real deal and in a long career playing for Chelsea,

Tottenham, Queens Park Rangers and Crystal Palace, Venables would become the first player to represent England at every level from schoolboy right through to full international.

Off the field of play, Venables would throw himself into a bewildering array of extracurricular ventures, some inspired, others harebrained and a few just plain perplexing. He had written novels and television detective series, he had devised board games and also fancied himself as a crooner in the mould of Sinatra (albeit a Cockney version). He ran his own private members' club in London's Kensington called Scribes West and had, briefly, been involved with fellow players George Graham and Ron 'Chopper' Harris in a tailoring business. Least memorably, he had also invented the 'Thingummywig', which, for the blissfully unaware, was a hat with a wig stitched inside that allowed ladies to leave home with their curlers still in, without fear of embarrassment or ridicule.

When he wasn't emancipating the housewives of Britain, Venables had also made a name for himself as one of the best coaches in the game, especially in his spell at Barcelona (1984–87) where he had won the La Liga title and the Spanish Cup and reached the final of the first post-Heysel European Cup, losing to Steaua Bucharest on penalties. (The sheer novelty of the Cockney in Catalonia was a gift for the red-top headline writers who soon dubbed him 'El Tel'.) Intriguingly, Venables had been interviewed for the position on the recommendation of the then England manager Bobby Robson, who had just turned down the Catalan giants' overtures for a third time.

Imaginative and progressive, Venables had cut his managerial teeth at his old club Crystal Palace, taking them from the old Third Division in 1976 to the First Division by the end of the decade. So impressive was the club's dramatic turnaround under Venables that the media began calling Palace the 'team of the eighties' and while the south-east London side would never quite live up to the hype, Venables's reputation as a coach was made. Indeed, as his Palace side rose up the league ladder, Venables

Caretaker England manager Joe Mercer shares a joke with the press ahead of his first game in charge against Wales in May 1974 (probably about the bloke's hair behind him).

England fail to beat Poland at Wembley in October 1973 and it's the beginning of the end for Alf Ramsey.

Ron Greenwood wisely decides against the perm and tight shorts for the 1982 World Cup squad photocall.

Bad luck and dodgy refereeing in the vital Holland v. England World Cup qualifier in Rotterdam in October 1993 would, ultimately, cost Graham Taylor his job as England manager. Well, that and the ugly tracksuits...

Bobby Robson looks on as Chris Waddle misses his penalty against West Germany and England are out of the 1990 World Cup.

England secure their place at the 1998 World Cup Finals after a staunch performance in Italy in October 1997. Rarely, has a goalless draw been greeted with such joy.

No amount of consoling from Terry Venables can ease Gareth Southgate's pain after his crucial penalty miss against Germany at Euro 96.

Another fine mess – Kevin Keegan does his best Stan Laurel impression after the defeat to Germany at Wembley in October 2000. Moments later, he would quit as England coach.

Sergeant Wilko to the rescue – Howard Wilkinson (second from right), steps in as England coach for the game against Finland in Helsinki in October 2000.

Aye, aye skipper – coach for just one game, Peter Taylor (right), still managed to make one of the biggest decisions of the decade, making David Beckham the new England captain.

Sven-Göran Eriksson is welcomed to the FA by the chief executive Adam Crozier in January 2001. Queues of swooning women just out of shot.

Wet, wet, wet – Steve McClaren's tenure ends in misery against Croatia at Wembley in November 2007.

Enter Fabio Capello – the £6 million man arrives for his first day at work as England manager in January 2008.

would even be appointed coach to the England Under-21 side, working alongside Dave Sexton.

Modern, forward-thinking football coach on one hand, wheeler-dealer on the other. Part genius, part Del Boy. Venables certainly had the ear of the players and, for the most part, the public. Moreover, having managed him terrifically at Tottenham, he was arguably the only coach who knew how to handle the wayward genius of the man England needed more than ever, Paul Gascoigne.

Jimmy Armfield and Terry Venables would eventually meet on four separate occasions, and each time the FA's headhunter became ever more convinced of his suitability for the England job. But not everyone concurred with Armfield. A BBC *Panorama* programme made by the reporter Martin Bashir in September 1993 had made numerous allegations surrounding Venables's business dealings, prompting Venables to issue a libel writ against the corporation. Moreover, having been a football pundit in the BBC's televised football coverage since the mid-1980s, Venables, angry and irritated, left the BBC and signed up for their rivals ITV.

With his name often in the papers for all the wrong reasons, the FA's international committee, especially Noel White, were wary of endorsing Jimmy Armfield's preferred candidate but, keen to see the matter resolved and England begin to move forward, they gave Venables the benefit of the doubt.

A chance was all Venables wanted and when he finally arrived for his interview on the seventh-floor offices of the Football League's commercial department in Old Marylebone Road, he did so confident that now was his time to finally land his dream job. Sat around a large mahogany table were the men of the FA's international committee who would decide Venables's fate. The interview went well. The atmosphere was relaxed and convivial and Venables was frank and open about all of the stories, rumours and hearsay that had populated the pages of the nation's newspapers in the last year. The committee was also impressed that throughout the courtship he had never once mentioned the salary on offer.

That said, he also knew when to bite his tongue. At one point in the interview, the FA's chief executive Graham Kelly became distracted by a woman standing on a roof opposite and threatening to jump. 'It just goes to show,' said Kelly, 'I bet she's got more problems than all of us.'

'Speak for yourself,' thought Venables. 'If she had my problems she would have jumped twenty minutes ago.' Mercifully, she didn't and was eventually talked down by the emergency services.

The FA had spent the weeks that had passed since the first meeting doing their homework on Venables, digging around to see if there were any more skeletons in his cupboard. Venables, meanwhile, had been fending off the advances of other international teams eager to pickpocket his services from England. Wales, for instance, had offered him the job of replacing Terry Yorath, while Nigeria had also expressed an interest in making him their new coach for the World Cup finals in the USA.

But there would be only one job Venables wanted – aside from his old one at Spurs, perhaps – and on Tuesday, 25 January 1994 he received the news he had been waiting for. With the committee finally in agreement, their scepticism as to their new coach's probity assuaged, as much as it could be, a contract had been prepared (complete with get-out clauses in case any serious allegation of wrongdoing on Venables's part was ever proved) offering England's new team boss a reported £170,000 a year. Initially, Venables had only been offered a one-year deal, but when he refused the FA extended the offer to take him through to July 1996 and the end of the European Championship. And in a move designed to show the world (and Venables) who still held all the power they even invented a new job title. No longer would this be the England manager. This would be the 'England coach', the idea being that this was purely a football appointment and had little or nothing do with a wider management role. Not that Venables really cared. Besides, all the best international teams, like Brazil and Italy, called their managers 'coach'.

The deal done, Venables called his wife Yvette, who, having had her piano lesson and done the shopping, was just about to start cleaning the kitchen floor. He told her the news. Delighted for her husband and relieved that the weeks of uncertainty had finally come to an end, Yvette Venables laid down her mop and put the kettle on.

With the official announcement of his appointment delayed by a day so as not to clash with the funeral of the legendary Manchester United manager Sir Matt Busby, Terry Venables strode out on to the Wembley pitch on Friday, 28 January 1994 as only the seventh permanent England manager, or the first ever England coach, if you believed the Football Association's spin. With a full-length overcoat protecting him from the winter chill and a mile-wide grin covering his face, Venables seemed taken aback by the sheer number of photographers and journalists who had arrived for his coronation. Behind him, Wembley's electronic scoreboard read, 'Congratulations, Good Luck Terry.'

Later, in the press conference, flanked by Millichip and Kelly, and with Jimmy Armfield standing in the wings, he told the media of his plans for England. 'Everyone feels very low at the moment, and it's about time we brought some fun back. The only way to do that, of course, is by winning games,' he asserted. 'We must have a system of play, and an alternative to it, which the players can understand and are familiar with, but the problem is that I'm going to have so little time with them. It's up to me to make it as simple as possible, so that they know exactly what they've got to do.

'I want to play in a way that will win the admiration of the public, which means good football. Not fantasy football where you play well and lose, you've got to have common sense. As the man said, we've got to go back to basics – stop goals, create in midfield and finish well.'

Though it had taken nine weeks to appoint Graham Taylor's successor, the FA chairman Sir Bert Millichip was convinced that the wait had been worth it. Besides, with two and a half years of friendlies ahead of the new manager, it wasn't like there was any great hurry. 'We have been criticized for being too urgent and we have also been criticized for delay,' said Millichip. 'I was very impressed with Terry's desire to be the coach, and the eagerness with which he wanted to get down to work.'

The formal press conference over, Venables worked the room for scores of additional media interviews. Same questions. Same answers. Same smile. Nothing was going to ruin this moment for Terry Venables – not even the umpteenth question about Alan Sugar ...

Sixteen Lancaster Gate was all mahogany and memories. Pictures of England's former glories – or rather glory – adorned the walls, the trophy cabinet glistened with the kind of unrecognizable baubles most fans would struggle to name and there, on the wall, was a photograph of the late Bobby Moore, proudly leading England out at Wembley Stadium. That one picture said more to Terry Venables than any of the trophies or the trinkets. That, he reflected as he entered the building for his first day at work on Monday, 31 January 1994, was what playing for England should be all about.

But when Venables reached his office on third floor, pushed opened the double doors, turned right and set about working, he was staggered. Far from a progressive, forward-thinking, thoroughly modern organization, the Football Association seemed stuck in a time warp. As the days went by, he soon discovered that there were no dossiers on England's opposition, no match or player records from former managers, not even a video library of past matches. And though England had been awarded the right to host the 1996 European Championship back in May 1992, precious few friendly games had been arranged for England in preparation for the finals. It seemed change wasn't just needed on the football pitch.

Venables's first task, other than bringing in a blackboard and a Subbuteo table to work on tactics, however, was to finalize his own team. Like Graham Taylor before him, he called in an experienced hand in the shape of former England assistant Don

Howe to act as a technical co-ordinator, combined with a younger hand, Bryan Robson (who had just taken over as player-manager at Middlesbrough), the idea being that the former England captain would be groomed for the role in the future as he split his duties between club and country. Venables would also appoint another vastly experienced ex-England international to his set-up by handing the responsibility of the Under-21 side to Ray Wilkins. He also ditched the two long-standing physios Fred Street and Norman Medhurst in favour of Dave Butler and Alan Smith.

With his first game, a midweek friendly against the reigning European Champions Denmark at Wembley, booked in for 9 March, Venables flew out to Rome, with the press in tow, to check on two of his most important players, David Platt and Paul Gascoigne. In Rome, he found Gascoigne in good form and in good spirits. Typically, Gazza was besieged by photographers and autograph-hunters wherever he went, but the two still managed a useful reunion at the Hassler Hotel at the top of the Spanish Steps. It was a different story in Genoa. Now with Sampdoria, David Platt, one of England's other World Cup heroes from 1990, met Venables at the airport himself, without a paparazzo or a pushy fan in sight. Such was the fickle nature of fame.

Even as his first game approached, Venables still had to deal with his off-field problems, with four court cases hanging over him. Then, on the very day of the game against Denmark, a moment the new England coach should have been cherishing, he discovered that one of his former lawyers had issued writs against him, claiming some £312,000 in unpaid fees. The more things changed in Venables's life, the more, it seemed, they stayed the same. 'I must be the only person who actually gets less publicity by becoming manager of England,' he said with a shrug.

Still, the reception he received that night from almost 72,000 fans inside Wembley certainly put a smile on Venables's ageing face. With debuts for Blackburn's attacking left-back Graeme Le Saux, and Tottenham's wide man Darren Anderton, and a recall upfront for the man cast aside by Graham Taylor, Peter Beardsley (now back at his native Newcastle), it was a side designed with goals in mind and with players noted for their creativity and imagination. And lest anyone should think that that side wasn't attacking enough, there would also be a debut, as a substitute, for Le Saux's fellow Channel Islander, Southampton's extravagantly skilful Matthew Le Tissier.

While the 1–0 win and, more importantly, an encouraging performance sent everyone home happy, the next game saw England run riot, putting five past a poor Greece side. Curiously, though, just 23,569 people turned up to watch at Wembley.

After games, Venables and his entourage would often repair to Scribes West, the club he owned in Kensington, and it would soon become a regular haunt for some of his team, as well as a kind of glorified drop-in centre or expensive soup kitchen for pressmen, football agents and assorted hangers-on. It would gain notoriety for some more unsavoury incidents too. In March 1995 the Chelsea and England midfielder Dennis Wise was prosecuted for assaulting sixty-five-year-old taxi driver Gerard Graham and smashing the glass partition in his cab after a night at the club in November 1994. He was sentenced to three months in prison but was later acquitted on appeal. Venables continued to select him, right up until his conviction. His club manager, Chelsea's Glenn Hoddle, though, stripped him of the captaincy.

The reputation of Scribes was such that the comedian Frank Skinner even toyed with the idea of pitching a novel business idea to the England coach. 'I was going to ask him what he thought of my idea for an El Tel theme nightclub called Wormwood Scribes,' he said, 'but I chickened out.'

A month before Wise's court appearance, Venables had taken his team across the Irish Sea to Dublin for his first away fixture as England coach against Jack Charlton's Republic of Ireland. After uninspiring and unspectacular games against Norway (won 2–0), USA (won 2–0), Romania (1–1) and Nigeria (won 1–0), Venables was in need of a performance first and a result second against a team they hadn't beaten for a decade. He got neither. Shortly after Wolverhampton Wanderers' David Kelly had put the home side ahead, trouble flared in the upper tier of the main stand. Singing anti-IRA songs and ripping out the seats and throwing them on to the Irish fans below, hordes of drunken English hooligans caused a suspension in play, prompting England skipper David Platt to run over to the side of the pitch and appeal for calm. Fat chance. Moments later, a piece of wood whistled past Platt's head. With no sign of the violence ending, the referee Dick Jol had little choice but to take the players off the field. After only twenty-seven minutes, the game was abandoned.

For the FA's Graham Kelly, it was the worst possible outcome. Trouble among travelling England fans may not have been a rarity, but now, with Euro 96 a little over a year away, the prospect of England's first major tournament in thirty years being disrupted by hooligans was suddenly at the forefront of everyone's minds. 'I am very distressed about it,' said Kelly. 'This is a very difficult situation for the authorities to deal with. I am very shocked at the callous disregard these people had for the safety of the people, the children, who were below them.'

In his book *Venables' England: The Making of the Team* (published before the European Championship), the England coach feared the worst come the summer. 'We mustn't make excuses for this kind of behaviour,' he wrote. 'If it is repeated during the European Championship finals, then, in social terms, we will be the disgrace of the world; it will all mean nothing if it is overshadowed by pictures of thugs throwing bits of iron down from the terraces and fighting in the streets.'

The spectre of hooliganism, insipid, tortuous performances and a public rapidly losing faith in this latest version of the England team, didn't augur well for Terry Venables. Whether it was the relief that Graham Taylor had departed or joy that Venables had been appointed (or maybe a bit of both), that initial enthusiasm, that zing, had dwindled and all but evaporated.

It got worse. After three mediocre performances in the Euro 96 dress rehearsal, the Umbro Cup, against Brazil (the 3–1 defeat was his first as England coach), Japan (won 2–1) and Sweden (3–3), even his arch-advocates, the tabloid press, were beginning to turn on him. Brian Woolnough, his long-time ally and the football writer for the *Sun*, was verging on the apoplectic. 'This is awful, terrible,' he wrote after the Japan game. 'What the hell is Venables playing at? This was the ninth game under his control and the reality was that England under Venables were no better off than when Graham Taylor was sacked.'

Most noticeable were the sorry attendances at Wembley Stadium. When I was working for the football magazine *90 Minutes* in the mid-1990s I was given the dubious pleasure of attending all of Venables's friendlies at Wembley in the run-up to Euro 96 and, as the months went by, the crowds got smaller and smaller, so much so that an attendance of over 30,000 became the exception, not the norm. At times, as I looked round the vast, endless sections of empty seats, the atmosphere in the old Empire Stadium often bordered on the funereal. Ordinarily, when the Wembley crowd is bored or unhappy they tend to start a Mexican wave. In 1995, when the wind whistling through the stadium was the loudest sound, there were never enough people to perform one.

By September 1995 and the visit of Colombia it was clear that England's fans were growing increasingly weary not just of Terry Venables's experimental sides and his much-vaunted 'Christmas Tree' formation but with the lack of any real competition in the games. The attendance that Wednesday night told its own story – just 20,000. Not 20,001 or 19,999 but exactly 20,000. It was as though someone, somewhere had decreed that no game at Wembley could ever be seen to be so poorly attended. That said, even if that was the exact attendance for the game, it still represented a depressing statistic for a team that was supposed to be surging into Euro 96 buoyant, brimming with confidence and with the public full-square behind them.

Still, at least those few, those happy few, got to see the Colombian goalkeeper Rene Higuita's astonishing 'Scorpion Kick'. Faced with a lofted cross-cum-shot from England's Jamie Redknapp, the keeper had dived forward and with the ball about to cross the line behind him, thrown his legs forward and cleared it back over his head in the most showboating and, well, pointless manner imaginable.

It's a different story at Wembley today, of course. Even the England games against countries most fans would struggle to locate on a map attract decent crowds, and this despite the ever-spiralling cost of a ticket. The World Cup qualifier against Kazakhstan in October 2008, for example, pulled in over 89,000 people to Wembley.

The new Wembley Stadium that opened in March 2007 is, of course, a magnificent structure, but then so it should be given that it cost almost £800 million and took four years to build, and fans will want to visit it, regardless of England's opposition, just for the experience. But the old Wembley was notoriously difficult for travelling fans to reach and, with its problematic seats, restricted views and shabby demeanour, was never going to be a big draw, not least when it was a midweek game and the opposition on show was as mediocre as the hosts.

There were few positives for Venables as he made his way through 1995. His myriad legal disputes continued to cast an ever wider shadow over his tenure and at times it seemed as though Venables spent more of his time lining the pockets of lawyers than he did talking tactics with his players. Claims and counter-claims flew around like confetti, writs would be served and cases contested, often at the most unfortunate and inconvenient of times. On Monday, 2 October, for instance, Venables had announced his squad for the forthcoming friendly against perennial party-poopers Norway in Oslo at midday at the Park Court Hotel near the FA headquarters at Lancaster Gate, before heading straight down to the High Court to contest a libel case brought against him by the former Tottenham Hotspur vice-chairman Tony Perry over allegations Venables had made against him in his 1994 autobiography. The two would eventually settle out of court, Perry receiving £20,000 as part of a £500,000 damages and costs settlement. Later, he admitted that an apology from Venables a year earlier would have satisfied him, but it was never forthcoming.

On the playing front, there was also mounting concern not merely over England's chances at Euro 96 but at their wholesale lack of firepower in attack. Just seventeen goals in the eleven games under Venables made a mockery of his reputation as one of the game's great attacking coaches.

At the heart of the problem was Alan Shearer. A prolific, irresistible goalscorer for his club Blackburn Rovers, Shearer seemed to be stymied by his lone-striker role in Venables's Christmas Tree formation, the net result being that he had now gone seven games without an international goal. Likewise Teddy Sheringham. A more creative player than Shearer but a striker nevertheless, he had scored just once in his eleven England appearances.

At least there were some positives for Venables to take solace in. Paul Gascoigne, the England talisman who now lit up Scottish football with his new club Rangers, was finally fit and back to something approaching his best, while new recruits like Liverpool's Jamie Redknapp and Steve McManaman were settling nicely into international football.

The goal drought, for England and Shearer, would continue in the dismal goalless draw against Norway, where Gazza (thigh strain) was again sorely missed. Not that Venables was unduly concerned. After all, his reputation within the game was still good, even if it was not without blemish off the field. He had even received an offer from Italian Serie A giants Internazionale to become their new coach on a salary more than three times that which he was receiving with England. While he politely declined Inter's offer, the news was enough to shake the Football Association into something resembling action over their coach's future.

During the trip to Norway, it had emerged that the FA officials Graham Kelly and Sir Bert Millichip had met to discuss what they were going to do with Venables, especially in light of the interest from one of European football's biggest clubs. Soon after, Millichip had publicly announced that Venables would have the FA's backing as coach not just up to the conclusion of Euro 96 but through to the World Cup finals in France in 1998. While the news came as something of a surprise, not least because England's performances hadn't exactly given any real reason to suggest that Venables was a coach worth keeping, it transpired that the decision had not been unanimous. While Kelly and Millichip were in agreement, the other two members of the international committee, Ian Stott and Noel White, remained to be convinced. Little did Venables know it, but what had seemed like the best news he had had in some time would actually prove to be the beginning of the end for the beleaguered England coach.

Trouble, it seemed, was only ever a headline away for Terry Venables. Even the first encouraging performance under him for some time – a 3–1 win over Switzerland at Wembley in November 1995 – would be overshadowed by yet more allegations in the tabloids. This time it was Harry Harris, the *Daily Mirror*'s chief football writer, having a go. Harris had long been a thorn in Venables's side, forever probing the coach's business dealings, much to Venables's chagrin. This time, the story centred on the £2.1 million transfer of Teddy Sheringham (a player who, co-incidentally, had just scored and had one of his best games for England against Switzerland) from Nottingham Forest to Tottenham in August 1992 when Venables had been in charge at White Hart Lane, and an alleged £50,000 cash payment to Venables's business partner Eddie Ashby.

There was more. Jeffrey Fugler, of the marketing company Fugler & Fugler, was suing Venables for monies owed to his consultancy. Fugler had alleged that Venables had encouraged him to inflate his fees for the work he was doing for Tottenham Hotspur rather than pursue the £20,000 he was still owed by Scribes West for work he had carried out for Venables's club. Moreover, Fugler also maintained that Venables had been involved in a marketing consultancy with the former Chelsea player David Webb and that he had requested payments be made to Webb for his part in the transfer of two players from Southend to Tottenham.

As 1995 dripped into 1996, it would prove to be anything but a happy New Year for Terry Venables. With the draw for Euro 96 looming, he had received notice from the Department of Trade and Industry that they had commenced proceedings to disqualify him as a company director for the alleged mismanagement of four companies (Scribes West Ltd, Edenote plc, Tottenham Hotspur plc and Tottenham Hotspur Football and Athletic Company Ltd). A few days later – and just three days after a 1–1 home draw with Portugal – the case with Jeffrey Fugler also reached its conclusion and it was more bad news for Venables.

Finding against the England coach, Mr Recorder Duncan Williams described some of the evidence offered by Venables as 'not entirely reliable to put it at its most charitable', and ordered that Fugler receive half of what he was claiming (£11,292.95, plus interest) and also half of his legal costs. That still meant a bill of around £100,000 for Venables and Scribes West. 'I am disappointed at today's result,' said Venables. 'However, I feel significantly vindicated in that the claim was almost halved. I wish this to be an example that I will not yield to such disgraceful tactics. Never.'

That weekend, Venables and the massed ranks of the Football Association convened at Birmingham's International Convention Centre for the draw for Euro 96. Publicly, the FA had brushed over Venables's latest appearance in court, arguing that it did not affect his ability to do his job. Privately, though, there was now grave concern about just where all of Venables's legal contests would ultimately end up.

On the Saturday night before the draw Venables met FA chief executive Graham Kelly at his hotel. He told Kelly that he was angered over public comments made by Noel White and Ian Stott in that morning's papers questioning the effect that Venables's off-field problems were having on his and the FA's reputation, and that he was going to quit after England's European Championship campaign had ended.

Just as all of Venables's many adversaries had seemed to orchestrate their legal battles so that they coincided with an

England game or a squad announcement, now Venables had chosen his moment with an almost wicked irony, just hours before the European football community assembled for the Euro 96 draw.

Conscious that if the news broke of Venables's decision, the European Championship draw would be not merely overshadowed but ruined, Kelly arranged a meeting at the Hyatt Regency Hotel with Sir Bert Millichip and Noel White the following morning so the three could discuss the rapidly deteriorating situation. Venables was also invited to attend.

That morning, the quartet aired their grievances, with Venables demanding to know if he had the full, unequivocal backing of the men in the room. When Noel White said he couldn't offer that reassurance, Venables confirmed his intention to leave.

At the draw on 17 December, hosted by the Little and Large of UEFA, Gerard Aigner and Lennart Johannson, Venables was, as ever, his usual self. Smiling, gregarious and clearly proud to be the coach of the host nation, he seemed a completely different person to the one who only that morning had handed in his notice. The draw itself, meanwhile, would throw up some enticing matches. As one of four seeds, England were drawn in the same group as Switzerland, Holland and Scotland (the first England–Scotland match in seven years), with the top two from the group qualifying for the quarter-finals. It was a route that gave them a possible semi-final showdown against Germany.

But as the countdown to 8 June and England's tournament opener against the Swiss began, a handful of men in suits in Birmingham knew that without yet playing a competitive match as coach, Terry Venables had called time on his England stewardship. Publicly, the Football Association claimed that negotiations over extending Venables's contract beyond Euro 96 and to the World Cup in 1998 were still ongoing. Sir Bert Millichip even told the press that he didn't 'want him [Venables] going into the European Championship thinking he is going to get the sack, because he is not'.

But Venables's mind was made up. The story itself would not break until 10 January, however, prompting another hastily arranged FA press conference, with the line offered that Venables would be leaving his post after Euro 96 to concentrate on clearing his name with regard to the court cases looming against Alan Sugar and the BBC and its *Panorama* programme. That Venables had chosen to leave simply because he didn't have 100 per cent backing seemed extraordinary. Few people, in any profession, enjoy that luxury. But did he even merit a new contract anyway? Legal issues aside, his record as England coach at the time he resigned was unspectacular to the say the least, with just six wins and one defeat to show from fourteen completed friendlies. 'It is a sad day for me because I loved being England manager,' he said, forgetting his correct job title. 'I loved it and it was something that I always wanted. But I had no option. I must clear my name and it was a decision, given all the circumstances, I had to make.'

Four days later, as if to prove that the life of Terence Frederick Venables could never be anything other than tense or taxing, he was banned by the High Court from being a company director for seven years.

CHAPTER 6

THE MAN IN THE WHITE SUIT

'I have never heard a minute's silence like that.'
Glenn Hoddle on the mark of respect shown for Diana, Princess
of Wales before the England v. Moldova game at Wembley on
10 September 1997

It's April 1987 and the BBC's flagship pop music programme *Top of the Pops* is featuring that week's number 12 record in the charts, 'Diamond Lights'. Performed by Tottenham Hotspur and England team-mates Glenn Hoddle and Chris Waddle under the imaginative name 'Glenn & Chris', it's a plodding, overproduced chunk of electro-pop rock by two men with rolled-up jacket sleeves and high-waisted jeans, coupled with the kind of heinous haircuts that could help build a solid case for the return of capital punishment.

It wasn't really their fault that they looked like stunt doubles from *Miami Vice*. This, after all, was the 1980s, the second decade in succession that fashion had managed to forget. The remarkable thing about Glenn & Chris's foray into pop music, though, was not that it somehow managed to scale the upper echelons of the charts, but that it was entirely at odds with the élan they both displayed on the football field, especially in the case of Glenn Hoddle ...

In the blood and thunder, guts and glory game of the 1970s, Glenn Hoddle's passing, touch and vision seemed to be from a different time and place. Spotted as an eleven-year-old by the Spurs striker Martin Chivers, he had signed for Tottenham as an apprentice in 1973 and made his debut at seventeen in August 1975. He progressed to the full England team by November 1979, scoring on his debut in a 2–0 win over Bulgaria in a European Championship qualifier at Wembley.

But while many marvelled at the vast invention and abundant skill of Hoddle – there was even an Eric Clapton-esque graffiti campaign in the 1980s proclaiming 'Hoddle Is God' – he was rarely treated with the same reverence when it came to the English national team. Despite his undoubted talent, Hoddle, like Tony Currie, Frank Worthington or Alan Hudson before him, found himself cast in the role of luxury player in the England squad, one whose flamboyant, expressive style of play was anathema to a succession of England coaches whose focus veered more towards graft and honest endeavour, rather than anything quite so flimsy as guile and imagination.

On the continent, national team coaches would doubtless have built a team around Hoddle, such was his ability to change the face of a game with an improbable goal or a defence-splitting pass. Indeed, the French legend Michel Platini once said that had Hoddle been French he would have won 150 caps or more. As it was, Hoddle had to content himself with fifty-three which, on reflection, was scant reward for one so undeniably gifted.

After a spell at French side AS Monaco where he worked under then manager Arsène Wenger (he called Hoddle 'the most skilful player I have ever worked with'), Hoddle took his first managerial position as player-coach of First Division club Swindon Town, guiding them to promotion to the Premier League via the play-offs in 1993. A little over a month later and with his star in the ascendant, Hoddle had left Wiltshire to return to the capital as the new player-manager of Chelsea.

In his three years at Stamford Bridge, Hoddle set in place the blueprint to change Chelsea's dwindling fortunes. Now, instead of being the 'sleeping giant' most observers were wont to refer to them as, they were a club heading back in the right direction.

They reached the FA Cup final in his first season and the semi-finals of the European Cup-Winners' Cup in his second. But while Hoddle's Chelsea failed to make any real impact in the Premier League – they had to settle for mid-table placings in his time there – his very presence at the club and the way the team were now playing suddenly made Chelsea a more attractive proposition for the game's bigger, better players and soon the likes of the former Dutch skipper Ruud Gullit, ex-Manchester United striker Mark Hughes and the attacking Romanian full-back Dan Petrescu would join.

Certainly, Hoddle had made a promising start to his managerial career but his lack of silverware – he had won just one Division One play-off final – didn't really suggest that he was an England manager in waiting. So when Terry Venables stepped down at the end of Euro 96, Hoddle, still only thirty-eight, was merely one of many names in the frame.

Again, the FA had tasked Jimmy Armfield with helping to find a successor and this time he formed part of a sub-committee along with the chief executive Graham Kelly, chairman Bert Millichip, Keith Wiseman, the FA vice-chairman Chris Wilcox and Noel White. The group first met on 15 January 1996, five days after Venables's resignation had been announced, by which time the likes of the Newcastle manager Kevin Keegan, the Spurs coach Gerry Francis and former England skipper Bryan Robson, the man being groomed for the role, had all ruled themselves out of contention. By the end of the month when the committee met again, the former England manager Bobby Robson and Everton's most successful boss and then manager of Sheffield United, Howard Kendall, had also been scratched from the list.

Rumour abounded. On Armfield's recommendation, the FA's Graham Kelly approached Manchester United's chief executive Martin Edwards to ask for permission to interview their manager Alex Ferguson but, not surprisingly, was turned down. Kenny Dalglish, the former Liverpool and Blackburn boss, was said to be interested. Ray Wilkins, Joe Royle and Howard Wilkinson were all linked with the job while Frank Clark, the man who had rejuvenated the former European champions Nottingham Forest, was even announced as the new England boss in the *Sunday Express*, a report dismissed by the FA's press officer David Davies as 'bollocks and garbage'.

As candidates fell by the wayside, the name of Glenn Hoddle gained favour. The Chelsea manager had been on Armfield's list from the outset – he had even noted his name down as one for the future during the search that ended in Venables's appointment – and with other, seemingly more qualified candidates distancing themselves from the job, he gave Hoddle a call.

What happened next was a series of clandestine meetings that wouldn't have been out of place in a John le Carré novel. The pair first met in London's Hyde Park. As the two sat in Hoddle's BMW facing the Serpentine, they spoke at length about the job and what Hoddle could bring to it. They parted that day with Armfield's concerns that the Chelsea boss was too young and too arrogant finally assuaged. They reconvened soon after over tea at Hoddle's Ascot home before finally meeting in an abandoned car park nearby. Sitting on the bonnet of Armfield's car, Hoddle answered all of the questions thrown his way. From coaching to the media, from his religion to the effect the job may have on his young family, Hoddle seemed to be a man in complete control of his career, a manager who knew what he wanted and how he could go about getting it. 'I went back home to Blackpool and I must admit I wrestled with the decision for a while,' revealed Armfied in his autobiography, *Right Back To The Beginning*. 'With Venables, I was convinced we had found the right man at the right time. With Glenn, I wondered if he would stay for four or five years, which is what we were looking for. But I warmed to him, and frankly, I didn't have a long list of candidates.'

The search was over. Armfield recommended Hoddle for interview and after meeting the international committee and some inevitable contractual wrangling with Hoddle and his agent Dennis Roach, his appointment was ratified. Later, Sir Bert Millichip would explain the FA's decision. 'The general opinion of the committee was that it was essential that we went for someone with international playing experience, and it was a bonus that Hoddle played abroad. He certainly played the type of skilful football all the committee appreciates and that we need at international level now.'

Moreover, after the much-publicized legal problems of Terry Venables, it was refreshing for the FA to have found a man who came to the job free from the kind of off-the-field business dealings that they could patently do without. 'We did ask Glenn before he signed the contract whether there were any skeletons in his cupboard,' said the FA's chief executive Graham Kelly, before adding, 'other than that dreadful record he once made with Chris Waddle.'

Crucially, the FA found themselves in the fortunate position of being able to appoint Hoddle without the need to compensate Chelsea. For months, Hoddle had been caught in the boardroom crossfire at Stamford Bridge where the chairman Ken Bates and his rival Matthew Harding were involved in an all too public power struggle. As a result, Hoddle had found himself awaiting a new contract as manager. When it finally came, in the shape of a £1.2 million four-year deal, it wasn't too little (in fact it would have made him one of the top earning managers in the country) but it was too late. England had come calling and Hoddle wasn't about to say no.

At 4 p.m. on 2 May 1996 Glenn Hoddle was announced as the next England manager, a little over a month before Terry Venables would lead his England team into the European Championship. At a press conference led by Graham Kelly and David Davies at the Royal Lancaster Hotel, Hoddle and Venables appeared side by side, both in grey jackets and wearing ties that warranted immediate disciplinary action. It was a show of unity designed to pre-empt any awkward line of questioning about how the handover would occur. Behind the scenes, though, Venables had already warned David Davies to keep Hoddle away from his training camps for fear of any distraction it might create. 'I am sure that he has the right credentials,' said Venables. 'I have enjoyed the job, Glenn will, it is well worth it. Do you know, if the time ever came again for me then I would definitely consider doing it again?'

If anyone ever doubted that Venables was walking away from the England job against his will, here was the conclusive proof. But this, for the time being, was Hoddle's day, the fulfilment of a childhood dream to one day lead his country. 'It has been a burning ambition of mine and the time is right for me. It is the pinnacle of my career and I had to take it,' he told the throng. 'People will say the England coach needs more experience but experience should not always be gauged by grey hair. I have played abroad and been a manager here for six years. I believe I am ready for this.'

While most of the media attention focused on his relative lack of success and/or experience, the thorny issue was just how the handover from Venables to Hoddle would happen, especially as the pair's roles would overlap for anything up to two months, depending on how far England progressed in Euro 96. It was a difficult, almost impossible situation. On one hand, there was the incumbent, focused on his one and only chance of success with England; on the other, the incoming man, with his own ideas, desperate to mould the players into his own team.

Against his better judgement, Venables conceded to allowing Hoddle a solitary visit to Bisham Abbey, the team's headquarters for Euro 96, to observe the current crop of England stars at close hand. Though results may have suggested otherwise, this was a squad good enough to go far in the championship. In David Seaman and Tony Adams they had a defensive backbone as dependable as any in world football. In the midfield they had the driving force of Paul Ince and the incomparable, irrepressible energy and invention of Paul Gascoigne, while upfront they had the 'SAS' themselves, Alan Shearer and Teddy Sheringham. Certainly, Venables was pleased with the great strides his team had made, not to mention the spirit in the camp. 'The openness of their minds was terrific,' he would say. 'Whatever I asked of them they responded to. They wanted to listen and learn.'

*

After all those months of meaningless friendlies, of tinkering and tweaking, Euro 96 was now just three weeks away. Faced with the prospect of playing top-class European opposition on home soil, the FA arranged a trip to the other side of the world to play the international minnows China and Hong Kong. It was a baffling decision. Not for the FA some casual rounds of golf and lazy afternoons spent relaxing by a pool in the Mediterranean, oh dear no. It had to be a 12,000-mile round trip to the Orient just for a couple of games that meant nothing aside from a few extra quid in the FA coffers. Here, though, was a final opportunity for the England team to enjoy a trip away from the glare of publicity back home and without the possibility of any crowd trouble ruining the games. The good news was that not even the most determined of football hooligans bothered to make the trip to the Far East. The bad news, though, was very bad indeed.

While the victories against China (3–0) and the Hong Kong Select side (1–0) were largely forgettable, the trip would nevertheless remain etched in every football fan's memory for all the wrong reasons. The trouble had started on the flight out, and, as with most of the shenanigans on the trip, centred around Paul Gascoigne. Having wrapped up a League and Cup double with Rangers the day before they left, Gascoigne had been celebrating in style and he was still at it when the plane was taking off. Eager to get another beer, Gascoigne had caught the attention of one of the stewards not by the internationally recognized gestures of a tap on the shoulder or word in the ear but by poking him in the back (although Stuart Pearce maintained he 'patted him on the bum'). A scuffle ensued, the pilot then got involved and Gascoigne was threatened with being dropped off in Russia unless he behaved himself. Faced with an unscheduled stopover in Moscow, Gascoigne backed down.

The games came and went and were noticeable only for the fact that the striker Alan Shearer failed to score again, making it a worrying 939 minutes without a goal for the national team. But with two largely irrelevant victories and no major injury scares (despite the team bus colliding with a taxi on the way back to the hotel), a contented Venables gave the team the green light to have a night out in Hong Kong to celebrate Gascoigne's twenty-ninth birthday, sending one of his coaches, the former England skipper Bryan Robson, along to keep an eye on proceedings.

That night, the party repaired to the China Jump Club in the Marco Polo section and as the drinks took their toll so the behaviour of England's players took a turn for the worse. Late on, Gascoigne and Liverpool's Robbie Fowler became embroiled in a juvenile argument about the quality (or otherwise) of the Liverpool striker's chat-up lines, the net result being a pint of beer poured over Fowler's head, courtesy of Gascoigne.

Fowler wouldn't be the only victim. Teddy Sheringham also got an impromptu shower, followed soon after by Steve McManaman. The evening ended with England players taking turns to sit in the 'Dentist's Chair', lying back while an array of spirits were poured straight down their throats. As Stuart Pearce, who wisely opted for an early night, later explained, Teddy Sheringham emerged from the carnage 'looking more like Ollie Reed than an international footballer'.

The following day, the England party set off for home, some of them nursing hangovers, others, like David Davies, blissfully unaware of just what had gone on the night before. Ahead of them was a thirteen-hour flight back to the UK which, in the other world of Paul Gascoigne, was more than enough time to make mischief, especially as the players were occupying the top deck of the Cathay Pacific 747 while the management and FA officials were dozing downstairs.

Myriad rumours exist as to what really happened on the flight home. Suffice to say, though, that Paul Gascoigne was heavily involved again. As the team slept in the first-class cabin, a tipsy Gascoigne was awoken by a slap to the face. Irked beyond belief, the Rangers midfielder marched up and down the aisle demanding to know who had hit him. With the red mist descending, Gazza laid waste to the cabin; the diminutive Dennis Wise even hid in an overhead locker to evade his wrath. Believing Steve McManaman to be his tormentor, Gascoigne punched the

Liverpool winger and kicked in the TV screen in his armrest and then, just in case it wasn't McManaman who was the culprit, did the same to Les Ferdinand's as well. Years later, Gascoigne would discover that it was none other than his fellow Geordie Alan Shearer who actually dealt him the initial blow.

Of course, team bonding was one thing, but binge drinking and public humiliation were another thing entirely. After a year of sub-standard performances the reaction back in England was predictably hostile. For David Davies, it was a PR fire-fighting exercise he could have done without, especially as the squad had all dispersed for a four-day break.

But if Davies had thought the fracas on the flight home was enough to be going on with, he was wrong. The day after they returned, the tabloids were awash with lurid photographs of the players on their ill-fated night out in Hong Kong, drenched in booze, their shirts ripped open. It was back-page news, front-page news and, for that matter, most of the pages in between. The images looked like a scene from any provincial city centre bar late on a Saturday night, not a group of elite professional athletes on the verge of a major competition.

Cue hand-wringing, hysteria and the kind of moral outrage usually reserved for cheating celebrity spouses and MPs on the make. That said, it was easy to see why a public starved of football success would take offence. Here, after thirty years, was the next best thing to the World Cup back on these shores and the players were showing all too publicly just how much they cared. Was it too much to ask for them to keep their heads down and concentrate on the job in hand?

What had started as a misguided money-making exercise had turned into a PR disaster beyond comprehension for the Football Association. So much for a low-key warm-up trip. The furore was unimaginable, the reaction unprecedented. A poll of *Daily Mirror* readers showed that some 86 per cent wanted Gascoigne expelled from Euro 96. There were even calls in Parliament to have the offenders thrown out of the tournament. 'This has happened at a time when obviously we are worried about what is going to happen over the next few weeks when the competition gets under way,' argued John Carlisle MP, vice-chairman of the Conservative Party's backbench sports committee. 'It sets a terrible example. The culprits should be identified, publicly exposed and thrown out of the squad at once. And if that includes Paul Gascoigne, then so be it.'

That was never going to happen. Paul Gascoigne was central to Terry Venables's strategy. Yes, he was singularly incapable of behaving himself in any given situation and yes, he was his own worst enemy, but here was a player blessed with the kind of talent that no team, especially England, could afford to forgo. Publicly, Venables told the media he would conduct his own inquiry, but the reality was that the coach was not about to jeopardize all the work he and his team had put in in the last two and a half years just to hang Gascoigne and his accomplices out to dry and start from scratch.

So Venables defended his players manfully, maintaining that no curfew had been broken and that the team had indeed been given the management's blessing to go out that night. Still, with legal action pending, the England players, led by Tony Adams, settled the bill for the damage to the Cathay Pacific aircraft collectively, with each player paying £500 whether involved in the vandalism or not. Quite a hefty bill, then, considering Terry Venables had described media reports of players' misbehaviour on that flight as 'grossly exaggerated'.

The truth, of course, was that standing four-square behind his players was Terry Venables's only option, but it had helped foster a siege mentality among the squad. Besides, to go on record and criticize his players would have done untold damage to his preparations for Euro 96, which was now a little over a week away.

It had been a long time coming but England had finally caught Euro 96 fever. Across the country, sales of England replica shirts rocketed – even the lamentable grey away kit the manufacturers Umbro had created was shifting – bookies took record amounts of bets, flags adorned houses and every other car and van seemed to have a cross of St George stuck on the windscreen or the bonnet.

The anticipation and excitement ahead of the event were perhaps best encapsulated by the official song of the England team. 'Three Lions' had been written by the man behind the band the Lightning Seeds, Ian Brodie, along with the comedians, presenters of the TV show *Fantasy Football League* and self-styled 'Rene and Renata of Euro 96', Frank Skinner and David Baddiel, and it had a chorus perfectly suited to the football terraces. Indeed, the refrain '*It's Coming Home! It's Coming Home! It's Coming! Football's Coming Home!*' would soon ring out across the pubs, clubs and schoolyards of the nation. 'The fact the FA let us do it at all shows a lot of balls on their part,' said Baddiel, 'but they felt that *Fantasy Football* was essentially a good thing.'

To which Skinner countered, 'Although we couldn't have done a song called "Let's All Go to Luxembourg and Set Fire to a Wine Bar".'

That said, the song wasn't received favourably when Baddiel and Skinner travelled to Burnham Beeches to play it to the squad and get them to take part in the accompanying video. 'We all laughed and shouted rubbish, rubbish,' recalled Stuart Pearce in his book *Psycho*.

The media too was awash with news of the competition. The *Mirror* newspaper, for instance, surveyed the great and not so good of the entertainment world ahead of the tournament. Everybody was chipping in with messages of goodwill for England and, of course, Scotland, who had been drawn in England's group along with Switzerland and Holland. The veteran rock band Status Quo had, they said, had rearranged a tour just so they could see the games (as if they hadn't had several years to plan it). Even the fugitive Great Train Robber, Ronnie Biggs, sent his support from his home in Rio de Janiero. 'I'm sure they'll win,' he insisted. 'It could be the best stick-up since the robbery.'

Central to the paper's coverage, though, was Uri Geller, the 'master of the paranormal'. Famous for, well, bending spoons, Geller had taken the orange ball that England had won the World

Cup with in 1966 and had 'energized' it ahead of the first game against Switzerland, the idea being that at 3.00 p.m. when the game kicked off, readers could rub a picture of the ball and concentrate on England winning. 'Just keep thinking "They can win, they can win," and you can help them to victory. You can even bend the ball towards the goal if you try hard enough,' said the Israeli. 'It will put them [the team] in a positive frame of mind. It will give them adrenaline, physical energy and increase their sharpness and speed of mind. It's an extra edge.'

At their base at the Burnham Beeches Hotel in Buckinghamshire, the England team took a walk after breakfast, gathering their thoughts ahead of the opening game, before boarding the coach and arriving at Wembley at 1.45 p.m., slap bang in the middle of the opening ceremony.

And what a ceremony. Laboured, awkward and predictable, it was designed to show English football through the ages and featured hundreds of volunteers re-enacting scenes such as 500-a-side peasant games, the advent of international football in 1872 and, unfortunately, one horseman falling off his mount and right into the advertising hoardings right under the Royal Box.

In the dressing room before the game, the captain Tony Adams, chosen ahead of David Platt, did what he could to prepare his team, motivating those that needed it and calming down those, like Gascoigne, that were in danger of boiling over. 'If a player looks edgy I'll have a word,' he said. 'Some players like omens. If I can I'll find one for them – and if I can't, I'll make one up.'

Terry Venables, meanwhile, had taken the weeks of negative press and the backlash from the ill-fated Far East trip and, to his credit, helped foster a new solidarity within the team. By the time they took to the field for the opener against Switzerland with the weight of the nation's (and Status Quo's) expectations on their shoulders, every last man knew what he had to do.

It was like 1966 all over again. The sun was shining, the world was watching and Wembley, a stadium starved of success for so long, was heaving. It would take just twenty-three minutes for England and Alan Shearer to answer all their many critics.

Taking a neat through pass from Paul Ince, Shearer took a touch before blasting the ball home off the near post. After twelve games and twenty-one months, the Blackburn striker had finally broken his international drought. Wembley erupted. England had lift-off.

Or so they thought. In the second half, England withered. It was as though the jetlag from the China trip had only just kicked in. Inevitably, the Swiss equalized through a Turkyilmaz penalty and but for a fine save from David Seaman to keep out Marco Grassi in the dying moments, it could have been the worst start imaginable to the tournament. As the English fans left Wembley that day fearing the worst, the Swiss fans, with their cow bells and comedy cheese hats, sang as though they'd just won the competition.

The following day, the Scottish newspaper the *Daily Record* revelled in England's stuttering start to the tournament, claiming that the 'English arrogance ... knew no bounds' and remarking on the irony of seeing the Swiss players 'dancing Nobby Stiles-like jigs around Wembley'.

The English papers, meanwhile, were concerned that England lacked any real spark or imagination going forward, maintaining that while it was a relief that Shearer had come good and that England hadn't lost, the lethargic performance of Paul Gascoigne in midfield gave Venables real cause for concern. 'Out of Gaz!' ran the headline in the *Mirror*.

Pilloried by the press and public alike for his antics on the trip to China, Gascoigne was now, more than ever, the focus of every-one's attention and this time he had failed to rise to the occasion. Substituted after seventy-four minutes, he had started brightly but faded badly as the game progressed. It was as if all the things that Uri Geller had demanded – adrenaline, physical energy, sharp-ness, speed of mind – were patently lacking from Gasgoigne's performance. But that, according to Venables, could have been said about several of the England team. 'We didn't play well in the second half,' he reflected. 'We were dead on our feet and it wasn't the result we were looking for. I'm very disappointed.'

All hype and no glory. After all the publicity, all the propaganda, all the expectation, England had failed to impress.

Come Monday morning, though, David Davies and the FA press team had something else to worry about. Opening the daily papers, he found reports of three more England players, Jamie Redknapp, Teddy Sheringham and Sol Campbell, seen out drinking in an Essex nightclub at 2.30 a.m. on Sunday, just hours after the frustrating draw against the Swiss. It was though the China debacle had never happened. But the very fact that the press had seen fit to report the story sent Terry Venables over the edge. Labelling some journalists as 'traitors', the England coach questioned why the press, like the public, weren't backing his team. 'The German and Italian players have wine with their meal. What would we make of that? We would call it progressive thinking,' he argued, ignoring the fact that, in all probability, the Germans and Italians didn't do it bare-chested sitting in a dentist's chair at 2.30 a.m. 'The criticism we get is awful. We are becoming hardened to it but do not understand it … We are the host nation but at the moment I feel we are throwing away the advantage of being at home.'

That Venables felt compelled to speak out against the press was a sure sign that he was beginning to feel the immense pressure of being the first England coach to host a major tournament since Alf Ramsey. But what was so baffling was that he didn't understand the extent of the scrutiny on him and his squad. In the *Independent*, Glenn Moore argued that the coach's defence of his players was admirable, but Venables had to see the incidents from the perspective of the supporters.

> You can get away with a lot if you are winning, but if the performance is poor the presentation must be beyond reproach. Night-clubbing into the early hours after such a jaded display as Saturday's is so obviously stupid it smacks of arrogance. Anyone who paid £25 to £100 to be at Wembley was bound to be piqued at seeing Teddy Sheringham, who looked so exhausted at 4 p.m., out clubbing at 2.30 a.m.,

boozing or not. The pity of it is those players who took the sensible option and kept a low profile are – as with the Cathay Pacific incident – tarred with the same brush. One wonders if this is really conducive to team spirit.

With the pressure mounting on Terry Venables and his squad, England repaired to Burnham Beeches to prepare for the next game against the Auld Enemy. If the Scottish tabloid press were to be believed, this was much more than just a football match. This was revenge for Culloden. This was Bannockburn II, the spirit of Braveheart, and the 'Battle of Britain'. This was one glorious opportunity to put an end to the thirty years of crowing about the World Cup win in 1966.

With the nation hooked as at no time in its sporting history – more even than in 1966 – and with a fired-up Paul Gascoigne once again the focus of everyone's attention, Venables hatched a plan to keep him out of trouble and out of the spotlight. Knowing that Gascoigne loved fishing, he arranged for the midfielder and the moustachioed England goalkeeper David Seaman (or 'Old Beaver Face' as Gascoigne called him) and the reserve keeper Ian Walker to go angling at a lake near the team's hotel. No nightclubs, no dentist's chairs, no photographers hidden furtively in the background. Just three men, some rods and the noble pursuit of trout. 'We go to get away from everything but it's serious stuff when we're fishing,' explained Seaman. 'We won't give our secrets away, such as the kind of flies we are using! I'm sure people will be surprised just how seriously Gazza takes his fishing. He is totally into it.'

On the day of the game at 11.20 a.m., Manchester city centre had been rocked by a massive IRA bomb that had caused widespread damage but, miraculously, had not taken any lives. Two hundred miles south, though, all eyes were on Wembley again. These days, the Tartan Army was a much better behaved, although no less boisterous, band of brothers than in former times. Officially allocated just 8,000 tickets (although there were probably at least three times that many in the stadium), they arrived in the capital confident of building on an unexpected but well-deserved draw against the Dutch in their opening game.

That week, as the row over Venables's 'traitor' comments rumbled on, Craig Brown's Scottish team also talked up their chances of pulling off a famous win. Their central defender Colin Hendry, for instance, was convinced that he could put one over his team-mate and the man he would be marking, Alan Shearer. 'Every dog has his day and I feel we can achieve something at Wembley,' he told the *Daily Record*. 'We could kill two birds with one stone by beating England and virtually knocking them out. It really couldn't be a better stage. I'll be able to live on a Scottish victory all next season and I won't be slow to mention it at every opportunity.'

Certainly, England were vulnerable. With just a point from their opening game against the Swiss, Venables knew anything but a victory against the Scots would leave his side facing the mammoth task of beating the group favourites Holland to qualify for the quarter-finals.

Fifty-three minutes in, though, and there was Alan Shearer again to break the deadlock, stooping to head in a Gary Neville cross at the far post. Shearer, his arms held aloft in front of the fans, was back to his swaggering best. Two goals in as many games had seen a resurgence of the confidence that was so clearly missing from his international displays. This was a different player.

The game's turning point would come with a little over ten minutes left to play. A Scotland penalty, awarded for a Tony Adams trip on Gordon Durie, was taken by Leeds United's Gary McAllister and brilliantly saved by David Seaman. But if the miss was enough to quash any hopes of a Scotland revival, what happened next would finish the game.

And how. With the England fans still celebrating Seaman's save, the keeper hit a long kick downfield that found Teddy Sheringham. Ever aware, Sheringham played the ball short to his Spurs colleague Darren Anderton on the left wing. Without taking a touch to control it, Anderton flicked the ball forward to the advancing Paul Gascoigne. Charging forward, Gascoigne collected Anderton's pass on the edge of the Scotland penalty area. As Colin Hendry endeavoured to intercept, Gascoigne flicked the ball over his head with his left foot, leaving Hendry prostrate on the turf, before volleying the ball low and hard past his Rangers team-mate Andy Goram in the Scotland goal. For Gascoigne, who had endured months of ribbing from his club-mates about the game, not to mention weeks of negative press, it was the perfect riposte. Here, in one flash of bewildering brilliance, the troubled midfielder had demonstrated why Venables and England chose to suffer his errant ways.

As Wembley roared its seismic approval, Gascoigne, with his peroxide-blond hair, ran behind the goal and lay on the pitch with his arms outstretched as Steve McManaman, Jamie Redknapp and Alan Shearer picked up some strategically placed drinks bottles and, in a parodic re-enactment of the now infamous Dentist's Chair incident, squirted the liquid down his throat. Game over.

The following day, the *Mirror*, a newspaper that had never shied away from criticizing Gascoigne's many excesses, printed an editorial entitled 'Mr Paul Gascoigne: An Apology', in which the publication admitted that 'Gazza is no longer a fat, drunken imbecile. He is, in fact, a football genius.'

After the game, Gascoigne had showered and left Wembley within half an hour, an exit widely assumed to be his way of snubbing the media. Truth was, he had other things on his mind. He had raced away from the scene of one of his greatest ever performances to go and see his girlfriend and the mother of his son, Regan, to ask her to marry him. For the record, she said yes.

That night, Venables gave the players the night off and this time nobody managed to find trouble. Well, apart from the short-haired blond man reported to the police by locals for running naked through the Burnham Beeches hotel gardens ...

A little under three years earlier, England's World Cup hopes and Graham Taylor's fate had been dealt a fatal blow by the Dutch in a World Cup qualifier in Rotterdam. Then, England had been undone by a combination of dubious defending and questionable officiating. Now, just a draw against the same opponents stood between England and the quarter-finals of the European Championship.

While the win over Scotland had afforded England the luxury of not needing to beat the Dutch to progress, it seemed as though the whole nation had now earmarked England as champions elect. It was, perhaps, premature. Holland, after all, were a class apart from the opposition England had faced so far in the competition. Coached by Guus Hiddink and based around a nucleus of Ajax players who had won the European Cup in 1995 and narrowly lost out on penalties to Juventus in the final just a month earlier, they were an archetypal Dutch side, adept at swift, incisive passing and capable of some breathtaking counter-attacking.

Buoyed by the victory over Scotland and, perhaps more importantly, the rejuvenation of Shearer and Gascoigne, Terry Venables was nevertheless advising caution ahead of the final group game. 'Holland won't play for a draw and we won't,' he said. 'I can't think for one minute my players would go for a draw. We've got to keep our feet on the ground to make sure we go into it in the right way. If we think we're through now it would be a big mistake.'

Venables needn't have been worried. Come match day on a balmy Tuesday evening at Wembley, England, inspired by Paul Gasgoigne, ran Holland ragged, racing into a four-goal lead within sixty-two minutes, thanks to two goals apiece from Shearer and Sheringham. Interestingly, Gascoigne's boot sponsor, Adidas, had promised the midfielder £10,000 for each goal he scored during the tournament, although it was a deal fraught with potential embarrassment. 'If he farts in front of the Queen,' said the company's Paul McGaughey, 'we get blemished.'

An incredulous crowd looked on in awe. This was England, the same England that had laboured against the very ordinary Swiss side, the same England that had spent the past thirty months struggling to account for teams like Japan, Colombia and Bulgaria, and here they were not just beating Holland but beating them at precisely the kind of game for which the Dutch had rightly become renowned. Moreover, England's four-goal lead also meant that Scotland, who were beating Switzerland in their final game, would also qualify for the next phase, making it past the group stage in a major tournament for the first time.

Twelve minutes from time at Wembley, though, Scottish dreams would be dashed yet again when the young Ajax striker Patrick Kluivert skipped through the English defence and slipped the ball past David Seaman, a goal which may not have taken the sheen off England's stunning victory but did mean that Craig Brown's team would be knocked out of the tournament on goal difference.

After the sluggish start against Switzerland and the hard-fought but largely unimpressive win against the Scottish, England had produced a performance that had convinced a sceptical public and a typically critical media that here, finally, was a team capable of emulating the class of '66. Certainly, Terry Venables, after two and a half years of dour, poorly attended friendlies in the lead-up to the tournament, regarded the game as vindication for all of his and his squad's work and even declared it to be the greatest moment of his football life 'because of the way we played, because of the opposition and because of the importance of the occasion'.

Only the weariest of cynics could have disagreed. It had, by some margin, been the greatest display by England at Wembley since World Cup Final in 1966, a wonderful, mesmerizing show-ing that confounded the team's critics and established the host nation as one of the favourites to take the trophy. In the Wembley dressing room after the game, the players threw each other in the cavernous communal bath, singing 'Football's Coming Home!' at the top of their voices. Soon, a fax would arrive from the Prime Minister John Major congratulating them on their performance.

In the press conference after the game, the defender Stuart Pearce, like everyone around the country that had just witnessed the game, was in a state of shock. 'I have never known an atmos-phere like it,' he beamed. 'The national anthem, for instance, is being sung by so many people. That is good. It is a party atmosphere. Winning helps, you know, it is a good feeling.'

Terry Venables, meanwhile, was a man suffering mixed emotions. On one hand, he had just orchestrated probably the finest England performance since 1966 and, as such, was enjoying the kind of publicity and popularity that England coaches over the years had rarely received. On the other, his was a face of regret, regret that he was soon going to walk away from the team he had built and the job he had started with England.

And therein lay the Football Association's problem. The further England progressed, the better they played and the more the nation became consumed in the championship, the more Venables's stock rose. Could England really be about to lose the coach who had turned them from international has-beens into potential world-beaters?

By contrast to the Dutch game, the quarter-final against Spain was a tense, nervy affair. On another day, England might have lost. Spain were dogged, resolute and dangerous going forward. They even had two goals disallowed (one of which should have counted) and also had reasonable appeals for two penalties turned down. After 120 minutes of goalless football, the game went to a penalty shoot-out.

If ever there was a sign that this was destined to be England's day it came with the very first kick of the shoot-out when Real Madrid's Fernando Hierro blasted his kick against the crossbar. With Alan Shearer and David Platt converting their penalties, up stepped Stuart Pearce, the man whose missed penalty in the shoot-out in Turin six years earlier had left him in tears and a nation distraught. That he volunteered to take a spot-kick was a testament to the man's indomitable spirit. That he thundered the ball low and hard to Zubizarreta's left was nothing short of astonishing. As the ball nestled in the corner and Wembley shook, Pearce turned to the crowd and punched the air, screaming uncontrollably, the ghost of Turin finally exorcized. With Paul Gascoigne scoring from England's fourth kick, it was left to the ever-dependable David Seaman to beat out the penalty from the so-called 'Beast of Barcelona', Miguel Angel Nadal, and take the hosts through to the last four.

By the time the semi-final against Germany came round on 26 June, national pride and jubilation had tipped into xenophobia and what the *New York Times*, no less, described as 'an orgy of nationalistic bashing'. Needless to say, the chief culprits were the tabloids. As the game approached, for instance, the *Daily Star* ran the headline 'Herr We Go, Bring On The Krauts!' while the *Sun* went with 'Lets's Blitz Fritz' and predicted that the contest would be a 'HUNdinger of a match'.

The newspaper that courted most controversy, though, was the *Daily Mirror* whose headline 'ACHTUNG! SURRENDER – For you Fritz, ze Euro 96 Championship is over', accompanied by mocked-up pictures of Stuart Pearce and Paul Gascoigne wearing First World War soldiers' helmets and a declaration of 'football war' on Germany, went further than any other newspaper. The man behind the headline was the newspaper's then editor, Piers Morgan. 'It seemed like a good idea at the time,' he recalls. 'I thought it was still allowed to take the piss out of the Germans, but apparently that was no longer the case.'

Amid reports that Morgan had even planned to drive a tank to the German Embassy in London and hire a Spitfire to fly over Berlin and drop insulting leaflets ('Kelvin MacKenzie talked me out of it – unbelievably,' he says), the editor found himself on the receiving end of a backlash so violent he was forced to make a public apology. 'I was amazed,' he adds. 'My apology went out on the BBC News between *'Allo 'Allo* and *Dad's Army* – the irony wasn't lost on me. I still find it funny today, and so do most Germans I've met.'

Not that the media coverage was entirely one-sided. In Germany the big-selling daily *Bild* responded to the taunts of the English media. 'If you are the homeland of soccer,' it asked, 'then why is it that you have never won the world championship?' Then came the knockout blow. 'Why do you look like boiled lobsters after one day at the beach?' Ouch.

Come match day, and the idea that the quarter-final against Spain had been the most nerve-racking England game in recent history was parked with almost indecent haste. Playing in their grey kit so as to avoid a clash with the Germans' traditional white shirts, England made the perfect start, a third-minute Gascoigne corner flicked on by Adams and nodded home by Alan Shearer for his fifth goal of the competition.

The lead didn't last long. Thirteen minutes to be precise. A shot from six yards out by the German striker Stefan Kuntz levelled matters. And so it stayed, through ninety nervy minutes and on through an excruciating half-hour of extra-time, in which Paul Gascoigne was a stud's length away from converting Alan Shearer's cross into the Golden Goal that would have ended the contest.

A week short of six years since the agony of Turin, here we were again. England now faced the prospect of another penalty shoot-out against a team renowned for their prowess from the spot. Back in Italia 90, Germany hadn't missed a single penalty, but this time England seemed better equipped than ever. Despite weary legs and shredded nerves all round, the ten penalties were traded, each one finding the net with accuracy and venom. Something had to give and with the recognized penalty specialists all having done their job, up stepped the Aston Villa defender Gareth Southgate.

One of England's most accomplished performers in the tournament, Southgate had impressed everyone with his assured displays at the heart of England's defence, so much so, in fact, that some commentators had even earmarked him as a future England captain. Articulate and level-headed, Southgate was the kind of defender you saw on the continent. Quick, skilful and comfortable at bringing the ball out of defence, he was one of a new kind of stopper, equally at home spraying fifty-yard passes across the field or launching desperate last-gasp tackles.

For all his undoubted skill, though, his penalty-taking, on this crucial night at least, wasn't up to the mark. Opting for placement over power, Southgate slid his penalty to Andreas Köpke's right but the German goalkeeper had guessed correctly, making a comfortable, routine save. Moments later, England's fate was confirmed. Andreas Möller stepped up and maintained the Germans' perfect record from the penalty spot, beating David Seaman with aplomb. Game over for England. Cue tears.

In the dressing room, Southgate was inconsolable. But then so was every other England player. To his credit, Tony Adams attempted to lighten the gloom, putting his arm round Southgate. 'But Gareth,' he said, 'it was a shit penalty, wasn't it?' Someone had to miss and that someone, inevitably, is usually English. This time it happened to be Gareth Southgate and his only crime was that he chose to put his name forward for a penalty when other, supposedly more senior players like Paul 'The Guvnor' Ince, looked the other way. Later, in a press conference, Southgate held back the tears as he spoke of his 'bitter disappointment' and revealed that his mother had asked him: 'Why didn't you just belt the ball?'

On the team bus back to Burnham Beeches, the silence was interrupted by Stuart Pearce. Taking the microphone at the front of the coach, the veteran defender confirmed what most people in the game had expected and announced to the squad that the defeat against Germany had been his last game in international football. Later, though, Pearce would be persuaded to play on by the new England coach, Glenn Hoddle.

Back at the hotel, the team gathered for a chance to reflect on what might have been. Some, such as Adams, stayed up all night, drowning their sorrows; others, like Venables and his coaching team, slipped away for a quiet drink. Paul Gascoigne, meanwhile, consoled himself as only Gascoigne could, by engaging in a tomato ketchup fight with Robbie Fowler in the kitchens, before returning to his room and bursting into tears.

Sadly, the spectre of hooliganism also reappeared after the final whistle at Wembley. In London's Trafalgar Square around 2,000 fans fought pitched battles with riot police, smashing shop windows and vandalizing vehicles. Stoked up by an undeniably partisan tabloid press, fuelled by alcohol and angered by the nature of another heartbreaking and premature exit from a major tournament, they even attacked a couple from Bournemouth whose German-made car got caught up in the melee. In total, over 200 arrests were made, while sixty-six people were injured and more than forty vehicles damaged.

It was a similar scene across the country. Near Brighton in East Sussex, a seventeen-year-old Russian student was stabbed in the neck and chest by attackers who mistook his accent for German, while in Bedford a gang of 300 rampaged through the town, looting shops and smashing windows. In Shirley in the West Midlands, meanwhile, hooligans threw bricks through the window of the German-owned Aldi supermarket.

For England and Terry Venables, though, Euro 96 was over. The Germans, stubborn, resilient, unbreakable, went on to take the title, defeating the Czech Republic in the final, to record their first European Championship title as a unified nation. This had been the month, the heady, sun-drenched month when football was meant to come home. So what if it didn't pan out the way everyone had planned, it had given people some memories that would last a lifetime.

As for Terry Venables, he bade farewell to the England job he loved so much knowing his reputation as a coach had been enhanced and that he had restored some much-needed pride in the English national team. And being the true performer he was, he had left the nation wanting more. At his last press conference, at noon on 27 June 1996, Venables spoke for one final time to the media, some of whom who had always believed in him, others perhaps less so. As he left the room, the press corps, to a man, applauded. It was as much a show of respect for his achievement with England as it was a sign of their gratitude for the memories he had helped manufacture. Suddenly, all the talk of Christmas Trees and court cases, of dentist's chairs and debauchery was forgotten. At least for now …

*

The 1996–97 Premier League season began on 17 August at Selhurst Park, where Wimbledon were hosting the reigning champions Manchester United. As the game entered the final moments and with the visitors winning comfortably, United's impressive twenty-one-year-old midfielder David Beckham received the ball just inside his own half and, spotting the Wimbledon goalkeeper Neil Sullivan off his line, hit the ball long and high over his head and into the net, effectively deciding the BBC's Goal of the Season competition on the very first day of the campaign.

With one audacious sixty-yard shot, David Beckham's life had changed for ever. One moment he was the ordinary working-class lad with floppy fringe from Chingford trying to forge a career in professional football, the next he was England's superstar in waiting. And given that it was the kind of goal that even the great Pelé had tried and failed to score in his long and incomparable career, it was a sure sign that here was a young player with the confidence and talent to make a real and sustained impact on the international stage.

Like everybody else in the country, the new England coach Glenn Hoddle had noticed the rise of David Beckham and as he set about finalizing his first squad for his first game as England manager, a World Cup qualifier away to Moldova in Chişinău, it seemed obvious that Beckham should be handed his chance.

If Hoddle saw something of himself in David Beckham it was entirely understandable as the comparisons between manager and player were clear. Both men had the kind of talent that could unlock defences with passes that other players just couldn't visualize. They were both gifted at dead-ball situations and both capable of scoring spectacular goals.

A settled, successful side and the post Euro-96 feel-good factor would afford Glenn Hoddle the kind of honeymoon period most England coaches would sell their family for. Indeed, he had assumed control at a time when everybody, from the tabloid press to the public, was behind the team, perhaps more so than they had been in decades. After all, short of winning the tournament or lengthening Paul Gascoigne's studs, there was little more England could have done in the summer.

Not that Hoddle would need a honeymoon period. The game against Moldova on 1 September, with Beckham starting in midfield, was won at a canter and was followed up with wins over Poland and Georgia. It was all going swimmingly. Helping Hoddle adjust to the most high-profile job in football was his long-term friend and his right-hand man at Swindon Town, John Gorman. Eight years older than Hoddle, the pair had first met when they were players at Tottenham Hotspur and had forged a firm friendship. Later, when Hoddle had moved into management he had often sought the assistance of the Scot as his right-hand man, but the offer of a job with the English national side still came as something of a surprise. 'I was at Bristol City and I didn't expect it,' he recalls. 'Glenn had left a message and said, "I want you to come and have a chat." I didn't think he was going to ask me to go to Chelsea again either because he had Graham Rix there doing a good job … Then of course he just threw it on me about the England thing which, as you can imagine, being Scottish, was a bit of a shock!'

England's progression towards the World Cup finals continued serenely, save for a sole defeat, at home against Italy in February 1997. With one game left, the return fixture in Rome on 11 October, England needed a point to secure their qualification for the finals. Ahead of them, however, was arguably the toughest test in European football. It would be one of those archetypal, backs against the wall English performances that seemed thirty years out of date. Blood – quite literally in Paul Ince's case – sweat and, for once, only tears of joy. For the first time in fifteen games, a visiting side had left the Stadio Olimpico with a point. Not only that, they had left with a guaranteed place at France 98. It was a night to remember. 'That was fantastic, because of the atmosphere, the tension and the build-up to the game,' recalls John Gorman. 'We knew what we had to get and we went out and put on a great performance and got it.'

With their place in the World Cup finals assured, Glenn Hoddle took a twenty-eight-player party out to that default choice for any football team seeking a few days in the sun, La Manga. The Spanish resort's Hyatt Regency Hotel would be the team's base for the final World Cup warm-up games against Morocco and Belgium in Casablanca, as well as hosting the now traditional England team-bonding pursuits like karaoke, golf and drinking. Crucially, the hotel would also be the venue for Hoddle to announce his final twenty-two. That, of course, meant that six of the players who had made the trip to Spain were going to be returning home to the UK disappointed. Or, to be more accurate, five would return home disappointed and one would return home apoplectic.

That man was Paul Gascoigne. Since his breathtaking arrival on the international scene at Italia 90, Gascoigne's name had moved increasingly from the back pages to the front. Paparazzi shots of late-night drinking sprees with his celebrity friends had suggested that his mind wasn't exactly on England and the World Cup. Compounding matters, meanwhile, was his ongoing relationship problems with his wife Sheryl.

Gascoigne's problem, of course, was that he wasn't his own man. Ever since he cried at Italia 90, he had become public property, a national treasure even. Of course, there were other players out and about in London's West End on the nights Gascoigne was, but they were lucky: the paparazzi weren't interested in them. He was his own worst enemy.

Indeed, the many issues in Gascoigne's personal life were such that Hoddle had even arranged for him to visit his trusted faith-healer Eileen Drewery at her home. Hoddle had first encountered Drewery when he was eighteen. Suffering from a hamstring strain and doubtful for a match that weekend, his then girlfriend, Michelle Drewery, suggested he visit her mother, who as well as being a publican was also a faith-healer. Grudgingly, he agreed. The hamstring injury disappeared. Hoddle was hooked. 'The experience had a profound effect on me,' he would say later. 'She explained that much of the gift she had was down to God, that she was just a channel. It was then that I really started to think along spiritual lines. My life started to change and really blossom in the sense that I started seeing it from a completely different – and much deeper – perspective.'

While Hoddle's relationship with Michelle Drewery ended after six months, his relationship with Eileen blossomed. Over the next decade, he would visit her whenever he fell foul of injury. She helped his recovery from an Achilles injury in 1984; a knee problem before the World Cup in 1986 was overcome; even Hoddle's dad's arthritis of the back was cleared up after some sessions with Drewery. Later, when Hoddle went into management, he recommended his players go and see her for physical and even mental healing. 'I've never forced anyone to go and see her,' he insisted. 'It's always down to them. But it's been intriguing sometimes to see hardened professional footballers come away from visiting Eileen having had a profound experience.'

When Gascoigne visited Drewery – he claims he only went because he thought Hoddle had said 'brewery' – he did so not with an open mind as Hoddle advocated, but with acute scepticism. Over the course of a forty-five-minute consultation, Drewery concluded that Gascoigne had demons emerging from his head (thoughtfully, she opened the window to let them out), and that if he was going to remain free from the bad spirits poisoning his mind he needed to stay away from the evils of tobacco and alcohol or risk letting them back in. In his book *Gazza: My Story*, though, Gascoigne revealed that, as he left Drewery's house that day, he looked round to see Hoddle's healer sitting in another room 'having a fag'.

Other players under Hoddle's charge had greater success with Drewery. The Spurs winger Darren 'Sicknote' Anderton, for example, had been suffering from a long-term thigh injury but had resisted visiting Drewery for a year before he finally gave her a try. Then, after an operation, Anderton began visiting her once a week, every week for seven months. The result? A fully fit Darren Anderton.

There was also talk of Hoddle's psychological warfare. Beckham has observed that while other managers play mind games with the opposition, Hoddle played them with his own players. He brought in his mentor John Syer, the sports psychologist, who asked players to speak into a pen at team meetings. The Biro was meant to simulate a microphone, and players were asked to vent their true desires as sportsmen. But their true desire as sportsmen was not to talk into a pen.

On the final day of the stay at La Manga, Hoddle prepared an interview schedule for each of his players, allocating them five minutes apiece in the Hyatt's Royal Suite to tell them whether they would be part of his final squad of twenty-two. The coach set the scene as though he were hosting a dinner party, rearranging the room's furniture and even putting the mellow mood music of the saxophonist Kenny G on what, in a moment that would have made even Alan Partridge cringe, he described as the 'superb CD system'.

The goalkeeper Ian Walker was the first to receive the bad news, followed by Phil Neville, Dion Dublin, Nicky Butt and Andy Hinchcliffe. That left Gascoigne and, depending on whose version you believe, it was either one haymaker short of a boxing bout or a difficult situation perfectly handled by a coach in complete control. Certainly, the contrast in the accounts is marked. Gascoigne maintains he burst into the room just as Phil Neville was being told he had failed to make the final squad; Hoddle says he was alone and waiting for the midfielder. Gascoigne says he had had a few beers but wasn't drunk (he did admit he was hungover from the night before, though); Hoddle maintains he was half-cut. Gascoigne contends that he barged into the room and set about rearranging the furniture in his own inimitable style; Hoddle says Gascoigne shook his hand, wished him all the best and *then* flew into a rage. Even the peacemakers are different. Gascoigne says David Seaman and Paul Ince restrained him. Hoddle says his assistants Glenn Roeder and John Gorman did the job.

Whatever the real story was (and Kenny G is enough to send any rational man into a violent rage, yet alone one with a temperament as fragile as Paul Gascoigne's), it may have been more politic for Hoddle to have named his squad, with reserves, prior to the trip, thereby saving himself and the discarded players the possibility of any flashpoints. But no. Later, Hoddle would say, perversely, that he thought the trip had gone well and that he 'felt satisfied with a job well done'. One can only imagine the carnage that would have ensued if the trip had gone badly.

Gascoigne wasn't the only player who hadn't exactly warmed to Hoddle's management style. Tony Cascarino, who played under him at Chelsea, was less than impressed with the manner in which Hoddle handled his squad. 'Grown men feel as if they are being treated as children,' he wrote in his book *Full-Time: The Secret Life of Tony Cascarino*. 'There is a coldness to him … If Chelsea won, it was because of his decisions, and if we lost, it was our fault – never his.'

Later, as manager of Southampton, he tried and failed to offload the striker James Beattie. 'Hoddle is a great coach,' Beattie would go on to say, 'but I know he annoyed some of the senior players. They were irritated by the way he treated them.'

Hoddle's squad for the World Cup finals would, nevertheless, contain few real surprises, save for the exclusion of Paul Gascoigne. It had a solid defence, marshalled by Gareth Southgate and Tony Adams, industry allied to invention in midfield with Paul Ince and David Batty, and options going forward with Shearer and Sheringham and the teenage Liverpool striker Michael Owen waiting in the wings.

With electrifying pace and a glut of goalscoring records for England's Under-15 and Under-17 sides, Owen's potential was such that he had virtually bypassed the Under-21 side, playing (and scoring) just once for them in a game against Greece at Carrow Road. When he made his full international debut for England in a 2–0 friendly defeat to Chile at Wembley in February 1998, he became the youngest full England cap in the twentieth century, less than two months after his eighteenth birthday.

Owen, however, would have to wait until the second match of the finals to get on the scoresheet. After a routine 2–0 win over Tunisia in the opener in Marseille, England found themselves a goal down against Romania in Toulouse, a deficit which was soon rectified by Owen's successful arrival as a second-half substitute and his goal on eighty-three minutes. Sadly, England's defence wasn't as adept. In the last minute Chelsea's Romanian midfielder Dan Petrescu rounded his Stamford Bridge team-mate Graeme Le Saux and steered home a winner.

It would be a costly defeat. Despite another win against Colombia and a first goal in an England shirt for David Beckham, England still qualified for the next phase, but their runners-up spot in Group G meant an encounter in the second round with their perennial foes, Argentina, and not Romania's next opponents, Croatia.

The game against Argentina in Saint-Étienne, the last of the second round matches, would be another nerve-shredding experience for England's long-suffering supporters and, by some way, the game of the tournament. In a first half with more incidents, accidents and controversy than in the rest of the tournament combined, England fell behind after just six minutes, when Gabriel Batistuta squeezed his penalty past David Seaman. Four minutes later, another penalty, this time hammered home by the England skipper Alan Shearer, brought Hoddle's side level. After sixteen minutes, the Liverpool striker Michael Owen, just eighteen years old, received a pass near the halfway line, before beating José Chamot and Roberto Ayala with his astonishing pace and then, just as it seemed that Paul Scholes might be in a better position to shoot, coolly maintained his balance and slotted the ball past keeper Carlos Roa for a goal that would propel the teenager from promising young striker to worldwide superstar. Once again, though, the teams would be level. Deep into injury time in the first half, a cleverly worked free-kick by the Argentinians found Javier Zanetti unmarked in the penalty area and in a flash, his left shot was nestling in the net behind David Seaman.

Any chance England had of truly forcing the issue after half-time, however, would be undone by a spot of juvenile petulance from the Manchester United midfielder David Beckham early in the second period. Clattered by the opposition's Diego Simeone, a prostrate Beckham had flicked out his leg and kicked the Argentine in full view of the Danish referee Kim Milton Nielsen. Simeone was booked for the foul. Beckham, though, was dismissed. 'The sending off of David Beckham was straightforward,' the official explained later. 'The rules are very clear about kicking or attempting to kick an opponent. Many people today forget that it is a red card offence. Some have said it was only a soft kick, but that does not matter. In that situation one person has to be punished. If I had not sent him off, I would have been punished for not following the rules. I was surprised by the reaction after the game. But the most important thing for me is I believe what I did was right.'

Remarkably, England continued to press and if a Sol Campbell goal had not been disallowed because Alan Shearer was adjudged to have obstructed the goalkeeper, they would have recorded a famous and thrilling victory. As it was, once more the match would require a shoot-out to break the deadlock. Surely England were not destined for a second helping of penalty heartache? Eventually, Hoddle settled on his line-up for the game of Russian roulette. Shearer, as ever, would lead off, followed by Paul Ince, Paul Merson, Michael Owen and culminating with David Batty.

Shearer went first and scored, in reply to the opening effort from Sergio Berti. Hernán Crespo missed, with Seaman saving low to his left, but Paul Ince's almost identical kick would meet the same fate. The two teams then exchanged successful penalties until the fifth and final kicks. When Roberto Ayala coolly converted his, it was left to David Batty to keep England in the tournament. It wasn't to be. His tame effort was easily saved by Carlos Roa and Hoddle's dream was over. 'My stomach,' he said later, 'felt as if it had been ripped out.'

In the dressing room after the game, Hoddle surveyed the scene. Alan Shearer sat silent and naked on the floor, Tony Adams cursed continually on his way to the shower while the villain of the piece, David Beckham, went round the room apologizing to each and every player for his dismissal. On their return, the England team and management would be lambasted for not practising penalties, although the truth, as was often the case, was a little different. 'We did practise penalties,' insists Hoddle's assistant John Gorman, 'we just didn't practise them that day.'

The tournament over and the nation deflated, Hoddle could not afford to dwell on what might have been. He returned to work to prepare for the upcoming qualifiers for the European Championship in Belgium and the Netherlands in 2000 and to quickly finish a World Cup diary book he and his agent Dennis Roach had already brokered with the publisher André Deutsch.

But for a few paragraphs criticizing David Beckham for his impetuosity, Hoddle's book, ghostwritten by the FA's Director of Public Affairs David Davies, would prove to be about as sensational, but nowhere near as useful, as the Yellow Pages. For many, though, it represented an absolute betrayal of confidence and an abuse of trust from the England manager. The players, especially, were less than enamoured with the publication. England's unofficial shop steward Gary Neville maintained the book should never have been written while his counterpart on the other flank, Graeme Le Saux, was equally critical, and this despite all the players being fully aware that the book was in the process of being written during their time away. 'Not one of them came up during France 98 to complain about what we were doing,' maintains David Davies.

That said, when the serialization of the book hit the pages of the biggest-selling tabloid in the UK, the *Sun*, and was treated with the kind of earth-shattering sensationalism it patently didn't warrant, it was as though Hoddle and Davies has betrayed not just the confidence of the England squad but the entire nation. It had seemed that while the players and the country were investing everything in the tournament, Hoddle (and Davies) were more intent on wringing whatever they could out of the World Cup. Yes, Bobby Robson had 'written' diaries during the major tournaments when he was in charge of England – he had also endorsed cigars when he didn't even smoke – but they hadn't provoked the kind of interest that Hoddle's had, not least because since the inception of the English Premier League, the media interest in the game had exploded beyond all reason. Had England won the World Cup then Hoddle (and Davies) could have written whatever he wanted, safe in the knowledge that gongs and untold glory would follow.

Still, the book was another shockingly dumb decision, not just by the manager but by David Davies and the Football Association. To do the diary was folly. To get the manager of the FA's media relations to ghostwrite it with the blessing of the chief executive Graham Kelly was nothing short of brainless. 'On reflection,' said Davies, 'writing the book was wrong. No ifs, no buts. Wrong, wrong, wrong.'

He had a point. This, after all, was the FA's very own spin doctor, not some hack on the make. This was an experienced journalist who must surely have known the ramifications that such a book would entail. Remarkably, it would signal the beginning of a change in fortunes for both men, but in quite different ways.

For Davies, who arguably escaped the sack only by virtue of Graham Kelly's approval of the project, it appeared that as the book's ghostwriter he was less culpable than the author Glenn Hoddle. To an extent, that was true. It was Hoddle's name on the cover, after all. It was *his* World Cup diary. But for Davies, a man whose very job was to control the news surrounding the England team, not be part of it, it was a dreadful lack of judgement.

Luck and timing would be on David Davies's side. No sooner had the furore of Hoddle's book started to subside when the very core of the Football Association seemed to implode. Soon, Graham Kelly, the chief executive who considered wearing a pink shirt as 'living dangerously', would resign over a plan to lend the Welsh FA £3.2 million in return for their support for the FA chairman Keith Wiseman's nomination to become FIFA vice-president. Within a couple of weeks, Wiseman too would go.

Years later, Kelly and Wiseman would be cleared of any wrong-doing, but now, with the tumbleweed blowing through Lancaster Gate, the scandal over a little World Cup diary had all but blown over.

If Glenn Hoddle's World Cup diary and his ongoing association with Eileen Drewery had put his job at risk, his interview in *The Times* would become the defining moment not merely of his time as England coach, but arguably his entire career in football.

England had begun the 2000 European Championship quali-fiers in patchy form. A defeat away to Sweden in September 1998 and a goalless draw at home to Bulgaria a month later had seen the team panned in the press and Hoddle, still reeling from the reaction to his book, without a team strong enough to keep him safe in his job. Poor results, dwindling team confidence and a coach seemingly out of favour with his players made for worrying times for the England boss. Keen to get the team and the nation behind him once more, Hoddle, Dennis Roach and the FA decided to embark on a media charm offensive ahead of a friendly with the reigning world champions France. One of the journalists granted an interview with Hoddle was the chief football correspondent of *The Times*, Matt Dickinson. Prior to the interview, Dickinson spoke to Martin Samuel of the *Daily Express*. In the course of the conversation, Samuel mentioned that while England's stuttering start to the qualifying campaign should be discussed, nobody had ever really challenged Hoddle on his religious and spiritual beliefs, especially in light of his reliance on the likes of Eileen Drewery and comments he had once made on Radio Five Live about reincarnation which had gone largely unnoticed.

When the interview began – it was conducted on the phone as the FA declined a face-to-face meeting – it did so like so many others, but when the football talk was done, Dickinson ventured a question about Hoddle's faith.

My beliefs [replied Hoddle] have evolved in the last eight or nine years, that the spirit has to come back again, that is nothing new, that has been around for thousands of years. You have to come back to learn and face some of the things you have done, good and bad. There are too many injustices around.

You and I have been physically given two hands and two legs and half-decent brains. Some people have not been born like that for a reason. The karma is working from another lifetime. I have nothing to hide about that. It is not only people with disabilities. What you sow, you have to reap.

You have to look at things that happened in your life and ask why. It comes around.

Dickinson was incredulous. 'Hoddle's done enough interviews and been in the game long enough to know when to decline to answer a question, but he didn't,' he recalls. 'And it wasn't like I had to tease it out of him. I'd always understood reincarnation to be something where you come back to the world to make it better, not some twisted view whereby it's some kind of punishment.'

The interview over, Dickinson double-checked his notes just to confirm that what he had just heard, from the England coach no less, was true, and suddenly, improbably, he had an exclusive unlike any other in his career. 'I thought at first it would obviously make a great back page lead but then it just snowballed,' he says. 'I didn't really think he'd lose his job because of it. I thought there'd be a statement and an apology and that would probably be the end of it.'

How wrong. When the interview was published in *The Times* on 30 January 1999, David Davies's mobile phone melted. That day, he took seventy-one calls about the piece. As January slid into February, the pressure on Hoddle mounted from every angle: from pressure groups, fans, sponsors, politicians. Even Richard and Judy got involved. During an interview with the Prime Minister on their daytime show *This Morning*, they asked Tony Blair whether Hoddle should go and, in a surprisingly frank response,

the PM simply said, 'Yes.' If Hoddle ever doubted the severity of
the situation, he could be assured that if the nation's favourite TV
couple were discussing his future, or lack of it, then his days were
surely numbered.

With the media clamour for Hoddle to quit growing ever
louder, David Davies (now acting chief executive following
Graham Kelly's departure in December 1998) hatched a plan
to try and save the beleaguered England coach. It involved an
unqualified apology, an agreement not to make any non-football
statements in the future and, most contentiously, to dispense with
the services of Eileen Drewery. No deal, said Hoddle.

With both sides standing their ground, Glenn Hoddle became
the ex-England coach on 2 February 1999. At a press conference at
the Royal Lancaster Hotel, in the same room in which Hoddle had
been unveiled as the new boss some thirty months earlier, David
Davies, in solemn tones, addressed the 200-strong media pack.

> After more than twenty-four hours of meetings and discus-
> sions, it became apparent to all those concerned that this was
> the right decision for English football.
>
> The position had become increasingly untenable for both
> the FA and Glenn. He accepts he made an error of judge-
> ment and, of course, he has apologized. The past few days
> have been painful for everyone involved but that is as
> nothing compared to any offence that may have been caused
> to disabled people in our country. We accept this was not
> Glenn's intentions. It is unquestionable, though, that the
> controversy over whatever was or was not said has damaged
> both Glenn and his employers.
>
> Glenn has served the England team with dedication and
> with loyalty but eventually all parties agreed that in the
> circumstances this was the correct way forward. Howard
> Wilkinson is being asked to take charge of the game against
> France on February 10.

As Davies spoke, though, he was interrupted by a man wearing a Liverpool away shirt who burst into the room and began hurling obscenities in Hoddle's direction. Twenty-nine-year-old labourer Gary Raines from London had a disabled nephew and he, like so many others, had been deeply offended by Hoddle's comments. 'Glenn Hoddle deserves what he's got,' he told the press later. 'What he has done is out of order, he's an absolute disgrace to English football.'

Hoddle, meanwhile, was a picture of contrition. 'I accept I made a serious error of judgement which caused misunderstanding and pain to a number of people,' he said. 'This was never my intention and I apologize.'

For Hoddle's critics, it was the logical and only acceptable end to this most unpleasant of situations. The Sports Minister and lifelong Chelsea fan Tony Banks said, 'It is a personal tragedy that Glenn Hoddle's career as England coach has ended in this fashion. He is a decent man but his views as expressed caused distress to many disabled sports men and women who have achieved so many triumphs for the country.'

Fellow Chelsea supporter, former Tory Cabinet minister and Football Task Force chairman David Mellor, meanwhile, was also glad the matter had been resolved. 'I take no pleasure in the demise of Glenn Hoddle but I do not think he gave the FA any choice,' he said. 'His personal beliefs have become inextricably linked with his job. English football was being dragged down by his bizarre beliefs.'

Later that day, the acting FA chairman Geoff Thompson confirmed Davies's announcement of a new caretaker manager for the England team, the FA technical director Howard Wilkinson, to take charge of the team for the friendly against France the following week.

Having guided Leeds United to the First Division title in 1992, Wilkinson at least boasted a managerial track record that was better than Hoddle's. Now fifty-five, he had seen at close hand what the England job could do to a man and was determined to rise above the pressure. 'I saw Ron Greenwood break out in sores,

Bobby Robson go grey and poor Graham Taylor double up in anguish.' He added, 'If I was single, with no kids, it would be no problem. But I've a wife and three children and I've seen the effect the job can have on your family. It won't happen to mine.'

The controversial faith-healer Eileen Drewery was also quick to leap to Hoddle's defence. 'It's been a complete witch hunt from the very beginning,' she raged. 'I am very upset. Who is going to help the thousands who believe in reincarnation? Glenn didn't offend anyone.'

That, of course, wasn't the case. By committing the cardinal sin in football management of talking about issues outside the game, especially those on which he held such controversial views, he had single-handedly scuppered any chance of continuing as manager of the national team. If the imprudent book and his much-publicized belief in the spiritual world had taken him to the brink of unemployment, the comments on people with disabilities had all but signed his P45. Even after his resignation and apology there was still some residual sense that here was a man who still regarded his beliefs as rational and right.

A year later, when Glenn Hoddle reappeared as the new manager of Southampton, Matt Dickinson was sent to The Dell to cover his first match for *The Times*. In the press conference, Dickinson sat by as another journalist asked Hoddle whether he regretted what he had said about disabled people. Again, Hoddle maintained he had been misquoted, even though he had previously accepted Dickinson's quotes as being accurate. 'So I thought, "I'm not having that" and I challenged him on it,' adds Dickinson. 'Sure enough, he got a bit chippy and we went at it again. Now he says he hasn't got a problem with *The Times*, just with one person who works there. I think he thinks I'll get mine eventually, and if that happens to be in the next life then I can live with that.'

In the acknowledgements in *My World Cup Story*, Glenn Hoddle concluded by saying that his book was 'the diary of a dream unfulfilled – until next time'. For Hoddle, though, there would be no next time. It was the end of the road. Maybe, just maybe, it was karma ...

CHAPTER 7

THE MAGNET

'People say you have to take your coaching badges to be a manager. I don't agree. When I went to Newcastle my only qualification was 1,000 rounds of golf in Spain, but it didn't do me any harm.'

Kevin Keegan, 2007

Listen to or read almost any interview with Kevin Keegan and you'll soon see how he nearly always refers to himself in the third person. It's a weird way to conduct an interview but one that not just 'Kevin Keegan' but many footballers employ when they're enduring the agony of the media and their never-ending questions.

We shouldn't be surprised. After all, Kevin Keegan has always been concerned with Kevin Keegan. Indeed, over the years, especially in his managerial career, Keegan had always been a man very much in control of his own destiny, even though for the most part, that destiny tended to be somewhere other than the club that employed him.

Late in 2008, of course, Keegan had walked out on his beloved Newcastle United for the second time, following disagreements with the club's multi-millionaire owner Mike Ashley over interference in team affairs. It was the latest in an increasingly long line of incidents where the former England skipper had left his club, seemingly at a moment's notice, and propagated the idea that when the going got tough, Kevin Keegan got going.

Schooled by two of the greatest managers in the English game, Kevin Keegan's managerial career had begun so promisingly. Nearly eight years after his final appearance for the club and his retirement from playing, he had returned to St James's Park in February 1992 as the manager. Taking over a team that were on the verge of falling into the third tier of English football, he had not only steadied the ship and avoided relegation but in his first full season taken the club up to the new Premier League as Division One champions. While Keegan would soon galvanize both players and fans alike, he would also display an aptitude for making clever investments in the transfer market. Backed by the club's owner, the millionaire property owner Sir John Hall, he brought another local hero, Peter Beardsley, back from Everton, he enlisted the composed Charlton midfielder Robert Lee and paid a then club record fee of £1.75 million for Bristol City's Andy Cole, a striker whose goals – 68 goals in just 84 games, a strike rate that is very rare in the modern game – would spearhead the Magpies' revival. Later, he would also smash the world record for a transfer fee by paying £15 million for Blackburn's England striker and local boy made good, Alan Shearer.

That said, Keegan could also court controversy. With the club in their best position in years – they had finished third in the Premier League in 1993–94 and qualified for the UEFA Cup – Keegan sold Cole to Manchester United in January 1995 in a shock £7 million deal, then the British transfer record. The club had won their first six games of the 1995–96 season and were leading the Premier League by a massive twelve points by January when Cole was offloaded. By the end of the season, Newcastle's lead had evaporated and the club would finish second to the club Cole had been sold to, Manchester United.

The sale of Andy Cole and the resultant slide down the Premier League table were the first signs that Keegan was perhaps ill-equipped to manage at the very highest level. While his Newcastle team were undoubtedly one of the most attack-minded in the English game, there were always doubts about the defensive quality of the side. In time, Keegan would even bring in a specialist defensive coach, the former Liverpool and Republic of Ireland centre-half and now television pundit Mark Lawrenson, but the role would be short-lived. 'Kevin's own words to me when he brought me in,' says Lawrenson, 'were that he had kind of neglected what had been happening at the back because he was so involved with trying to make Newcastle an unstoppable force going forward.'

Adventure and energy going forward coupled with lapses and leaks at the back would, inevitably, make Newcastle United games in the Keegan era some of the most entertaining matches to watch in any league. More great attacking players would arrive too: the French winger David Ginola, the England striker Les Ferdinand and the Colombian forward Faustino Asprilla, to name but three. Sure enough, the goals continued to flood in – only at both ends of the field.

The pressure of coaching the team and matching the expecta-tions of the success-starved Newcastle fans would eventually get the better of Keegan. As Manchester United closed the gap on Newcastle and then overhauled them, Keegan gradually lost his grip not just on his team but on what passed for his reality, culminating in the famous anti-Manchester United rant, live on Sky television, where he announced that he 'would love it if we beat them! LOVE IT!'

On New Year's Day 1997, the rotund astrologist and non-league football aficionado Russell Grant published his predictions for the year in the *Daily Mirror*, drawing tarot cards for some of the great and the good of the sporting world, including Kevin Keegan. Drawing the 'Tower' card, Grant predicted the New-castle manager would experience 'disruption and change' as well as 'unexpected events which can create a mass of problems'.

Just one week after Grant's predictions were published, that 'disruption and change' arrived like a wrecking ball. Following discussions with the Newcastle board, Keegan announced that he was leaving the club with immediate effect. 'I feel I have taken the club as far as I can,' he said in a statement, 'and that it would be in the best interests of all concerned if I resign now."

Later, in the updated version of his autobiography, the imaginatively titled *Kevin Keegan: My Autobiography,* published in 1998, Keegan explained that he 'felt as though I was on a train and had enjoyed the journey. But my station was coming up and it was time I was getting off.'

But if Newcastle's passionate fans felt aggrieved by Keegan's flit, they would have more reason when he re-emerged just eight months later at Second Division Fulham, especially as the statement given by Newcastle when he left had said that Keegan no longer wished 'to continue in football management at this stage in his life'. The Cottagers had just been taken over by the Egyptian multi-millionaire owner of the Harrods department store, Mohammed Al Fayed, in a deal worth £30 million. With his aim to take the West London club to the Premier League within five years and make them 'the Manchester United of the south', Al Fayed had pledged another £20 million to redevelop their ageing Craven Cottage ground as well as substantial funds to spend on new players. The only question was which man was going to oversee Al Fayed's revolution.

The existing coach, Micky Adams, had saved the club from dropping out of the Football League in the 1995–96 season and then, in the following season, guided them to promotion to the then Second Division. It was an incredible achievement, given the club's perilous finances and lack of resources, but not, it seemed, sufficient to keep him in his job, at least not while Kevin Keegan was waiting in the wings.

After meeting Al Fayed at Harrods and discussing the position of Chief Operating Officer (and the not inconsiderable matter of a reported £500,000-a-year salary and a 5 per cent share in the club's parent company Fulham Leisure Ltd), Kevin Keegan announced his return from his self-imposed exile to take control at Craven Cottage, appointing Ray Wilkins as team manager and leaving poor Micky Adams seeking alternative employment.

As it had with Newcastle United, Keegan's influence on Fulham was dramatic. On his arrival at the end of September 1997, the club were languishing seventh from the bottom of Division Two. By the end of the season, they had reached the play-offs only to be knocked out by Grimsby Town. The following season, when he had taken over the coaching duties from Ray Wilkins, Keegan took the team up again, this time to the First Division, where they bulldozed the rest of the division, winning 101 points out of a possible 138.

Though Keegan was still in charge of a team in the second tier of English football, albeit one with the wherewithal to go much higher, and had yet to acquire his formal coaching qualifications (something which concerned the FA's technical director Howard Wilkinson), his name was still held in high regard at Lancaster Gate. Moreover, as the search for a new England manager to succeed Glenn Hoddle stuttered along without result, the name of Keegan gradually became a genuine contender, especially when Arsène Wenger, Arsenal's French manager, rebuffed the FA's advances.

When Wenger ruled himself out of the running, declaring that the job wasn't one for a Frenchman, Keegan announced that it was also the 'wrong time' for him to do it, even if he did 'fancy having a go', as though it were a fairground ride. Within two weeks, though, Keegan had not only become the bookies' favourite to take the job, but now had a rabid football public intent on installing him as the new England manager.

Keen to help his country but reluctant to leave Fulham and risk more accusations of walking out on his club, Keegan and the Football Association brokered an extraordinary deal for the forty-eight-year-old to become the first part-time manager of England, with the arrangement to be reviewed after England's next four matches, three of which were crucial European Championship qualifiers.

But Kevin Keegan would never make that appraisal meeting. After his first game in charge on 27 March 1999, a convincing 3–1 win over Poland in front of an ecstatic Wembley crowd (and featuring a hat-trick by Paul Scholes), the clamour for Keegan to take the job on a full-time, permanent basis was such that even his employer, Mohammed Al Fayed, announced that he was prepared to release Keegan from his contract at Fulham and give him as 'a gift to the nation'. For many observers it appeared to be a thinly veiled attempt by Al Fayed to curry favour in his long-standing battle to get a British passport.

A month later, ahead of England's friendly with Hungary in Budapest and now with the green light from Fulham, Keegan confided to the Football Association's acting chief executive David Davies that he was ready to take the job on a full-time basis. 'We've got to stop messing around,' said Keegan. 'I've needed time to think about it and weigh it up, but the more I've worked with the players, the more I've wanted to do it.'

On 14 May, David Davies confirmed that Kevin Keegan had signed a three-year contract to become the England manager, worth a reported £3 million, or over six times the amount Terry Venables had received just four years earlier. Alongside Keegan would be his long-time assistant Derek Fazackerly and, controversially, the sixty-year-old former Newcastle manager Arthur Cox, whose full-time role was vetoed by the FA in favour of a part-time position. He also gave his former charge at Newcastle, Peter Beardsley, a role as an assistant coach.

Yet the outpouring of public love, the euphoria that greeted Keegan's coronation, would soon fade. A series of lacklustre performances in the European qualifiers (a goalless draw against Sweden at Wembley and a 1–1 draw away in Bulgaria) left England needing two wins from their remaining qualifiers to make the finals in Holland and Belgium. The first, against Luxembourg, would be a formality with Alan Shearer scoring a hat-trick in a 6–0 rout, but the final game of the campaign, a disappointing goalless draw in Poland – so often an obstacle to England's progress – left England's hopes of qualification reliant on Sweden beating Poland in the concluding group game to send England through.

Anxiety soon turned to relief for Kevin Keegan, though, when the Swedes, already through as group winners, defeated the gallant Poles 2–0 in Stockholm, giving England second place in the group (at the expense of the Poles and by virtue of a better head-to-head record in their two matches), and setting up a two-leg play-off against Scotland, the first meeting of the two nations since the unforgettable encounter at Wembley at Euro 96. The *Sunday Mirror*, meanwhile, declared that the 'Swedes Have Saved The Turnips'.

There was relief elsewhere in the Football Association. Following Graham Kelly's resignation at the turn of the year, David Davies had filled the role of chief executive in the interim while the search for a new boss continued. And while the idea of appointing a non-English coach was still something of an alien concept to most of the FA's international committee, the same could not be said when it came to the position of chief executive. Thus on 20 October 1999 the FA announced that Graham Kelly's successor would be young, gifted and Scottish. Thirty-five-year-old Adam Crozier was the joint chief executive of the advertising agency Saatchi & Saatchi and had beaten a clutch of high-profile candidates to the job, including the Liverpool chief executive Rick Parry and the man who made Euro 96 such a success, the former FA official Glen Kirton.

The new chief executive couldn't have been more different to his predecessor. Young, dynamic and with discernible cheek-bones, he arrived at the Football Association with a remit to give the organization a much-needed makeover, both structurally and commercially. Conveniently, though, Crozier would not officially join the FA until January 2000 – after the two-legged European Championship play-off between England and Scotland had been decided.

When the play-off arrived, it was England who started as favourites. Scotland, meanwhile, had secured second place in their group behind the runners-up at Euro 96, the Czech Republic, who had won all ten of their games, scoring twenty-six goals and conceding just five. In the lead-up to the first leg at Glasgow's

Hampden Park, the tabloid press once more went into overdrive, predictably billing the game, as they do any match between teams from either side of the border, as the 'Battle of Britain'. It was, if some reporters were to be believed, so much more than a football match. It was Bulldogs versus Bravehearts, it was a 'tribal blood-feud'; the *Mirror* went even further, declaring the game to be 'bigger than Bannockburn'.

What it would be, however, was a compelling contest. In the first game at a hostile Hampden Park on 13 November, England secured a 2–0 victory with both goals coming from the ever-dependable Manchester United playmaker Paul Scholes. That said, it had been anything but comfortable. A total of ten yellow cards would be issued by the Spanish referee Diaz Vega, five for each side.

The contest was now England's to lose and, with a healthy advantage to take back to Wembley for the second leg, the odds were stacked against Scotland. Not that it showed. Four days later, on a chilly Wednesday night, the visitors took the game to England and went one ahead approaching half-time with a head-ed goal from the Everton midfielder Don Hutchison. With the pressure mounting on England, Scotland continued to press and with only a few minutes remaining the Blackburn Rovers centre-half Christian Dailly met an in-swinging corner which, but for an astonishing reaction save from England's David Seaman, would have sent the game into extra-time. As it was, England – and Keegan – had ridden their luck yet again to make the finals of Euro 2000 and Scotland's revenge for Euro 96 would have to wait. It had been close, closer than anyone, not least the FA who had had to change jockey mid-race, had wanted, but England were through.

In the aftermath of the contest there was scant praise for Keegan and his team's achievement of reaching Euro 2000. Instead, it was Craig Brown's Scotland side that took the plaudits for a performance, especially in the second leg, which more than warranted a place in the finals. Getting to Holland and Belgium was one hurdle that Keegan had overcome, albeit with the kind of luck that had largely deserted the likes of Graham Taylor. Now, though, Keegan had realized the magnitude of the task confronting him. In a little over seven months and with the prospect of only four friendly games in which to experiment before the European Championship began, the England coach had to find a way of turning his team into genuine title challengers – and it would take more, much more than a personable nature and a seemingly inexhaustible supply of enthusiasm.

The pre-tournament friendlies in 2000 would merely confirm Keegan's predicament. A goalless draw against Argentina at Wembley and a 1–1 result against Brazil offered little to suggest that a revival was under way, nor did the 2–0 win over the Ukraine, although it did mark the debuts of two of England's most promising young midfielders, Aston Villa's Gareth Barry and Liverpool's Steven Gerrard. And quite what England were doing playing the part-timers of Malta on a dirt track of a pitch in Valletta just five days before the finals started is anyone's guess. The result there, a shambolic 2–1 win, was arguably the worst performance of Keegan's reign to date and, at a time when confidence should have been high, it was going rapidly in the opposite direction. Not that Keegan seemed to notice. 'Call me romantic,' he said after the game, 'but yes, we have a good chance of winning Euro 2000.'

For 'good', read 'none'. Drawn in a group with Portugal, Germany and Romania, England twice surrendered leads in the first game against the Portuguese where they went two goals up within eighteen minutes only to lose the game 3–2, a result compounded by David Beckham's reaction to some of the England fans who had never forgiven him for Saint-Étienne. As he left the pitch, his shirt draped over his shoulders, a small section of the crowd hurled abuse in his direction, insulting his pop star wife Victoria, and Beckham, who, ironically, was one of the few England players to have played well on the night, responded by giving them a one-finger salute.

Matters got worse against Romania in the final group game. Having been 2–1 ahead at half-time England had contrived to concede an equalizer straight after the break and then, with seconds left on the clock, conceded a penalty when the Manchester United full-back Phil Neville made a brainless excuse for a tackle on Coventry City's Viorel Moldovan inside the eighteen-yard area, and Ioan Ganea slotted in the penalty to send England home without even getting past the group stages. Remarkably, England had even beaten Germany 1–0 in their second game but the nature of another spineless capitulation had rendered that otherwise memorable outcome instantly forgettable.

Results aside, it had been another shocking tournament for England and, especially, the Football Association. Keen to present to UEFA and FIFA the image of a modern, progressive association, more than capable of staging the 2006 World Cup, they found that their bid for the tournament would take an almost fatal blow, not because of England's dire displays on the field, but from the all too predictable behaviour of their supporters off it.

Even before the game against Germany – always a game with the potential for trouble – nearly 400 English fans had been arrested in Brussels for rampaging through the streets, vandalizing cars and hurling anything they could get their hands on through shop windows. Later, ahead of the match in the southern Belgian town of Charleroi, police would use water cannons to disperse the rival sets of fans that had been clashing repeatedly in the town's Charles II Square. No matter who the manager was or how well the team were doing, it seemed destined that the so-called 'English disease' would always present itself.

The Euro 2000 inquest began soon after, both inside the meeting rooms at Lancaster Gate and, of course, in the press. At the Football Association there was mounting concern that Kevin Keegan was not the right man to guide England to the World Cup finals in Japan and Korea in 2002. While he was liked and respected, the fact that England had collapsed so spectacularly – against Romania, for instance, they only managed eight shots on goal, compared to Romania's twenty-four – and seemed to have little idea how to contend with even the most average of European opposition didn't augur well for the World Cup qualifying campaign due to start in early October.

Kevin Keegan, meanwhile, laid the blame for the team's exit squarely at the feet of Kevin Keegan. 'It has been a struggle out there to get our passing game together but this is fairly basic and can be put right,' explained the England manager. 'We're not saying they can't pass the ball. I see it in training, at their clubs, and they do it in the Champions League, but it was not in this tournament to the standard required. I am not blaming the players. It is my problem to make them pass it better.'

Not so, said the team captain Alan Shearer. 'The players take responsibility,' said Shearer, who had played his last game for England after announcing his international retirement. 'The manager puts the players out on the pitch but it was our own fault. There are no excuses. We got what we deserved because we were not good enough.'

Ultimately, it mattered not who was to blame, and besides, it wasn't as though the players were going to get sacked. Despite another depressing tournament, the Football Association continued to back their manager, even though it might have been the ideal time to replace him, given that an entire World Cup qualifying campaign lay ahead of them, with opportunities to make one or two mistakes along the way. Soon, though, that decision would be taken out of the FA's hands.

For seventy-seven memorable years, to play at the Empire Stadium at Wembley represented the pinnacle of achievement for footballers the world over. Now, though, it was beginning to show its age. Tired, uncomfortable and frayed around the edges, the powers that be at the Football Association had obtained planning permission to raze the famous old stadium and its iconic Twin Towers and replace it with a stadium fit for the twenty-first century, and what the FA hoped would be a venue that would convince FIFA that England was the perfect choice to host the 2006 World Cup finals. But by July 2000 those hopes were dashed and the tournament was awarded to Germany. The FA had no option but to plough on with their stadium project, which continued despite massive delays and cost overruns.

It wasn't the only building work the Football Association had commissioned. In an attempt to drag the game's governing body kicking and screaming into somewhere approaching the new millennium or, failing that, the 1970s, the chief executive Adam Crozier had overseen the FA's move from the antiques showroom that was Lancaster Gate (their home since 1929) to their swanky new offices at 25 Soho Square, in the heart of London's West End. 'Lancaster Gate is not suitable for a top-performing modern organization,' Crozier said, forgetting that, for the most part, the FA were anything but that. 'We've run out of space. Leaving Lancaster Gate is another step in enabling us to create an organization of which we can be proud.'

Wembley's farewell game before the bulldozers moved in would be the World Cup qualifier against Germany on Saturday, 7 October 2000. There couldn't have been a more appropriate opponent. But as Kevin Keegan finalized his squad for the game and the away fixture in Finland four days later, he received news that his mother Doris had passed away in hospital at the age of seventy-six. Keegan was devastated. Suddenly, from preparing for arguably the most crucial game in his time as England manager, Keegan was now concerned with something far more important to him.

Personally and professionally, Kevin Keegan was struggling to cope. Come match day, his very demeanour suggested that the pressure on him was finally beginning to tell. As the rain lashed a near full house at Wembley, he seemed distant, preoccupied. When Germany's midfielder Dietmar Hamann squeezed a long-range free-kick low and hard under David Seaman's body to open the scoring, Keegan's disposition, like the dismal north London sky above him, darkened still further.

Seventy-six goalless minutes later, the referee Stefano Braschi of Italy finally put Wembley Stadium out of action and England out of their misery. Another defeat. Another feeble, unimaginative, uninspired display on this day of all days. The day when

Wembley said goodbye. As Keegan and his team trudged off the sodden pitch and toward the tunnel, the crowd turned on them again, just as the prearranged (and now entirely inappropriate) farewell firework display kicked in. Moments later, though, the real fireworks would begin.

After the final whistle, the FA's executive director David Davies made his way to the dressing room to console the manager and players. Keegan, though, was beyond consolation and when Davies entered the room he knew exactly what had happened. Taking him aside, Keegan confirmed that he was quitting as England coach with immediate effect. Not even the combined diplomatic skills of Adam Crozier and the FA chairman Geoff Thompson could persuade him to stay. Keegan was going.

Shocked into silence and now without a manager for the game in Finland just four days later, the FA management began making some quick-fire contingencies, with Crozier installing Howard Wilkinson as the temporary coach for the match in Helsinki.

Keegan, meanwhile, would give his one and only interview live on television. Soaked to the bone and looking more composed and at ease than he had in weeks, Kevin Keegan explained his decision as Kevin Keegan always did – in the third person. 'Kevin Keegan has given it his best shot. I don't want to go on and outstay my welcome,' he said, in an address that was strangely similar to the one he gave when he walked out on Newcastle United in 1997.

> It's the end of the road for me. If I carried on, it would be for all the wrong reasons ... I told the players first that that's me finished. I just feel that I just fall a little bit short for what is required of this job and the first person I've got to be honest to is myself. I sat out there first half and I could see things weren't right but I couldn't find it in myself to solve the problem. I've had a fair crack from the FA and the fact they have been so supportive makes it very difficult to leave the job. Nevertheless, because I'm the sort of person who is always honest with myself, despite ten to fifteen minutes of talking [after the match], I am going.

I thanked the players for their efforts, because they've been tremendous for me; I thanked them for the performance because, particularly second half, they put on a performance that any coach would be proud of. As I have said, I just feel I fall short of what is required for this job. It is a massive job – there were parts of it I could do adequately and parts of it I hopefully did very well, but as for the key part of getting players to win football matches, again today I failed. After Euro 2000 a lot of managers bit the dust; some of whom had done a lot better than me and I always felt I had to start this campaign off well. But we haven't done that, so …

'There was an effort made to try to dissuade me from going but, although it may not seem so to you, I think that the timing is right. I feel in my heart of hearts that I'm not up to it. Last game at Wembley, and against Germany. For Kevin Keegan, there's nothing more I want to do.

In a shocking, almost surreal moment, Kevin Keegan had walked once more, leaving England and the FA searching for their fifth coach in just seven years. The truth, however, was that had he, and not Howard Wilkinson, gone to Helsinki with the team and returned without anything resembling a favourable result, it was unlikely that he could have survived in his job, especially with England's hopes of qualifying for the 2002 World Cup so seriously jeopardized.

Kevin Keegan left behind a team that was eminently capable of achieving something in the international game but had spectacularly failed to do so. Nice guy though he was, Keegan, by his own admission, had simply found this level of football too much for him. Tactically bereft and without the answers to the innumerable questions that the international game posed, he had relied on those age-old English failsafes – enthusiasm and luck – to see him through, but in a game that had moved on, a game where even the smallest of nations were progressing with almost indecent haste, Keegan and his team were only ever going to be exposed. His record as coach merely reinforced that notion. With a win ratio of just 38 per cent from his eighteen games in charge, Keegan was, and remains, the least successful full-time England manager of all time.

CHAPTER 8

THE LADYKILLER

'A master in the art of love-making.'

Sven-Göran Eriksson's former lover, Faria Alam

After Kevin Keegan's latest vanishing act, England began the search for their third manager in two years. With Howard Wilkinson taking charge for the qualifier against Finland, Adam Crozier and the FA international committee compiled a shortlist of potential candidates. On it were some familiar names: Bobby Robson, Arsène Wenger, Alex Ferguson, even Terry Venables, but there was also a clutch of younger English coaches such as Bryan Robson and Peter Taylor. This was also the first time that the idea of a foreign coach leading the England team had been broached, with David Dein, the Arsenal chairman, suggesting the name of Sven-Göran Eriksson, the Swede in charge of Italian Serie A champions Lazio.

Certainly, Eriksson had the pedigree. The first coach to win league and cup doubles in three countries (Sweden, Portugal and Italy) and the winner of the UEFA Cup and the Cup-Winners' Cup, he had a track record as impressive as any other coach in Europe. Moreover, he was clearly interested in the opportunity. According to David Davies, Dein and Eriksson's adviser Athole Still had been in contact within an hour of Kevin Keegan tendering his resignation after the defeat to Germany. It was then that the idea of England's first foreign coach had taken seed.

In the short term there was not only the tricky World Cup qualifier to negotiate in Helsinki but an upcoming friendly in Turin against Italy. With Howard Wilkinson's agreement only extending to the Finland game – he would return from Scandinavia with a scoreless draw from a game they were unlucky not to win – the FA needed to act to find another stand-in. Initially, a plan to have Bobby Robson, now managing Newcastle, assisted by the Leicester City boss Peter Taylor and Manchester United's assistant manager Steve McClaren, was seen as the perfect stop-gap, but while Leicester and United both acceded to the FA's request to release their men, the plan was scuppered by Newcastle's chairman Freddy Shepherd who, fearing that Robson might get a taste for the international game again, refused to sanction the deal.

Peter Taylor, though, was highly regarded within the Football Association. A successful coach of the England Under-21 team, he had vacated the position when Howard Wilkinson had been appointed the FA's technical director and decided to run the team himself. After a year at Gillingham, Taylor had been appointed manager at Leicester City in July 2000 when Martin O'Neill had headed north to take over at Celtic. He had hit the ground running too, taking the unfashionable East Midlands side to the top of the Premiership and earning him the Carling Manager of the Month Award for September. Coincidentally, he had also been in the crowd at Wembley the day Keegan had quit.

On 21 October, Taylor was returning home from a narrow 1–0 defeat away at Liverpool when his mobile phone rang. It was Adam Crozier. He wanted Taylor to take control for the Italy game. 'Was I surprised? Yes, but I was over the moon too,' he recalls. 'I never dreamt I'd manage my country, whether it was for one game or not. It was just a fantastic feeling.'

Without any of the associated pressure or intense media scrutiny that faces permanent England coaches, Taylor resolved that while there was little point in making radical changes to the team or the set-up, he was determined to make his England side younger and, as such, selected a squad where no outfield player was older than thirty. 'Maybe it would have been different if I was the permanent manager but I just felt that the older players could have done without a trip to Italy and that the youngsters deserved an opportunity,' he adds.

Perhaps the key decision Taylor took, though, was selecting twenty-five-year-old David Beckham, the villain of the piece at the World Cup in 1998, as the new England captain. 'I knew how much it meant to him to play for England,' explains Taylor. 'I also knew how well he had handled the sending off against Argentina and the amount of stick he received after it. I just thought that he has tremendous character. There was only a couple of possibilities, like Gareth Southgate, but I decided to go with David and the way that he performed as captain both on and off the pitch made it the right decision. There are certain players who don't enjoy that kind of responsibility but you could always see how much David enjoyed playing for England.'

As England, led by David Beckham, took to the field in Turin, eventually losing by a single Gennaro Gattuso goal, the search for Kevin Keegan's full-time successor continued. Back home, rumour, hearsay and plain old claptrap filled the newspapers, day in and day out, but the idea that the England team could soon be managed by a foreigner nevertheless gained momentum, not least because, Venables and Robson aside (and both, for differing reasons, were never going to get the job again), there were no English managers with a CV that showed anything other than mere promise, an engaging personality and an occasional cup win or promotion. That, after all, was how England had ended up with Glenn Hoddle. That was how they ended up with Kevin Keegan.

The FA were at a crossroads: continue with the age-old approach of appointing the best English coach available, even if that meant someone who was singularly ill-equipped to do the job, or appoint the best person they possibly could, regardless of nationality and their mammoth salary demands. The BSkyB-fuelled boom years of the Premier League, and the consequent and unstoppable influx of foreign talent to Britain, had changed the face of the national game irrevocably. Bigger stars, bigger wages, bigger egos. It was a difficult time for football managers, and, for the most part, the English coaches had failed to adapt. Moreover, the professional game, in the higher echelons at least, had reached such an unprecedented plane that many of the game's stellar players now had no need to pursue a career in club management once their playing days had ended. After all, why put yourself through the pressure and the risk to your reputation when a) you could opt for a cosy career in the media saying what you wanted when you wanted, without ever having to face the brickbats of 40,000 fans every Saturday, and b) you already had enough money to see you through your retirement.

With no English coaches fitting the bill, attention returned to Sven-Göran Eriksson. Certainly, Adam Crozier, the man charged with modernizing the Football Association, was signed off on hiring the Swede, as was David Dein, and they convinced the international committee that here was a manager of rare talent and unquestionable pedigree, a man who not only spoke fluent English but, thanks to Lazio president Sergio Cragnotti's blessing, was also now available. Crozier and Dein set off for Rome, determined to get their man. After a meeting at Dein's daughter's flat with Eriksson and his agent Athole Still, a deal was struck to make the Swede the new England manager.

At 8.02 a.m. on 2 November 2000 at the Sopwell House Hotel near St Albans, the Football Association's Adam Crozier and David Davies unveiled the first foreign 'head coach' of the English national football team. Wearing a smart suit with a poppy in his lapel, Sven-Göran Eriksson spoke of his pride at his appointment. 'I am very honoured and very pleased to be here,' said the fifty-two-year-old. 'This is a big job, the biggest challenge I have faced in my life. I was surprised when the FA approached me but it only took me a matter of hours to make up my mind. When England ask, you don't say no. If I had turned down this opportunity I would not have slept well for the next two years.' He added, revealing a touch of dry humour that surprised many observers, 'I haven't come here for the money – or the weather.'

Of course, as Eriksson spoke on a grey Hertfordshire morning, there could be no denying that the British climate had not played a part in his decision to leave Lazio, but many were taken aback by the size of the package he had secured. With a five-year deal worth a reported £3 million a year, he was, by some distance, the highest-paid manager in the world.

On his appointment, the only other famous Swede resident in the country, the former GMTV weathergirl Ulrika Jonsson, said, 'If he should need any acclimatizing, I'm here waiting on his call.' Little did anyone know at the time, least of all Jonsson herself, but it would transpire that there was nothing Sven-Göran Eriksson happened to like more than a long, one-on-one session of acclimatization.

While the consensus seemed to support Eriksson's appointment there was still a vocal minority that viewed the decision as entirely alien to the natural order of football in England. Predictably, the *Daily Mail* accused the FA of selling the nation 'down the fjord' and considered the appointment an 'insult' to all Englishmen, before charging headlong into some petty national stereotyping. 'England's humiliation knows no end,' it said. 'In their trendy eagerness to appoint a designer foreigner, did the FA pause for so much as a moment to consider the depth of this insult to our national pride? We sell our birthright down the fjord to a nation of seven million skiers and hammer throwers who spend half their year living in darkness.'

The *Sun*, meanwhile, also devoted its editorial to the matter, saying: 'The nation which gave the game of football to the world has been forced to put a foreign coach in charge of its national team for the first time. What a climb-down. What a humiliation. What a terrible, pathetic, self-inflicted indictment. What an awful mess.'

Jack Charlton, the Englishman who managed the Republic of Ireland, meanwhile, was aghast. 'I'm very upset. The French are managed by a Frenchman, Germany by a German and the Italians have one of their own.'

When the hue and cry had subsided, however, it was patently clear that with World Cup qualification hanging in the balance and a paucity of home-grown coaches qualified to remedy that, Crozier and the Football Association didn't really have a choice. They had to go for the best, and that meant paying for it.

Sven-Göran Eriksson had assumed control of a team which faced an uphill struggle to make the World Cup finals. Even Howard Wilkinson, the FA's technical director and stand-in manager, was taking a long-term view. After the drawn game in Finland, Wilkinson had responded to a question from the *Evening Standard*'s Michael Hart about England's bleak prospects, suggesting that England might not need 'to worry about qualifying for 2002 and build a team for 2006' instead.

Some considered Wilkinson's words to be nothing short of treachery. Others felt he had a point. Whatever the argument, the very fact that the debate was even happening, and after just two out of the eight games in qualifying, was a certain sign that England were in real trouble. For his part, Eriksson seemed philosophical about the task in hand. 'If we don't get results, they will try to hang me,' he said. 'But if I was an Englishman, they would also try to hang me.'

Sven-Göran Eriksson was a markedly different character to his predecessor Kevin Keegan. Not for him the card schools and race nights, the tomfoolery and the wisecracks. Quiet, considered and taciturn, he preferred to keep the players at arm's length, relying heavily on his coaches to do his bidding on the training field. Even when he was on the touchline during matches, he couldn't be more of a contrast with the excitable, almost childlike bundle of nerves that was Keegan. 'If you want someone shouting, you will have to change the coach,' he once said. 'I will never do it.'

Off the pitch, Eriksson was equally reserved, often to the point of reclusiveness. His private life was exactly that, or so he thought. With his long-time partner, an impossibly glamorous Italian lawyer by the name of Nancy Dell'Olio, Sven enjoyed the finer things in life, with a passion for Tibetan poetry, a penchant for expensive restaurants and homes across Europe, a property portfolio that would be expanded by his purchase of a £2.5 million Georgian home in London's Regent's Park.

'Svennis', as his friends called him, had come a long way. The son of a bus conductor, Sven Senior, and his wife Ulla, he had suffered a serious knee injury while playing for the Swedish second division side Karlskoga in 1975 and was forced to retire at the age of just twenty-seven. The following year, on the advice of his friend and fellow professional Tord Grip, he accepted an offer to coach third division Degerfors, and took the club into Sweden's second division within three years.

As his coaching improved, Eriksson immersed himself in the methodologies of renowned coaches across Europe, particularly those in England. He was a keen student of the Liverpool 'boot room' of the 1970s and 1980s and visited Ipswich Town during their memorable triumphs under Bobby Robson. A move to IFK Gothenburg soon followed and by the end of the 1982 season he had wrapped up a UEFA Cup win, a Swedish championship and two Swedish cups.

Eriksson's success with Gothenburg would prove to be his passport to untold riches in the European game. Headhunted by the Portuguese giants Benfica, he soon steered the Lisbon club to a league title, a cup win and a runners-up spot in the UEFA Cup. From then on, it was just a matter of waiting for the phone to ring.

There was no shortage of takers: Roma, Fiorentina, Benfica for a second time, Sampdoria and, finally, Lazio where, thanks to seven trophies in three seasons, he managed to drag a club known for its underachievement out of the shadows of its city rivals Roma and to only its second *Scudetto* in almost a century of existence.

With a few notable exceptions, there weren't many jobs left in the game that could have tempted Eriksson away from the near legendary status he held at Lazio, and with an impeccable record in club management a move into international football seemed like a sound career move.

Eriksson would have nearly four months to idle away before his first game in charge of the national side. In the meantime, the Football Association had announced that as the builders were enjoying their tea breaks and red tops at what was Wembley Stadium, England would now begin their very own roadshow, taking their talents around the country's regional grounds while the new national stadium was being built. It was a politic move. For too long England had seemed like a team for London and the South-East. Now, everyone from Liverpool to Leeds, Southampton to Sunderland would have the chance to see their favourites in an England shirt.

With time on his hands, Eriksson decided to see just what talent he had to work with, turning up at Premier League games across the country, signing autographs and then leaving ten minutes early to beat the traffic. He was a busy man. Up to the announcement of his first squad for the friendly against Spain at Villa Park, Eriksson, and his long-time assistant Tord Grip, had attended twenty-five games in just forty-one days. Contrast that with his predecessor Kevin Keegan. Before he named his first squad, Keegan, still tied down by Fulham, managed to see just one Premiership game.

Breezing into the Villa Park press room, Eriksson turned on the charm. 'Nice to see you,' he said.

Suddenly, a voice piped up at the back of the room. 'Not for long ...'

Eriksson's first squad, an expanded thirty-one-man version, would signal the end of the line for many of England's old hands. Out went Paul 'The Guvnor' Ince, Dennis Wise and Graeme Le Saux, never to play for their country again. Tony Adams, meanwhile, had perhaps sensed his days were numbered and had already announced his international retirement.

There would be three Coles in the squad: the Manchester United striker Andy, the West Ham midfielder Joe and the uncapped Arsenal left-back Ashley, and three other new faces in Sunderland's Gavin McCann, West Ham's Michael Carrick and the one genuine bolt from the blue, Charlton Athletic's left-back Chris Powell. Surprisingly, the Aston Villa left-sided player Gareth Barry was sent back to the Under-21s despite starting three of the last four full internationals.

As for the game itself, Eriksson was looking forward to his international debut. 'I'm nervous about meeting so many new people,' he explained. 'It's like when you go out with a woman for the first time – you're bound to wonder how it will end up.'

With a sense of expectation not really felt since Terry Venables took control of the England team, everybody seemed keen to do their bit, not least to help erase the memories of the previous regime. Even the players were determined to impress. Realizing that here was a new broom, and a foreign one at that, they announced a self-imposed alcohol ban to be implemented when they began playing their games around the country. Ordinarily, the players would congregate after each match in the Players' Bar to have drinks with sponsors, guests, friends and family. Now, though, they were insisting that their bar should be dry. It was a move that surprised and delighted Eriksson. Concerned with the increasing numbers of salacious stories appearing in the Sunday papers, the drink culture among professional footballers had long been one of his bugbears and something he had been determined to eradicate.

Eriksson's first game as England coach would be an uplifting 3–0 win over Spain at Villa Park, Birmingham, on 28 February 2001. With goals from the Liverpool duo Nicky Barmby and Emile Heskey and a third from the Middlesbrough centre-half Ugo Ehiogu, it had been a game notable only for the number of players that Eriksson had employed. As it was his first game, nobody really cared that he had used eighteen of the twenty-six players at his disposal and handed three debut caps to Gavin McCann, Michael Ball and Chris Powell, but, in time, Eriksson's predilection for using friendlies as little more than extended training sessions would be called into question.

The victory over an average Spain side nevertheless set England up nicely in their bid to salvage something, anything, from their World Cup qualifying campaign. The good news for Eriksson was that it could hardly get any worse than it had been under Kevin Keegan. Gradually, though, England's players responded to the Swede's thoughtful, more considered approach to the game and a hat-trick of wins in their qualifying games, first against Finland at Anfield (2–1), followed by away wins against

Albania in Tirana (1–3) and Greece in Athens (0–2), saw England not only restore some pride to their performances but also give themselves an excellent opportunity of securing the second place needed to make the play-offs.

With two games left in the group for Germany and three for England, though, Germany were clear favourites to win the group and take the sole automatic place, not least because their record in qualifying was so outstanding. Beaten just once in sixty qualification games and undefeated at Munich's Olympiastadion since 1973, a win against Eriksson's England would seal their place in the World Cup finals, while even a draw would leave them just requiring another draw from their final game at home to Finland to progress. Indeed, so confident were the German Football Association of qualifying automatically that they had even arranged friendlies for Germany on the days of the play-off. England, meanwhile, were six points behind their opponents, with an inferior goal difference and seemingly destined to enter into that play-off if they were to reach Japan and Korea.

The vast majority of the 63,000 people in the Olympiastadion on 1 September expected another steamroller of a German performance. England got off to the worst start imaginable, Carsten Jancker tapping an Oliver Neuville header past David Seaman to give the hosts a lead after just five minutes. From then on, though, it was all England. The goals simply rained in.

The scoreboard at the Olympiastadion said it all: Deutschland 1 England 5. It was the kind of scoreline that bookies don't even have odds for. An unpredictable, unfathomable one-off and, it was argued, England's best performance since they beat West Germany in the World Cup final in 1966, although the 4–1 win over Holland at Euro 96 must have run it close. The *Independent* newspaper would call it one of 'the least believable results in international sporting history'. It was difficult to disagree.

Confidence oozed from each and every one of the players. There was a virtuoso performance by the hat-trick hero Michael Owen who seemed to score every time the ball crossed his path. Steven Gerrard, meanwhile, suddenly found his club form for his country, scoring a terrific goal and even nutmegging his Liverpool colleague and England's conqueror at Wembley a year earlier, Dietmar Hamann, just for the hell of it. It was unbelievable. For a nation so starved of success, so reliant on the vain hopes of a decent run in a major tournament, it was as though England had finally won the World Cup again.

An incredulous nation watched on. Could this really be the same England team that had lost to Germany just a year earlier? The answer was yes and no. Sure, the personnel involved were the same ones that had been so disappointing under Kevin Keegan, but they had been galvanized by a manager intent on proving his worth and the worth of his players on the international stage.

Now, any argument the press, or the supporters, may have had over the appointment of a foreign coach to the England manager's job had been rendered redundant. Not only had Eriksson overseen a memorable victory over England's bitterest rivals, but he had put England firmly back in the race to qualify for the World Cup finals in Japan and Korea.

Even Sven-Göran Eriksson seemed bemused. 'I can't believe that we can beat Germany 5–1 away, it seems like a dream, it's unbelievable. I said to the players: "I don't know what to say to you." I told them before the game, if you play football as you can play we can beat any team, even Germany away. But I can't believe it was 5–1.'

It was a view echoed by the man who masterminded Germany's 1990 World Cup win, 'Der Kaiser' himself, Franz Beckenbauer. 'I have never seen a better England team and I have never seen an England team playing better football. They had pace, aggression, movement and skill. It was fantasy football. When they scored their third goal they started to play football that would have beaten anyone in the world. Michael Owen was simply unstoppable. Our defenders were slow and they just could not handle his pace, while his finishing was unbelievable.'

The praise for Eriksson and England was truly fulsome. The *News of the World* led the way declaring that 'There's no doubt now that the Swede, doubted by some when he arrived, is a fully fledged Englishman. So arise, Sir Sven.' Hugh McIlvanney in the *Sunday Times*, meanwhile, described Eriksson as 'the master of a renaissance'.

In time, the victory would even be voted the third most popular event in a Channel 4 poll to find the *100 Greatest Sporting Moments*, one place behind England's World Cup win in 1966, and two places behind the top-ranked event, Steve Redgrave's fifth gold medal at the 2000 Olympic Games in Sydney.

Across the continent in Germany, however, the reaction was close to despair. This was the first time that Germany had conceded five goals or more since their 6–3 loss to France in 1958, and only the third time in their rich, successful history that they had lost by four goals or more. Amid the gloom, the newspaper *Welt am Sonntag* reflected that 'The German team received a severe lesson … As last night's events showed, football in this country is in baby shoes.'

While the nation celebrated long and hard, it was easy to forget that Germany were nevertheless still three points clear in the qualifying group and that England's hopes of pipping them to the automatic place rested on their final two games, both of which were at home. The first, against Albania at Newcastle's St James's Park, would prove to be a routine 2–0 victory – thanks to goals from Michael Owen again and Robbie Fowler – and, inevitably, it seemed there was a hangover from that starry night in Berlin. It mattered not that the performance was average and uninspired. At that stage in qualification and having dragged themselves back into contention, the result was everything.

Now sitting on top of Group 9 on goal difference, England went into the final game of their campaign knowing that a victory would in all likelihood, given their now vastly superior goal difference, award them and not the Germans the automatic place.

On paper, it had seemed like a walk in the park for England. After the triumph in Germany and the workmanlike win over Albania, few predicted any problems for Eriksson's England. Greece, after all, had never beaten England in their seven previous meetings and, moreover, had yet to win a game on their travels in the group.

But if England's trouble-free passage to the World Cup finals was all but assured, somebody had forgotten to tell the Greeks. At a full Old Trafford on 6 October, they took the game to England, grabbing the lead in the thirty-sixth minute through Angelos Charisteas. It would be over half an hour before England finally drew level. Teddy Sheringham, on for Robbie Fowler, scored with virtually his first touch, guiding a back header into the Greek net from six yards.

Just as England's World Cup balloon was about to be set free on a fair wind to the Far East, along came the Greeks and punctured it. Within sixty seconds of England's equalizer, the visitors had re-established their lead, with Demis Nikolaidis slotting the ball home from close range. As the ball rolled past Nigel Martyn in the England goal and the happiness turned to horror, all of England and Eriksson's endeavour in seizing the initiative in Group 9 seemed to have been for nought.

With seconds to spare in injury time and England facing the prospect of their first competitive defeat under the Swede – they had lost to the Netherlands in a friendly in August – and what they thought would be an awkward play-off against the Ukraine, England were awarded a free-kick some twenty-eight yards out when Sheringham went down from a challenge by Costas Konstantinidis. Having tried and failed with six earlier free-kicks in the game and with the clock ticking down, Beckham curled a delicious, unstoppable shot high into the Greek goal. And with rivals Germany failing to beat Finland at home, it meant England were through to the World Cup finals without a play-off and without a problem. Well, almost.

As Beckham ran to the corner flag, his arms outstretched in triumph and his team-mates in hot pursuit, Eriksson's face, so cold, so steely, finally cracked. He ran down the steps from the Old Trafford dug-out, laughing like a kid who had just chanced upon the keys to the tuck shop. At last, some emotion. At last, a sense that Sven was finally feeling what the rest of the nation were going through.

Eight years on, people remember the Greece game as the one where Beckham scored *that* free-kick but, if anything, the whole ninety-four minutes was dominated by him. Rarely had anyone seen such a tireless, breathless display of attacking midfield play. Football pundits often say that energetic players are 'box to box' types or that they 'cover every blade of grass' on the pitch. On that Saturday afternoon in October, Beckham was all of those things and a whole lot more.

But then he had needed to be. After the majesty of the performance in Germany, and the disciplined but unspectacular display against Albania at St James's Park, the majority of the England team had seemed paralysed by the fear of failure. With Michael Owen out injured, replaced by Liverpool's Robbie Fowler, the team had turned in their worst performance under their new manager. Paul Scholes and Nicky Barmby were largely anonymous while Steven Gerrard, a player who had been reprimanded by Eriksson after being caught enjoying an early hours drinking session with friends in Southport just a few days before the game against Greece, was predictably uninspired. Only the second-half substitutes, the ageless Spurs striker Teddy Sheringham and his former Manchester United team-mate Andy Cole, came close to matching the efforts of the one-man show that was David Beckham.

Finally, the burning effigies of 1998 were gone, replaced by awards, gongs and silverware. That year, David Beckham would win the BBC's coveted Sports Personality of the Year award and would finish runner-up to Luís Figo of Portugal in the poll for the FIFA World Player of the Year. In London, Madame Tussaud's would reveal their new Beckham waxwork while across the world in South-East Asia, the Pariwas Buddhist temple in Thailand would even commission a gold statue of the England captain. From devil to deity in three whirlwind years. And, lest we forget, there was already a course in 'Beckham Studies' at Staffordshire University.

With five out of six wins in his qualifying games, Eriksson had somehow taken a disparate assembly of individuals that was devoid of confidence and imagination and, with a football version of the loaves and fishes miracle, transformed them into one of the most improved teams in world football, difficult to break down, dangerous going forward.

With qualification assured, the England squad kicked back. They even had a drink or two to celebrate, all with the manager's blessing. As befitted their status as the first couple of football, the Beckhams hosted a £350,000 World Cup party in the Japanese garden of their 'Beckingham Palace' mansion in Hertfordshire. Billed as a 'sushi and Gucci' event, it attracted stars like Elton John, Cilla Black and the men behind England's official World Cup song, Ant and Dec, as well as Sven-Göran Eriksson and the England squad.

There's always a palpable sense of national relief when England qualify for the World Cup. Plans can be made, weddings rearranged and family holidays scrapped, safe in the knowledge that come the summer, there's something far more important to occupy one's time. In 2002 'World Cup fever', as it's called, would once more take over the nation, only this time the country's retailers had truly lost their marbles. The supermarket chain Asda started selling England gazebos and World Cup pizzas, complete with a halfway line made out of cheese. The menswear chain Burton was offering England suits, a snip at £175. Even Sven was getting in on the act, releasing his own CD – *The Sven-Göran Eriksson Classical Collection*. If you wanted World Cup tat, you really were spoilt for choice.

That Christmas, Eriksson accepted an invitation to attend the fiftieth birthday party of Richard Desmond, the owner of the Express Newspapers group and such cult magazines as *Asian Babes* and *Big Ones*. Also at the event at The Roundhouse in Camden, north London, would be the woman who had so graciously offered to help England's new manager 'acclimatize' when he first arrived in the UK. According to the *Daily Mail*, the idea to invite them both to the function had come from Prime Minister Tony Blair's spin doctor, Alastair Campbell, who suggested Sven-Göran Eriksson and Ulrika Jonsson would get along well as 'they were both Swedish'. If anything, they got on too well. Within days, the pair would become an item, albeit one that operated under the radar of the national media and Sven's long-term partner, Nancy Dell'Olio.

Personally and professionally, Christmas 2001 would be a busy time for Eriksson, juggling work commitments like attending the World Cup draw in South Korea, as well, of course, as the women in his life. Prior to the draw in Busan, the FIFA president Sepp Blatter announced a change to the qualification rules for the 2006 tournament that had been awarded to Germany. Breaking with a tradition that dated back to the inaugural World Cup in Uruguay in 1930, it had been decided that the winners of the World Cup, starting with the 2002 competition, would have to qualify for the next tournament, with only the host nation being afforded automatic qualification.

The following day, England received one of the worst draws imaginable: Group F, alongside Nigeria, Sweden and the seeded team, Argentina. This was quickly nominated, by whoever decides these things, as the 'Group of Death'. If Sven-Göran Eriksson had thought that international football was a breeze, now he would find out the true reality of the task on his hands.

England's World Cup plans, however, would be thrown into disarray by an injury to the pantomime-villain-turned-national-hero, David Beckham. On 10 April 2002 Beckham had broken a metatarsal bone in his left foot in a Champions League match for Manchester United against the Spanish side Deportivo La Coruña. The injury was problem enough but soon the press seized on the fact that it had been caused by Deportivo's Argentine international Aldo Duscher and that maybe it was part of a wider, deliberate plan to scupper England's chances ahead of their group game in the World Cup.

The news of David Beckham's injury was greeted with the kind of hysteria usually reserved for power cuts. In Chingford,

Essex, where he was brought up, the story had rocked the town to its very core. 'All the publicity around this injury is a bit silly but it shows how much the country cares. He knows his country needs him,' said a worried Sean Hawkes, the Beckham family's milkman. A local surgeon, George Olivelle, saw the press photographs of Beckham's foot and was taken aback, saying, 'I don't know about the injury but from the pictures he should go and see a chiropodist. His toenails look awful.'

Perhaps the clearest indication yet that Beckham's metatarsal was a matter of national importance came not when the Prime Minister Tony Blair demanded to be given regular reports on the England skipper's progress, but when Uri Geller got involved again. Within forty-eight hours of the news breaking of Beckham's broken bone, the spoon-bending Israeli psychic – sometimes referred to as a 'mentalist' – was already imploring the nation to touch their television sets and send healing waves straight to the England skipper.

With the national obsession with a small broken bone in a footballer's foot taking precedence over such comparatively minor world events as the so-called 'war on terror' or the uncertainty in the Middle East, it was clear that it would take a news story of earth-shattering importance to evict David Beckham and his metatarsal from the front and back pages. When it did happen, though, nobody could have guessed that it would have involved his manager.

In late April the *Daily Mirror* beat the *News of the World* to the exclusive that the England manager Sven-Göran Eriksson, fifty-five, had been having an affair with the TV presenter and ex-partner of the former England international Stan Collymore, Ulrika Jonsson. What had started out as a casual fling had turned into a relationship and now it was out in the open. As the bookmakers offered odds on which of the England manager's women would finally win his hand in marriage – Jonsson was at 33–1 with Dell'Olio at 16–1 – suddenly David Beckham's faulty foot was forgotten.

For the tabloid editors, it was a revelation. Behind Eriksson's grey suits, rimless spectacles and impassive manner, lurked a brooding, hot-blooded man, full of molten passion. Soon, all the sordid details of their affair would reach the public domain. There were illicit meetings, clandestine conversations and even conspiracy theories that Jonsson was a Swedish agent provocateur intent on extracting all of England's team strategies ahead of the two nations meeting at the World Cup.

Certainly, the story provided a major distraction ahead of the World Cup finals. At times, the revelations were pretty sordid. How, for instance, would the England squad respond to a manager when all they could think about when they looked at him was how he left his platform shoes outside Jonsson's bedroom to warn her nanny of what was going on behind the door?

The scandal, if two single adults having a relationship could be deemed a 'scandal', was still in the papers when, on 9 May, Eriksson announced his final twenty-three-man squad for the World Cup finals. While there were no major surprises, except perhaps the omission of Andy Cole, who announced his international retirement soon after, all anyone really wanted to know was whether David Beckham – the man his wife called 'Golden-balls' – was fit and ready to led England's World Cup campaign. Now, whether it was the magical, mystical intervention of Uri Geller or merely the combination of time coupled with expert medical treatment, David Beckham duly declared himself fit for the tournament. It was the resurrection that England fans had been praying – or touching TV screens – for.

Aside from the fairer sex, Eriksson's other primary motivation in life appeared to be money. Despite the fact that he was already the highest paid coach in world football, the Swede seemed to be less than discerning when the opportunity for some easy cash came his way. In the lead-up to the 2002 World Cup, for example, Eriksson was inundated with offers, most of which he somehow seemed to squeeze into his hectic schedule. There was a television advert with the chef Jamie Oliver for Sainsbury's, there was his classical compilation CD on the Naxos label, there was a football manager game with PlayStation and, in the weirdest fit of all, there was another commercial, this time for Cirio Del Monte pasta sauce. When Alf Ramsey was manager of England he got £3,000 a year.

And if proof were needed about the increasingly commercial nature of the Football Association since Adam Crozier took over, it came at a press conference where journalists were told they would not be allowed access to the England manager unless they promised to include the 'branded image' of the new PlayStation game – *Sven - Göran Eriksson's World Cup Challenge* – alongside their reports.

It wasn't just the manager who was cashing in. The players also stood to make substantial bonuses from England's successes. Just by being part of England's World Cup campaign in Japan and Korea, each squad member stood to earn around £200,000 from the team's sponsors, like Umbro and Coca-Cola, regardless of how far they got in the competition and irrespective of how much they were receiving from their own endorsements for boots and clothing.

Not that they needed the money. Since the birth of the Premier League and the resultant billions that Rupert Murdoch's BSkyB had pumped into the English top flight, players' wages had spiralled ever upward. Where once a sixteen-year-old earned less than £30 a week on the youth-training scheme, now they, or rather their agents, were negotiating contracts running into the hundreds of thousands or even millions of pounds. At the other end of the scale, the game's top earners, like David Beckham, had gone beyond being mere footballers and become multi-millionaires, brands even, whose club salaries were dwarfed by their off-field earnings.

That May, on the final day of a season which had seen Arsène Wenger's Arsenal win the Premier League and FA Cup double, and just a month before the England squad left for the Far East, David Beckham and his now healthy foot signed a new three-year contract with Manchester United said to be worth a basic £5 million a year, complete with an additional £3 million signing fee.

Three weeks before the World Cup began, England's million-aires, accompanied by their partners and families, travelled to Dubai for what the FA's director of communications Paul Newman called a 'holiday, not a training camp'. Put up at the lavish Jumeirah Beach Club, the Football Association, keen to ensure their prized players were rested and refreshed ahead of the World Cup, footed the bill for thirty-five private villas and the entire party of 123 people that took advantage of the offer. They would even pick up the tab for the week's laundry bill as well. Within twenty-four hours of touching down in Dubai, seven of the players would show their gratitude by leaving the luxury of their resort and being caught in the Planetarium nightclub in Wafi City at three a.m. With memories of the infamous Dentist's Chair episode on the ill-fated trip to Hong Kong prior to Euro 96 still fresh in the memory, it seemed as though even a new genera-tion of England players had learned nothing from the PR disasters of years gone by.

Awarded the finals in May 1996, the World Cup in Japan and Korea was the first time in the competition's history that a joint bid had been successful. For the English players, the main problem they would encounter would be the strength-sapping heat and humidity. For the English fans, at least the ones that didn't make the 6,000-mile trip to the Far East, however, the trouble was fitting in the most important event on the football calendar around such everyday irritants as work, school and family life. With tourna-ments in Europe, you knew where you stood. With Eriksson's squad based in Japan, it meant that England's games would kick off at the wholly inconvenient times of 0930hrs, 1130hrs and 0630hrs. It was Beckham for breakfast and Butt for brunch.

Although they were missing Liverpool's Steven Gerrard with a groin injury and Manchester United's Gary Neville with the dreaded broken metatarsal, Eriksson's squad looked strong, confident and ready to face the challenge ahead of them. Curiously, Neville's injury, though almost identical to David Beckham's, didn't receive the kind of hysterical press attention that the England skipper's did. Nor, for that matter, did Uri Geller get involved.

Mercifully, the opener against Sweden in Saitama didn't suggest that Eriksson had been whispering team tactics as well as sweet nothings during his pillow talk with Ulrika Jonsson. That said, Sven still couldn't help himself calling his former girlfriend on her mobile phone on the day of the match and leaving what Jonsson would later describe as a 'jolly message'. After that call, though, there would be no more contact between the two. 'I really believed I'd get another call, because he was insistent to me that his relationship with Nancy would end,' added Jonsson.

England, meanwhile, would be fortunate to emerge with a 1–1 draw and but for some smart saves from the ever dependable David Seaman, they could even have lost. To compound matters, David Beckham, the man an entire nation was pinning their hopes on, was taken off after an hour, clearly tired, clearly unfit and complaining that his left foot was hurting.

A draw against Sweden had given the game against Argentina added importance, if that were possible. With the squad on edge, Eriksson acceded to his captain David Beckham's request to allow the players to ignore the strict meal plan prepared for them in advance and to fill up on McDonald's instead. In the not so distant past, that tension would have been relieved by a night on the tiles, but not now.

Ever since the World Cup draw had been made, the Sapporo Dome had been the focus of media interest, primarily because of its retractable playing surface. Capable of hosting baseball as well, its USP was that its pitch could be slid out of the stadium and replaced with a different one for a different sport at a moment's notice. It was part stadium, part spaceship.

Under the Dome's vast fibreglass roof, England were a different team to the one that had laboured against Sweden. Singleminded and organized, the team gave a display that belied their second seeding in the group and made Argentina, the top seeds, look ordinary. Sol Campbell and Rio Ferdinand seemed solid and composed, Michael Owen was full of running and the Manchester United midfielder Nicky Butt had arguably his best game for his country, tackling endlessly and linking the play.

With just a couple of minutes remaining in the first half, Michael Owen went down in the penalty area under the softest of challenges from Mauricio Pochettino. It was a debatable decision at best, but England had a penalty. As a clutch of enraged Argentinian players surrounded the referee, Italy's Pierluigi Collina, David Beckham walked over, picked the ball up and put it on the penalty spot. Here, then, was a chance to finally put paid to the misery of 1998, to finally write a new chapter in the never-ending conflict that was England versus Argentina.

As Beckham waited for Collina's whistle, ignoring Diego Simeone's juvenile attempts to distract him, the ITV commentator Clive Tyldesley said, 'It doesn't get much bigger than this next kick of the football.' He was right. The weight of responsibility on Beckham's shoulders was immense. Score, and his status as national hero was assured in perpetuity. Miss, and he would be right back where he was after France 1998.

One thumping crisp drive down the middle later, and Beckham was running towards the corner flag, kissing his shirt and with a mile-wide grin stretching across his face. England had a precious lead, which they would have little trouble in maintaining right through to the final whistle. For Beckham, so vilified after the defeat to Argentina in 1998, it was revenge of the sweetest kind. 'As soon as I hit that ball, as soon as it went into the net, I went blank,' he said after the game. 'It was the release of everything that had gone on since 1998. The feeling was wonderful.' Certainly, under Sven-Göran Eriksson, David Beckham had become a much better player for his country. After just one goal in his first thirty-seven games for England – the free-kick he scored against Colombia at the 1998 World Cup – Beckham had added six goals in fourteen games under Eriksson, making him one of the team's most prolific goalscorers.

What made England's display all the more satisfying was that Argentina, like the pre-tournament favourites France, were on their way home without making it past the group stages. A goalless draw with Nigeria in the final group game sent England through, along with Sweden who topped the group by virtue of the extra goals they had scored.

That goal difference would prove crucial to England's chances. While the tournament had opened up, especially with the absence of two highly fancied sides like Argentina and France, England were now scheduled to meet Brazil in the quarter-finals, assuming they could get past Denmark in the second round. Sweden, meanwhile, faced games against France's conquerors Senegal, followed by the winners of Japan and Turkey in the last eight. England would have little problem overcoming Denmark. Three first-half goals from Rio Ferdinand – his first for his country – Michael Owen and Emile Heskey sent Eriksson's team through to a quarter-final against the Brazilians in Shizuoka.

Again, England made the ideal start, Michael Owen guiding the ball over the Brazilian keeper Marcos to claim a deserved lead after twenty-three minutes. England's fortunes, however, would be decided either side of half-time. Following an injury to the goalkeeper David Seaman, the game had gone into added time at the end of the first period when David Beckham, perhaps thinking of his injured foot, pulled out of a tackle on Brazil's flying full-back Roberto Carlos, allowing the opposition to break. When Ronaldinho moved the ball to Rivaldo, the ball was in the back of the net in a flash.

Five minutes after the interval, England found themselves a goal down. A free-kick from forty yards out on the right flank was taken by Ronaldinho who had spotted David Seaman wandering across his goal in anticipation of a cross to the back post and simply curled it high over his head and into the net. The brilliant Paris St Germain youngster had not only given Brazil the lead but embarrassed the England keeper Seaman in the process, which was no mean feat, given that this was a thirty-eight-year-old man with a ponytail.

Seven minutes later, Ronaldinho would be sent off for a studs-up challenge on the man who had replaced Gary Neville, Leeds United's Danny Mills. Now was England's chance. Down to ten men, the Brazilians should have been there for the taking, but England, with more than half an hour left to play, had nothing to offer. It was as though a different team had taken to the pitch. This one was tired, lifeless and bereft of ideas. The Brazilians encountered few problems in holding on to claim their semi-final place and send England home.

After the euphoria that had greeted the victory over Argentina, it was a toothless, exasperating way to go out of the tournament. England had had the best possible opportunity to beat Brazil and they hadn't so much blown it as not even tried. Much of the blame would be laid squarely at Sven-Göran Eriksson's feet. Famously, one unnamed player would later comment on Eriksson's inability to stir his troops against Brazil, arguing that 'We needed Churchill but we got Iain Duncan Smith.'

Another day, another bombshell. On 31 October 2002 the Football Association's chief executive Adam Crozier announced his resignation. While the official press statement from the FA chairman Geoff Thompson accepted the Scot's decision with 'great regret and sadness', it was the lack of support that Crozier received for his opposition to a new Professional Game Board that was behind his decision. Proposed by the Premiership clubs, the Professional Game Board was designed to administer not only their division but those in the then Nationwide League as well. Crozier's concern was that by having such a body, the professional game would become largely autonomous from the Football Association and possess greater power over income generation and distribution. That, he concluded, was something he could not support.

The impact Crozier had on the Football Association cannot be underestimated. Disregarding the move to their plush, new, open-plan offices in Soho Square, he not only managed to get the controversial Wembley Stadium build back on track and presided over the plans for the new National Football Centre, but transformed the FA into a commercially driven and surprisingly dynamic operation. Crucially, Crozier had also scrapped the age-old FA board of ninety-one members and replaced it with a streamlined twelve-strong version, so that decisions could be made more efficiently and results obtained more quickly. Yes, he rubbed some of the estate agents and bank managers on the FA board up the wrong way, but then there were always going to be casualties in the battle for modernity.

It may have been boredom or maybe simple, unashamed avarice, but Eriksson was also exploring new opportunities, especially ones from billionaire Russians whose chief hobby was football. Roman Abramovich was the thirty-six-year-old billionaire who had taken over Chelsea Football Club for £140 million with the express intention of making them the most powerful team in European football. Certainly, he had the means at his disposal. With a personal fortune estimated at over £7 billion, gleaned from the privatization gold rush of Russia's oil industry after the fall of Communism, he was a man who was used to getting what he wanted. Whereas the millionaire Fulham owner Mohammed Al Fayed had 'given' Kevin Keegan to the nation, Abramovich seemed intent on making his side the most successful in European football and if that meant prising the England coach away from Soho Square and into Stamford Bridge, then so be it.

But that, of course, wasn't the real story, not according to Eriksson at least. When asked what he was doing meeting Abramovich, the England manager conceded that the speculation was 'unfortunate' but all he had been doing was having tea with his new-found friend.

It wasn't the first time he had been tempted. Just a few months into his contract, before he had even led an England team into a game, Eriksson was alleged to have conducted negotiations to take over from Alex Ferguson at Manchester United. 'I think they'd done the deal all right,' said the Manchester United boss in an interview in *The Times Magazine*. 'I don't know for certain, but I'm sure it was Eriksson. I think they'd shaken hands. They couldn't put anything on paper because he was still England manager.' Like one of those people you meet at parties that's always looking over your shoulder to see if there's someone or something more interesting elsewhere in the room, it seemed Eriksson was ready and willing but, because of the small matter of his job as the England coach, unable to accept another offer.

England's qualification campaign for Euro 2004 continued apace. Victories over Slovakia and Liechtenstein at home and over Macedonia away had given Eriksson's team a healthy advantage at the top of their qualification group. Now all that stood between them and unbeaten passage through to the finals in Portugal was an away fixture against their nearest rivals in Group 7, Turkey.

Joining them on the trip to Istanbul in October 2003 would be the new darling of the English press and the team's supporters. The Everton striker Wayne Rooney was just seventeen years old but looked thirty-seven. Short and stocky but blessed with pace, strength and an indecent amount of skill, he had become the youngest ever full England international, aged seventeen years and eleven days, when he appeared as one of eleven second-half substitutes in a friendly against Australia at Upton Park in February 2003. Here was one of those rare, naturally gifted players, one who appeared to have a long and glittering career ahead of him, both for club and country, especially as Teddy Sheringham had played his last game for England, while the strikers jostling to take his place, such as Aston Villa's Darius Vassell and James Beattie of Southampton, hadn't really mounted a compelling case for regular inclusion. Certainly, the kid from Croxteth could play.

England's preparations for the game, however, would be interrupted by an incident so seemingly incongruous with the flamboyant lifestyles of England's millionaire players that it beggared belief. On 23 September the central defender Rio Ferdinand had been asked to take a routine drugs test at Manchester United's Carrington training ground, but had left without carrying out the procedure. Ferdinand insisted that he had then contacted the club in an attempt to rearrange the test but was informed it was too late. The test was then taken two days later and the result was negative. When the Football Association learned of Ferdinand's case, the chief executive Mark Palios decided to ban Ferdinand from playing for England until his case was resolved – and that meant missing the crucial European Championship qualifier.

When the news reached the rest of the England squad there was mutiny. The players were aggrieved that Ferdinand's fate, though still pending, already seemed to have been decided by the FA and that banning the Manchester United central defender from representing England was, they argued, a case of guilty until proven innocent. The case would end in a tense and unprecedented stand-off between the England players and not just the FA but FIFA itself. If the team decided not to travel to Turkey, they would not only forfeit the game but be disqualified from the tournament as well.

Led by the 'shop steward', Manchester United's Gary Neville, the players held a vote on the Tuesday prior to flying out to Turkey the following day, and decided to boycott the game unless the FA altered their stance on Ferdinand and permitted him to rejoin the squad. Even the coach was said to be quietly sympathetic with the players' plight.

For the new chief executive, Mark Palios, this was the first real test of his authority and one that he would win. With the national side in danger of being thrown out of the European Championship and the players facing a backlash from the general public, they finally relented and agreed to play the match in Turkey. Later, Neville would explain how close the England team came to striking. 'We were brassed off – we still are,' he told the press. 'It was just frustrating for us, we didn't like what had happened to him [Ferdinand] and still don't like what has happened to him. We just did what we felt was right ... There definitely were thoughts in my head that it [the game] would not go ahead. It was such an injustice – they could have done it to any of us next time.'

The only positive to be drawn from the saga was the new-found solidarity among the England team. When the talking stopped and the match finally got under way at Fenerbahce's hostile Sukru Saracoglu Stadium in Istanbul, the side looked resolute and determined. Despite a missed David Beckham penalty, who slipped as he took his kick and spooned the ball up and over the crossbar, England comfortably claimed the draw they needed to qualify for Euro 2004.

The man at the centre of the storm, Rio Ferdinand (not Mark Palios), meanwhile, would eventually be fined £50,000 and banned for eight months for missing his drugs test, meaning he would not only miss the rest of the season for Manchester United but also the European Championship in Portugal.

For Sven-Göran Eriksson, it must have been a welcome interlude out of the headlines and away from the prying eyes of the press. Not that it would last. Within a few months, Eriksson would be spotted leaving the Chelsea chief executive Peter Kenyon's west London home and, once again, the idea that Eriksson was ready to jump ship raised its head. With mutinous players, turmoil at HQ and the never-ending fascination with his private life, the idea of taking the reins at Stamford Bridge, especially with the vast resources that Chelsea now boasted, must have been extremely tempting.

As it transpired, Eriksson had little to worry about. In their eagerness to resolve the situation and show the watching world that they simply would not stand for their national team manager being courted by other teams, the Football Association outwitted everyone, not by sacking Eriksson or even reprimanding him, but by extending his contract by a couple of years and giving him an extra £1 million a year just to show how much they really valued him.

There were perhaps two ways to look at the situation. Either Eriksson was guilty of betrayal (or even treason if you believed the tabloids), or he was merely listening to a potential employer interested in securing his services. But this, of course, is football, where human nature is largely irrelevant, where right often passes for wrong and where day is sometimes night. In the eyes of that most blinkered of species, the football fan, a player or manager cannot leave a club unless they do so with a clear conscience and the blessing of the supporters. People expect loyalty, expect honour, even when the bottom line, literally, is that it's not in a player's or coach's interest to stay at any one club, not when there are huge sums to be made in signing-on fees and improved contracts elsewhere.

Misjudging the public's disdain for his constant, clandestine negotiating, Eriksson failed to see what he had done wrong. 'From where I'm coming from there is nothing wrong in listening to other people, other clubs, in England as well as other countries. But it's best to kill the rumours,' Eriksson told the media. 'I was not close to joining Chelsea. I was listening. When clubs come and you have ambition you listen to other jobs. You should be allowed to even if you are England manager.'

Virtually the only thing that could improve the waning popularity of Sven-Göran Eriksson would be a win, or failing that, a strong showing for England at Euro 2004 in Portugal. It wasn't to be. Despite the emergence of Wayne Rooney as a genuinely world class attacker – he scored four times before his tournament was ended by injury in the quarter-final against the host nation – England suffered another unfortunate and 'brave' exit on penalties to the Portuguese, a team coached by the man who had overseen Brazil's win over England at the 2002 World Cup, Luiz Felipe Scolari.

Another infuriating exit for England had done little to suggest that Eriksson was capable of taking the national side that all-important step further in major tournaments. But if the frustrating lack of success and/or progress had seen Eriksson's position as England coach weakened, it would be his eye for the ladies that would take him to the very edge of unemployment.

On 17 July, less than a fortnight after the end of Euro 2004, David Davies had called Eriksson to warn him of a story that the *News of the World* were planning to run on his relationship with an employee at Soho Square called Faria Alam. When Davies asked him whether there was any truth in it, Eriksson issued a flat denial. A week later, though, the England coach had backtracked. After the scandal of the Ulrika Jonsson saga, here was another lurid tale that the tabloids couldn't get enough of, not least because it also involved the top man at Soho Square, Mark Palios.

Faria Alam was a £35,000-a-year personal assistant at the Football Association. Born in Dhaka, Bangladesh, a few weeks after England had won the World Cup in 1966, she had joined the FA on 21 July 2003 having impressed David Davies in her interview. She was lively, outgoing and personable. Intriguingly, she was also the kind of typewriting temptress that could lead the steeliest of men astray, including the England coach.

The first to fall for her abundant charms would be another July 2003 recruit to Soho Square, namely Mark Palios, the FA's new chief executive. Some eight months after the departure of Adam Crozier, Palios arrived with a reputation as a shrewd negotiator and all-round tough cookie. In his playing career he had been a footballer with a career path that didn't involve running country pubs or sports shops when he retired. A graduate of psychology from Manchester University, he had enjoyed a long and largely anonymous playing career with Tranmere Rovers and Crewe Alexandra but had trained as an accountant with Coopers & Lybrand Deloitte and, having retired from the game, become a partner in the Arthur Young accountancy practice. Later, he would move to Pricewaterhousecoopers to become their head of business regeneration.

Despite the attention of Eriksson, Alam only had eyes for the FA chief executive. 'I really fancied Palios. I loved his deep, strong, sexy voice and he had an aura of power. But he was only interested in pleasuring himself and was so mechanical he left me totally unsatisfied. It was a huge letdown. Then he pulled up his trousers and said abruptly, "I've got to go." I felt like a piece of meat. It was awful.'

With Palios's prowess in the bedroom as unremarkable as his playing career, Alam turned her attentions to the England coach.

In the *News of the World* on 8 August 2004, Alam spoke of her affair with Eriksson at length, professing her love for him and describing the Swede as a 'master in the art of love-making'.

Recalling their first night of passion, Alam, who was paid a reported £200,000 for her exclusive story, explained how the two had consummated their relationship at Eriksson's house in Sweden, making it sound like the denouement from a Mills & Boon novel. 'He then peeled off my jeans and shirt. As I lay on the sheets, he took off my thong and told me, "You are incredibly beautiful." He stroked my back and ran his hands through my hair. We made passionate love. It was beautiful. He was not concerned about me getting pregnant. He put his arms around me and we fell asleep in the spoon position.'

Hilarious and humiliating in equal measure, it was the kind of unedifying exposé that the Football Association were growing increasingly used to dealing with. For many supporters, meanwhile, it was another bewildering story to take in, not because of the damage it may have caused to the FA's reputation or the deleterious effect it could have on the performance of the England team, but because the mere thought of the balding, bespectacled head coach engaged in matters of the flesh was enough to put people off not just their Sunday breakfasts but possibly the national game itself.

Though he looked and often behaved like a bank manager, Eriksson had stunned everyone with his way with the opposite sex. From Nancy to Ulrika to Faria, here was a man who was punching way above his weight in the dating game and a man, a manager, whose love life was manna from heaven for the nation's tabloid editors. Indeed, the contrast between the public perception of Eriksson as this cold, conservative Scandinavian and the private reality of what the tabloids would have everyone believe was somewhere between Casanova and Barry White, could not have been more marked. The FA's director of communications, the former BBC war correspondent Paul Newman, would say, 'The Gulf War was a cakewalk compared with Eriksson's love life.'

He had a point. In 2005 the Swedish theatre company Millon Fred's Productions opened their new play at Stockholm's Dramaten Theatre, entitled *A Play In Swedish, Italian and English*, about a Swedish manager known simply as 'Coach' whose love life threatens to derail his successful career as a football manager. 'It may be that some of the inspiration has come from a certain England manager,' said the theatre's artistic director, Stefan Larsson. This was not so much a case of life imitating art, but art doing its best to keep up with life.

Soon after the *News of the World* story broke revealing Eriksson's dalliance with Alam, Mark Palios decided enough was enough and announced his resignation as chief executive, just thirteen months after he had taken the position. 'I am very sad, but I feel this is necessary,' he said. 'Personally, I do not accept that I have been guilty of any wrongdoing.'

With Palios gone and David Davies stepping in once again as acting chief executive, the pressure on Eriksson to stand down increased. Other resignations would follow. The director of communications Colin Gibson, (who had succeeded Paul Newman in 2003) would go (for offering the *News of the World* the full story of Eriksson and Alam's affair in return for not running the Palios story), as would Alam herself, who would later mount an unsuccessful wrongful dismissal case against the Football Association. Eriksson, meanwhile, would be cleared of any wrongdoing at a five-hour meeting of the Football Association's board. Though he refused to comment on the outcome at the time, Eriksson would eventually speak out. 'When I meet English people, going to games and restaurants, then I like them. What I can never understand is that there is a sick interest in people's private lives,' he said. 'Sometimes I feel in this job that you should be a saint, at least a monk, you shouldn't earn much money and you should win every football game.'

The never-ending obsession with the England coach's private life, of course, was largely his own fault. Even at his first press conference on taking the job, Eriksson had been fully aware of the scrutiny he would placed under for the duration of his term. One look at how happily married, family men like Bobby Robson and Graham Taylor were treated would have shown him the kind of bumpy ride he was in for, but it was just naive to expect the people and, more importantly, the papers to leave him alone when he got himself involved with TV presenters on the one hand and in bizarre FA love triangles on the other.

So the FA began searching for another new chief executive officer and Eriksson went off to patch things up with the woman the press were now calling his 'long-suffering' girlfriend, Nancy Dell'Olio. Whatever you thought of Eriksson's qualities as a football coach, it was hard not to find the real-life *Carry On Soho Square* that he was starring in absolutely compelling viewing.

The Football Association was lurching from one crisis to another. Leaderless, embarrassed, humiliated even, it was, if anything, business as usual at Soho Square. Domestically, the game was in rude health, even though in 2004 the Football League had, somewhat confusingly, rebranded their three divisions so that the old Second Division (which had become the First Division) was now 'The Championship' while the old Third Division which, in turn, had become the Second Division, was now League 1. League 2, therefore, was the new name for the old Fourth Division.

Elsewhere, Chelsea, under their charismatic Portuguese manager Jose Mourinho, claimed their first top-flight title in fifty years while Arsenal would defeat Manchester United on penalties to take the FA Cup at Cardiff's Millennium Stadium. And, twenty years after the horrors of Heysel, Liverpool had won the European Cup for a fifth time, claiming the 2005 Champions League title with a stirring comeback against the Italian giants AC Milan in Istanbul. More was to come. That summer, England's cricketers would even regain the Ashes for the first time since 1987. Things, it seemed, could only get worse.

With the nation on a high, it was, of course, entirely predictable, inevitable even, that England's football team would throw one almighty wet blanket over proceedings. A 4–1 defeat in a friendly against Denmark in August – England's heaviest defeat for a quarter of a century – had been only partially mitigated by a lucky 1–0 win over Wales in Cardiff. As every game passed, and each England performance drew terrible reviews, it seemed as though Sven-Göran Eriksson's time as England manager was running out.

Come the World Cup qualifier against Northern Ireland at Belfast's Windsor Park on 7 September, there could be no doubt, especially in Eriksson's mind, that England fans were not merely turning against him, but wanted him out of the job as soon as was legally possible. Losing for the first time to Northern Ireland since Terry Neill scored the only goal against Alf Ramsey's team at Wembley in 1972, Eriksson's men had plumbed new depths. Northern Ireland, after all, were the 116th-ranked team in world football and were rated by FIFA as worse than Rwanda, Turkmenistan and Gabon. They hadn't even scored against England since 1980, let alone beaten them. As for England, they hadn't lost in Belfast since the 2–0 Home International defeat in 1927.

Although it was Eriksson's first ever defeat in a World Cup or European Championship qualifying match and did precious little to dent England's chances of qualifying for the World Cup in Germany, the writing was on the wall for the England coach. It was, without any argument, a desperate, dire performance and had it been another coach in charge in another era, it's unlikely that he would have survived. But this was Sven, the man with the biggest, most lucrative contract an England manager had ever enjoyed and to sack him now, with over two years left on the deal, would cost the Football Association more money than they cared to consider. With the FA refusing to countenance Eriksson's dismissal, it was left to the *Sun* to 'sack' the England coach. The day after the defeat in Belfast, the tabloid delivered their own P45 to Soho Square. Eriksson, however, wasn't in.

Eriksson's future would be high on the to-do list for the Football Association's new chief executive. On Thursday, 25 November it was announced that fifty-year-old Brian Barwick would be taking up the position on 31 January 2006. In contrast to the sharp suits and trim waists of Crozier and Palios before him,

Barwick was bald of head, generous of frame and heavy of moustache and looked liked he belonged in a 1970s TV sitcom or ordering reluctant kids round a school cross-country course.

But appearances were deceptive. Here, after all, was a football man through and through. A Liverpool fan, he had been the producer on BBC's *Football Focus*, a senior editor on their World Cup finals coverage in 1990 and 1994 and also the editor of their flagship football programme *Match of the Day*. In February 1998 Barwick had joined ITV to become their controller of sport where, under his tenure, the channel recorded its biggest ever audience of 23.8 million people for the match between England and Argentina at the 1998 World Cup finals. 'It's been a momentous day for me,' said Barwick, who was set to earn a reported £275,000 a year (or around half what Crozier had been paid). 'I'm looking forward to leading the FA into its next era.'

Brian Barwick had barely had time for his Health and Safety induction at Soho Square when he discovered just what the job of chief executive of the Football Association really entailed. On Sunday, 15 January 2006 the *News of the World* ran a story that would lead to the end of the Sven-Göran Eriksson England era.

Mazher Mahmood was an investigative reporter for the newspaper and the man renowned for his so-called 'Fake Sheikh' character, a disguise he had often employed to snare errant celebrities and politicians. In his career, the Sheikh had claimed some notable scalps, including the Countess of Wessex and the England rugby player Lawrence Dallaglio. The Sheikh had also exposed the Newcastle United directors Freddie Shepherd and Douglas Hall whom he had taped belittling fans of their football club and calling their star striker Alan Shearer the 'Mary Poppins of football' while they were holidaying in Marbella.

Under the guise of the Sheikh, Mahmood had contacted Eriksson's lawyer Richard des Voeux with a plan to enlist the England manager to help out with some consultancy work for a fledgling sports company, AJ Sports, that was setting up a football academy in the Middle East. Having checked the company's credentials – Mahmood had even gone to the trouble of setting up a company website, complete with corporate motto 'Test Your Limits, Taste The Glory' – Eriksson had asked for the FA's blessing to talk to the company, which, surprisingly given Eriksson's track record, they consented to.

A meeting was arranged at the world's only seven-star hotel, the Burj Al Arab in Dubai, but was cancelled twice by Eriksson and once by Mahmood, who had to return to the UK at short notice. 'The fact that I was forced to fly back from Dubai to attend a court case, and so cancelled my first meeting with Sven, only served to add to my credibility,' he explains. 'Which journalist would turn down a prearranged dinner with Sven in Dubai?'

When the pair finally agreed a date, the England coach and his agent Athole Still were given first-class flights and a £1,500 a night suite at the hotel for their trouble. They would even be fast-tracked through immigration and taken away in the back of a white Rolls-Royce. Eriksson's lawyer Richard des Voeux, meanwhile, would pay for his trip out of his own pocket.

Over a lobster dinner and £900 bottles of champagne, the Sheikh spoke of his ideas for Eriksson and soon talk turned to the Premier League and which clubs were ripe for a takeover. The names of Sunderland and Aston Villa were suggested. Eriksson agreed. 'Sven was desperate to impress me, to persuade me to buy Aston Villa and appoint him the manager,' recalls Mahmood. 'It wasn't too surprising that he used his friendship with Beckham to try and convince me it would be worth paying £25 million for the club. He bragged that he would be able to persuade Beckham to return to Britain to play for my new club. [But] as he reeled off his unashamed sales patter, dragging in Beckham, Sven was simply gifting me yet more headlines.'

Later, the group also met on a 72ft luxury yacht to continue their discussions. 'The only time I felt any danger of being rumbled was when my Arab headscarf kept slipping off my head.' he recalls. 'It's not easy to keep your composure at times and my weekend with Sven and his cronies was nothing short of a French farce.'

While Eriksson's desperate desire to engineer for himself a new, well-paid position – the figure of £5 million a year after tax was discussed – he compounded matters by also divulging personal information about many of the England players. He told the Sheikh of Michael Owen's unhappiness at Newcastle and how the striker had told him that he was only there for the money. He described Wayne Rooney as coming 'from a poor family'. And he had labelled Rio Ferdinand as 'too talented for his own good' and 'lazy sometimes'.

Eriksson's agent Athole Still called it 'disgraceful entrapment' but it had been a classic sting and one that, given Eriksson's wandering eye (professionally speaking), was almost bound to happen. The Football Association would be quick to issue a statement about the latest instalment in Eriksson's ever-growing catalogue of indiscretions. 'The FA can confirm that England's head coach, Sven-Göran Eriksson, continues to have the full support of the organization. This follows conversations between FA chief executive, Brian Barwick, and Sven, and subsequent conversations involving Brian with FA chairman, Geoff Thompson, international committee chairman, Noel White, and senior FA figures.'

Eriksson too was toeing the party line, despite the wealth of evidence against him. 'I would like to assure everyone, especially the fans, that I'm 100 per cent committed to the England job. I've told the FA this and value the great support I have received from them. I have spoken with the players concerned today and I have been very pleased with their reaction and am confident my relationship with them has not been damaged.'

But there would be no saving Sven. The following Monday, after a six-hour meeting between Eriksson and his employers at Soho Square, a compensation deal was agreed (although no specific amount was revealed) that would see the England coach stand down after England's participation in that summer's World Cup had ended. 'The FA and Sven felt it was important to clarify his future,' said the FA's chief executive Brian Barwick. 'There has been so much speculation surrounding this matter in recent weeks and months, it was important to resolve it now. This is the right outcome and I would like to thank Sven and his advisers for their tremendous cooperation. Our main objective is giving Sven and the England team the best chance of achieving success at the World Cup and Sven is definitely the man to lead us in Germany.'

Barely a tear was shed when Eriksson announced his intention to quit after the World Cup. Football fans had long since tired of his constant dalliances with potential employers, and it had seemed that the Swede's mind was always on his next big job or his next big salary, and not really on the dwindling fortunes of the England team.

Asked if he ever felt sorry the part he played in Eriksson's demise, Mazher Mahmood, the Fake Sheikh himself, is unrepentant. 'Not at all,' he says. 'Besides delivering results the basic requirement for an England manager is loyalty. Here was the manager in the run-up to the World Cup when his mind should have been focused on the team and tactics, selling himself to me in Dubai over a £1,714.73 dinner. If that weren't enough, he shamelessly slagged off England players. It was nothing short of treachery.'

CHAPTER 9

NOWHERE TO GO

'They'll have to drag me kicking and screaming out of Soho Square.'

Steve McClaren, 2007

With Sven-Göran Eriksson counting down the days to his farewell party, the Football Association's chief executive Brian Barwick began the search for the Swede's successor, pledging to announce the new manager before the 2006 World Cup finals in Germany. As in the case of Terry Venables and his successor Glenn Hoddle, there seemed to be no obvious reason as to why the announcement had to be made before the tournament, apart from to pre-empt any accusations that the FA were dithering again. Still, Barwick was a man on a mission. At the end of April 2006 he flew to Lisbon to discuss the job of England manager with the Portugese national coach and the man who had guided Brazil to World Cup glory in 2002 and Portugal to the final of Euro 2004. Certainly, Luiz Felipe Scolari possessed the kind of track record that was as good as, if not better than, Eriksson's and immeasurably more impressive than any of the other candidates mooted in the media.

Dark, brooding and full of menace (and moustache), Scolari was the archetypal tracksuit manager, a sergeant-major whose bite was every bit as bad as his bark. That said, he also possesses a unique line in motivation and man management. During the

World Cup finals in 2002, for instance, he presented every player in the Brazilian squad with a copy of Sun Tzu's *The Art of War*, a sixth-century BC Chinese military treatise. The fact that Scolari looked like a trucker on a tea break was irrelevant; he got his players to play for him *and* for each other.

As negotiations progressed with Scolari and his management and the likelihood of a deal grew ever closer, so the English media began their now customary pursuit. Yet this time it seemed more invasive, more pernicious, than usual. Scolari's children were abused at school, reporters went through his rubbish and even entered his house trying to find something, anything, on the prospective new England coach. For Scolari, his every move now the subject of intense media scrutiny, it was a fleeting glimpse of what life would be like if and when he committed himself to the impossible job. And, as he revealed soon after, it wasn't the kind of life he wanted. 'I don't like this pressure. It may be part of another culture, but it's not part of mine,' he told the press. 'The FA has a list of names it will choose its next manager from, but mine isn't one of them because I am closing this matter now. I am happy that they considered me but I don't want anything more to do with this because for two days my life has been invaded and my privacy destroyed.'

Two years later, however, with Scolari now the manager of Premier League club Chelsea, the Brazilian revealed that while the media intrusion undoubtedly played a part in his decision to reject the England job, it was actually Brian Barwick's impatience in insisting he sign the contract before the World Cup finals that extinguished any hopes of a deal. 'If they [the FA] had agreed [to announce it] after the competition, I would have signed a pre-contract [agreement] before the competition,' he said. 'They did not agree because they needed to tell the press who was the coach.'

It was a view later reinforced by the former Arsenal chairman and FA international committee member, David Dein. 'My experience of doing deals in football is if you want somebody, you never leave the scene until you have the guy signed up. Never let the guy leave the room,' he reflected. 'When you are eyeballing somebody, you have to keep that going, camp there, until you finish the deal. If you think you have a chance, you put the lid on the bottle.'

The failure to land Luiz Felipe Scolari was another ignominious chapter in the FA's history. While it was right and proper that Brian Barwick should be seen to be pursuing one of the game's pre-eminent coaches, it was humiliating in the extreme to be seen returning from Portugal with the contract unsigned and the England team still seeking its next manager.

Barwick, his plan in tatters, returned to work and the search for Eriksson's successor continued. While Scolari had, by some distance, been the most impressive candidate on the shortlist, the remaining runners lacked the international experience and track record of the Brazilian. Now, there were no World Cup winners, no box-office names, just a disparate assembly of domestic managers who had already been rejected earlier in the selection process. There was Martin O'Neill, the charismatic Ulsterman who had enjoyed success in Scotland managing Celtic; there was the Bolton manager Sam Allardyce and the Charlton boss Alan Curbishley. And then there was the Middlesbrough coach and Sven-Göran Eriksson's right-hand man, Steve McClaren.

Viewed as the continuity candidate, McClaren had been at Eriksson's side throughout England's near misses under the Swede. With an in-depth, first-hand knowledge of the players available and some experience of international tournament football (although not in a playing capacity), McClaren was also an FA employee already and could slip seamlessly into the role. In time, Allardyce, O'Neill and McClaren would all win second interviews. The decision now rested with Brian Barwick, the Premier League chairman Dave Richards, the chairman of the international committee Noel White, the FA director of football development Sir Trevor Brooking and the Arsenal vice-chairman David Dein.

On Thursday, 4 May 2006 Steve McClaren was duly appointed the new England coach. The eleventh man to hold the position on a full-time basis, the forty-five-year-old arrived at Soho Square for his first press conference in charge of the national team. Accompanied by Brian Barwick, McClaren soon found himself defending his appointment just moments into his tenure. 'I knew the process from the very beginning and I was quite comfortable with it,' he said. 'It didn't affect my job at Middlesbrough and it didn't affect the players. The outcome was the important thing. I don't see it as a case of first choice or second choice. I am *the* choice and I sit here as the next England coach.'

It was then left to Barwick to deliver one of the most remarkable and perplexing statements made during his time as chief executive. 'Steve did two fantastic interviews. He was my first choice, the FA board's unanimous choice,' he insisted. 'My first choice was always Steve. That might be difficult for people to get their heads across.'

For Barwick to stand in front of the nation's media and maintain that the Carling Cup winner McClaren, not the World Cup winner Scolari, had always been the man he and the Football Association had wanted for the job was nothing short of insulting. Certainly, the reaction to McClaren's appointment was less than rapturous. While, generally, the press seemed prepared to give him a chance (something most England managers had been afforded), the reaction among the fans was one of anger and bemusement. On internet forums, polls and message boards, the consensus was that McClaren's appointment did not represent anything like progress and that awarding the job to a man who had spent the majority of his coaching career acting as a number two (albeit to some undeniably successful managers) was hardly the ideal way to extract the very best out of some of the most talented players in world football.

Eriksson's final tournament in charge would prove to be another forgettable episode in England's miserable modern history. With a squad notable only for the inexplicable selection of Arsenal's seventeen-year-old Theo Walcott, a lad who wasn't even a regular in the Arsenal side, it was less a case of what might have been than where do we go from here? Not even Wayne Rooney's miraculous recovery from yet another metatarsal injury, sustained when he was playing for Manchester United in a Premier League match against Chelsea at Stamford Bridge at the end of April, could help England. Ultimately, though, Rooney's joy would end in despair as he was sent off for stamping on Portugal's Ricardo Carvalho amid some juvenile goading from his brilliant yet infuriating clubmate Cristiano Ronaldo.

The script was wearily familiar: Quarter-final. Penalty shoot-out. Heartbreak. It simply wasn't funny any more. Once again, it was Luiz Felipe Scolari's Portugal who put England to the sword. Goalless after extra-time, the game went to penalties, bloody penalties, only this time England's spot-kicks were worse than ever. Frank Lampard, Steven Gerrard and Jamie Carragher all missed and only England's player of the tournament, Owen Hargreaves, held his nerve to convert his. As for the boy Walcott, he spent the entire competition on the bench, despite being one of only two fully fit forwards.

It was the worst of tournaments for England, not merely for the depressing and predictable exit but the tacky circus that surrounded the team. With the players' wives and girlfriends in constant tow – the so-called 'WAGS' – it soon ceased to be a football competition and turned into some vulgar fashion show, as the gaggle of pop star partners, part-time models and assorted shopaholics hogged the limelight. One report in the *Mirror*, for example, revealed how a number of WAGS had downed seven bottles of Moët champagne, twenty-three lemon vodkas, twelve glasses of beer, four Sambuccas, five orange liqueurs and one Bacardi & Coke as they drunkenly celebrated England's narrow 1–0 win over Paraguay until four o'clock in the morning. It was crude, tasteless and unnecessary.

The day after another heart-breaking but not entirely surprising exit on penalties, David Beckham sat before a press conference at England's training camp and, after fifty-eight games as captain of the team, announced his decision to stand down. 'I came to this decision some time ago but I had hoped to announce it on the back of a successful World Cup. Sadly that wasn't to be,' he said, reading from a statement. 'This decision has been the most difficult of my career to date. But after discussing it with my family and those closest to me I feel the time is right.'

As he left the room, with tears in his eyes, the massed ranks of the media broke into a spontaneous round of applause. Soon after, Sven-Göran Eriksson gave his final press conference as England coach. 'I'm going on holiday, perhaps for a couple of weeks, perhaps for a year, I don't know,' he said with a shrug. 'I didn't have any intention during the World Cup to talk to anyone else, but tomorrow I can start to do that.' With only the sound of cameras clicking to accompany his exit, Eriksson made his farewells to the impossible job.

While England's performances in major tournaments were perhaps just enough to keep Eriksson in his job, it was his roving eye and, more crucially, his pursuit of even greater riches that would prove to be his undoing. For all his faults, though, Eriksson had succeeded in turning Kevin Keegan's directionless England into serial qualifiers, a team that progressed comfortably to the final stages of major tournaments without any of the heart-stopping drama seen under previous coaches. But for a bit of luck here and there and, as ever, some better penalties, who knows what he might have achieved with the national team. All England fans wished now was that he had been half as successful with the team as he was with the women.

With the ink still drying on a four-year deal worth a reported £3 million a year, McClaren set about creating his backroom team. In came one of his former coaches at Middlesbrough, Steve Round; meanwhile, the goalkeeping coach Ray Clemence was retained, and the sports psychologist Bill Beswick, who had also worked with McClaren at Middlesbrough, was hired again. But most strikingly, the move that took most observers by surprise was the appointment of the former England coach Terry Venables as his right-hand man. In the years since the near miss of Euro 96, Venables's managerial career had been unspectacular. As coach of the Australian national team, he had taken the Socceroos to the brink of the 1998 World Cup finals but had lost out to Iran in a play-off. His reputation still intact, he had then taken over at his old club Crystal Palace but left within a year; he had co-managed Middlesbrough with Bryan Robson and then lasted just eight months at cash-strapped Leeds United.

Yet before any of his backroom staff had been appointed and before any squads had been picked, McClaren had already made one key appointment. Max Clifford was the PR guru who had handled the affairs of such seemingly disparate figures as the Harrods owner Mohammed Al Fayed on the one hand and the American magician David Copperfield on the other. He had also assisted Faria Alam when her affairs with Sven-Göran Eriksson and Mark Palios had become known and had a reputation as the self-styled king of spin, a man who could turn tragedy into triumph, catastrophe into column inches.

Crucially, Clifford had already worked with Steve McClaren in April 2006, managing the revelation of an extra-marital affair that McClaren had had while he was separated from his wife, all with minimum fuss or comeback for the future England coach. 'Knowing what Sven had been through when he was England boss and all those dramas, Steve was very conscious of the important part that image and the media played in the job and that was why he contacted me,' explains Clifford. 'At the time, the image of football was all about money so as well as trying to protect his back and steer him through the media minefield, we tried to do a lot of charity stuff too where all the players would be involved so that everyone was doing their bit. The benefits of this were that hopefully it would have made journalists less antagonistic towards the players and the fans more supportive of them.'

Clearly, McClaren was already concerned with how England's supporters and, more importantly, the nation's media would take to him, especially given his perceived culpability in England's underachievement under Eriksson. Now Clifford had been cast not so much as a public relations adviser but as a bodyguard in the face of a savage tabloid press seemingly intent on getting someone else, someone better equipped, into the most important job in the game.

Within three months, however, Clifford would walk away from the role, leaving the England coach to fend for himself in the face of what would, eventually, be some typically hostile press coverage. 'The problem was that ... I just wasn't included in anything that was going on,' says Clifford wearily. 'You can talk to me about any of the clients I've been involved with over the years and I can tell you exactly what was going on and when but not with the FA. I will always say what I feel and I don't think the FA liked that. They didn't have control. It was maybe naive of me to think it could go somewhere. I told Steve that the FA might not like me being involved but he said, it's my decision, it's what I want. But clearly it wasn't what the FA wanted.'

Certainly, McClaren would need every ounce of fortune if he were to succeed. Win and win with style and it wouldn't matter how he appeared in front of the television cameras. In his favour was a squad as strong as any that his predecessors had enjoyed. With Gerrard and Lampard, Rooney and Owen, Ferdinand and Terry, he had at his disposal what the press had termed the 'Golden Generation', an assembly of players that were perhaps the best equipped since the team of 1970 to emulate the success of Alf Ramsey's 1966 World Cup winners.

Against him, though, was not just his less than spectacular managerial track record – a solitary League Cup success and a defeat in the UEFA Cup final with Middlesbrough – but a residual feeling that whatever McClaren did would always be tainted by his part in the failures of the Eriksson era. Lacking the experience of Bobby Robson (or for that matter Venables), the club successes of Eriksson or even the brutal honesty of Kevin Keegan, McClaren would also find it difficult to inspire an England team in real danger of spurning their chance to become one of the great England sides.

In a move that brought back memories of Bobby Robson's decision to drop Kevin Keegan or Graham Taylor's to omit Paul Gascoigne, Steve McClaren announced his first squad for the friendly against Greece at Old Trafford in August 2006 – and it didn't include David Beckham. When Beckham had resigned as England captain after the World Cup in Germany, he had expressed his desire to carry on playing for England. Now, though, he hadn't just been dropped from the starting eleven but from the entire squad. From England captain to outcast in one fell swoop.

Here, then, was a manager who was clearly intent not just on making his mark in his new job but on distancing himself from the previous regime, where the relationship between manager and captain had been so close, perhaps even too close. 'I told David I was looking to change things, looking to go in a different direction, and he wasn't included within that,' he said. It was the first major call of McClaren's tenure. That he had chosen to leave out a name as big as Beckham's showed courage but also a surprising lack of forethought. Surely, after all, David Beckham was still one of the best twenty-two English players available to him?

For his part, Beckham was dignity personified, although even the tone of his response suggested he had played his last game for his country. 'Having spoken to Steve McClaren this week I can fully understand that a new manager should want to make his mark on the team and build towards the next World Cup. I'm proud to have played for England for ten years and my passion for representing my country remains as strong as ever.' With his England career seemingly at an end, Beckham would also call time on his career with Real Madrid soon after, opting to move to the United States and sign a five-year, £125 million deal with the Major League Soccer side LA Galaxy at the end of the season.

Initially, Steve McClaren's bold decision seemed to have been vindicated. A 4–0 win against the reigning European champions Greece was followed by a 5–0 victory over Andorra in his first European Championship qualifier at Old Trafford. Slowly, though, the cracks would appear. After the narrow 1–0 win in Skopje against Macedonia in September, the two teams played their return fixture at Old Trafford a month later. Curiously, in a match where England were expected to win and win comfortably, McClaren chose to install Manchester United's £18 million midfielder Michael Carrick as the holding player in front of a four- man defensive line. With such a lack of ambition it was little surprise that the game ended in a wretched goalless draw.

Four days later, McClaren took England to Zagreb to face their main rivals in Group E, Croatia. Led by the charismatic former West Ham and Everton defender Slaven Bilić, the Croatian home record was exceptional, having remained undefeated for twelve years. Technically and tactically, they were also a class apart from the rest of England's opposition in the group. They had organization at the back, creativity in the centre and goals going forward. All of which made McClaren's decision to field a side in an untested 3-5-2 formation even more perplexing.

In fact, it beggared belief. Against Macedonia at home, a game they should have walked through, McClaren had taken the precaution of playing Carrick as extra cover for the defence. Now, against England's main threat in their group, they were virtually inviting the Croatians to attack them. Not that Bilić's side needed any invitation. One up on the hour thanks to a header from Eduardo da Silva, they doubled their lead eight minutes later with a goal that will live long in the memory of anyone who has seen it, not least Paul Robinson.

As Croatia pressed, the Manchester United full-back Gary Neville played the ball back to the England goalkeeper but as the Tottenham man went to clear it, the ball hit a small turf divot, bobbled up and over Robinson's foot and dribbled agonizingly into the net. After eleven years wearing the Three Lions, Neville finally had his first goal. Sadly, it was at the wrong end.

Bizarrely, when the goal went in, McClaren didn't punch the dug-out or, for that matter, a member of his backroom staff, nor did he storm to the edge of his technical area to berate those involved. Instead, he just got out his pen and his notepad and began making some notes. Quite what he wrote is a mystery. Whatever it was, it wasn't a letter of resignation.

*

Seven years, £798 million, five England managers and several FA chief executives after work had commenced, the new Wembley Stadium was ready and finally open for business. It had been a long, tortuous process, beset by delays, spiralling costs and rows between contractors, but it was, by anybody's reckoning, an astonishing piece of design and engineering. With its huge 133-metre arch visible right across the capital, its retractable roof and the most toilets of any public building in Europe, it was, by some margin, the most expensive stadium ever built. They had even erected a statue of Bobby Moore right outside the main entrance.

The last time a full England side had played at Wembley, of course, was the same day that the reluctant Messiah, Kevin Keegan, had decided that he wasn't England's saviour after all. Now, on 1 June 2007, following their nationwide roadshow, England were back at their spiritual home, preparing to welcome Wembley's first international visitors. As a friendly ahead of a European Championship qualifier against Estonia, just five days later, the match was a chance for Steve McClaren to tweak and fine-tune his side for the crucial game in Tallinn. The fact that it was against Brazil, arguably the best side in the world, however, suggested that maybe it wasn't the time to start experimenting.

If the game itself represented a new era for England, Steve McClaren found himself harking back to an age that he had tried to consign to history. With just one win to show from his last six games – and that was against the punchbags of the qualifying group, Andorra – the doubts about McClaren's ability had already put his position in jeopardy. In a move that took almost everyone by surprise, however, McClaren swallowed his pride and recalled the former captain David Beckham to his twenty-six-man squad for the two games. When it had seemed that he had ended Beckham's international career, now McClaren was begging him to save his own. 'Everyone knows David's attributes and he's a big-game player who can help us win in Estonia,' explained McClaren. 'We've a very important game in Estonia, we need to win it and it is a squad that can win it.'

The combination of a gleaming, shiny stadium, some genuinely high-class opposition and the prospect of David Beckham's first game in an England shirt in over a year, saw the new Wembley Stadium full for the visit of Brazil. With a debut for Reading's promising left-back Nicky Shorey and with Manchester United's Alan Smith partnering Michael Owen in attack, it was, inevitably, Beckham who stood out. In the first half, he would be involved in most of England's more promising attacks, while in the second, his ever-reliable dead balls nearly created a goal for Michael Owen and then did so for John Terry on sixty-eight minutes, as the captain powered a header past Helton in the Brazilian goal.

It would so nearly be Steve McClaren's finest hour but two minutes into stoppage time, the Brazilian substitute Diego stole in to head the latest of equalizers for the visitors with just fifteen seconds left to play. As for the Man of the Match, David Beckham, he would leave the pitch to a standing ovation, saying, 'I'm not sure if I knew I'd ever get this moment again but I'm happy to be part of a historic night.'

The reinstatement of Beckham, and the generally positive showing from England against the world's best, had the desired effect on team morale. When the team travelled to Tallinn, they returned comfortable 3–0 winners, with Beckham again providing assist after assist. There was no toying with tactics. No experimental formations. No drama. No danger. It had been one of those rare England games. A straightforward, businesslike win and one that had gone some way to restoring the smile to Steve McClaren's face.

Not everyone was entirely happy with the way the England team was developing. The versatile Liverpool defender Jamie Carragher, for instance, had rightly become disillusioned with being overlooked for the starting line-up, despite some heroic performances for his club, and the fact that other, less established players were getting games ahead of him. Tired of waiting and unable to see any change to his situation, Carragher announced his retirement from international football.

It wasn't the first time McClaren had encountered difficulties keeping his players happy. At Middlesbrough the young Italian striker Massimo Maccarone had found McClaren to be almost impossible to work with. 'Only in England could a man with such limited abilities be made into the national coach,' he said later. 'The ever-smiling McClaren is without doubt the most two-faced, false person I've had the misfortune to meet in football.'

Maybe it was his relative youth or some unnecessary desire to be one of the boys, but McClaren also seemed to be growing too close to the players. In fact, he had become irritatingly chummy in a manner that Ramsey or Robson would never have countenanced. In interviews and in training it was all 'JT', 'Stevie G' or 'Lamps'. There was no healthy distance between him and his players, none of that crucial detachment that all leaders need from their troops.

The win, however, would revitalize England's European Championship hopes. After a 2–1 friendly defeat to Germany at Wembley, they would embark on three consecutive 3–0 wins at home, against Israel, Russia and Estonia. Confidence, that most elusive of feelings in the England camp, was higher than it had been in months. Qualification now seemed inevitable.

Or at least it was until the visit in October to Moscow's Luzhniki Stadium for the crucial qualifier against Russia. Led by a man with an international managerial track record to compare with the very best in the game, the Dutchman Guus Hiddink, the match would be contested on a state-of-the-art synthetic surface, and at times, given the hysterical media reaction to the news, one could be forgiven for thinking that it was the same kind of plastic pitch that blighted British football in the early 1980s.

England started the game confidently and in control. Wayne Rooney volleyed his team into a twenty-ninth-minute lead and the prospect of the European Championship finals grew more tangible. Four minutes after the interval, however, Liverpool's Steven Gerrard contrived to miss the simplest of chances to double England's advantage and from then on, the game turned on its head. First, England's goalscorer, Wayne Rooney, conceded a dubious penalty, converted by Roman Pavlyuchenko, then just four minutes later, Paul Robinson would suffer another of his aberrations, gifting what would be the winning goal to Pavlyuchenko again.

England and McClaren's future now depended on Israel, one of the weaker sides in the group, obtaining a result against the team that had just beaten them, Russia. It was, as McClaren concluded correctly, a 'bad position' and if he needed an idea of just how bad the position was he only needed to read a copy of the *Racing Post*. Now they weren't offering odds on England's chances at Euro 2008, they were offering odds on his successor.

Remarkably, Steve McClaren would be granted a stay of execution. Against those odds, Israel had snatched a late 2–1 win against the Russians in Tel Aviv, giving Croatia a place in the finals, even though they had just lost in Macedonia, and England an unexpected route through to join them. Back at England's training camp, Steve McClaren's relief was palpable. 'What a night. Absolutely fantastic news for us all,' he told the Football Association's website. 'I would like to pay tribute to Israel for the professional way they went about their job. They showed what a proud nation they are and they deserve a lot of praise for their efforts.'

With Russia losing and Croatia through, it now left England needing just a draw in their final game against Croatia at Wembley on 21 November to qualify or a 2–0 win to ensure they finished top of Group E. Bizarrely, ludicrously even, England had gone from favourites to miss out, to favourites not just to qualify but to win their group. It was the kind of luck that had largely deserted the England coach during the campaign and the kind of luck that would have Scotland fans beating the walls in despair. It was, by some margin, the most successful night of the England manager's tenure, even though he had spent the evening watching TV in his hotel room.

It was a remarkable, fortuitous turnaround for McClaren and his team, even if McClaren himself had seen it coming all along. 'I always believed it would come down to the Croatia match. Thankfully it has,' he said. 'I know we've made things difficult for ourselves by dropping points early on but we have played a lot better during the second half of the campaign and I've got every confidence the players will do the job at Wembley.'

But the brand new Wembley was suffering. In their efforts to recoup some of the near £800 million they had spent on the new national stadium, the Football Association were keen to rent it out for music concerts and other sporting events. One such event would be the first ever NFL regular season game to be played outside of North America, between the New York Giants and the Miami Dolphins on 28 October 2007. But while gridiron fans in the UK seized the rare opportunity to watch two of the world's best American football teams in action, the impact on the Wembley pitch was disastrous. By the time England's final qualification game against Croatia came round just three weeks later, the Wembley pitch was still cutting up.

The condition of the playing surface was just one of many headaches for the England coach, and his chief concern appeared to be the position of goalkeeper. With Paul Robinson's confidence was still shattered from the game in Zagreb, and David 'Calamity' James perceived as too error-prone to risk, McClaren opted for Aston Villa's Scott Carson as his goalkeeper, even though it would be the on-loan keeper's competitive debut for England. Then there were England's long-suffering fans who now found themselves in the invidious position of wanting Steve McClaren to go, purely because he wasn't up to the job, but only as and when he had ensured that England had qualified for the European Championship.

England versus Croatia would be one of those nights that would start in farce and end in humiliation. Prior to the kick-off, the teams had lined up across the pitch for the traditional singing of the national anthems, with the English opera singer Tony Henry being drafted in to lead the singing. First, he tackled the 'Croatians' *Lijepa Naša Domovino*' (Our Beautiful Homeland) but instead of singing '*Mila kuda si planina*', which translates as 'My dear, how we love your mountains', Henry sang, '*Mila kura si planina*' which, unfortunately, translates as 'My dear, my penis is a mountain'. Any nerves the Croatians may have had ahead of the match would soon disappear in fits of schoolboy giggles.

In the new Wembley Stadium that night, there would be precious little else to laugh at. Within fifteen minutes of the kick-off, England found themselves two goals down. The first, after just eight minutes, was proof that McClaren's gamble on Scott Carson was folly indeed. Faced with an innocuous long-range shot from Niko Kranjčar, Carson failed to gather the ball and instead helped it into his net. Later, the *Sun* argued that 'we may as well have gone with Willie Carson' as the England goalkeeper.

Exceptional times required exceptional measures. On came David Beckham for his ninety-ninth cap, and the striker Jermain Defoe came on for the midfielder Gareth Barry. With Beckham providing some much-needed service to the forward line, England rallied. Soon Defoe would win a penalty, tugged back by his marker Josip Simunić, and Frank Lampard dispatched the spot-kick to give England hope.

Nine minutes later, England would draw level. Another unerringly accurate centre from Beckham on the right was controlled beautifully by Peter Crouch who fired past Pletikosa in the Croatian goal to give England an equalizer and, if the scoreline stayed the same, a place in the European Championship finals. It didn't. Thirteen minutes from time, as the heavy November rain poured down, the Croatian substitute Mladen Petrić sent a low skidding shot from twenty-five yards arrowing into the far corner of Scott Carson's goal. England 2 Croatia 3.

As his team conspired to lose their grip on the game and the group itself, McClaren stood on the touchline, sheltering under a Football Association golf umbrella and nursing what looked like a coffee. This wasn't football. This was a parent watching their kid play for the school team. This was a man more worried about getting what little hair he had wet than doing whatever it took to get his team, the nation's team, back in the game and back in the European Championship. It was an image that would come to define the tenure of Steve McClaren. Inevitably, in time, he would become known as the 'Wally with the Brolly'.

As McClaren took cover, his Croatian counterpart Slaven Bilić, meanwhile, was pacing up and down the touchline, with a beanie hat on his head, a stud in his ear and a cigarette in his hand, demanding more from his side, even though they had already qualified for the finals. The contrast could not have been more pronounced.

With its sodden pitch, the rain teeming down and England all at sea, it brought back memories of Kevin Keegan's final game in charge of the national team, when the fireworks fizzled out against Germany at Wembley. That day, Keegan resigned immediately after the final whistle. Steve McClaren, by contrast, vowed to stay on, maintaining that now was 'not time for recrimination'. As ever, though, he was wrong.

For the Croatian coach Slaven Bilić, who had spent four years of his playing career in the English Premier League with West Ham United and Everton, there were some words of comfort for Steve McClaren. 'Wake up,' he said, 'you didn't lose the game because of the tactics … We were simply the better team.'

Yet in an age of long, lucrative contracts and big money, it wasn't in McClaren's interest to resign. Go voluntarily and he could forget about having the rest of his contract paid up. Hold out and wait for the push and he could walk away from the biggest job in English and arguably world football with a settlement running into millions of pounds. 'I'm not stepping down. I'm not thinking about my future,' he shrugged. 'I'm thinking about the game. It's a huge disappointment.'

'Huge' was an understatement. This was first time in fourteen years that England had failed to qualify for a major tournament, and the first time in nearly a quarter of a century that they had not qualified for the European Championship. It had been a shocking result.

The end came swiftly. Immediately after the Croatia game, Brian Barwick had spoken with the FA's director of corporate affairs Simon Johnson, the FA chairman Geoff Thompson and the chairman of the international committee Noel White, and agreed that McClaren should go. With the decision yet to be ratified, Barwick convened an emergency meeting at Soho Square for early the following morning.

At 6.30 a.m. on Thursday, 22 November Barwick arrived at FA HQ, followed soon after by the other board members. The meeting was brief, just ten minutes, the vote unanimous, and less than twelve hours after the final whistle had blown at Wembley, and after eighteen matches, 1,620 minutes of football and 457 days in something resembling control, Steve McClaren became the former England manager.

At a press conference soon after, televised live on all the major networks, five of the board faced the media and it was left to Geoff Thompson to announce McClaren's departure. 'At a meeting of the FA board this morning the FA board unanimously decided to terminate the contract of England head coach Steve McClaren with immediate effect. We have also terminated the contract of assistant Terry Venables, also with immediate effect,' said Thompson, adding, 'I would like to thank Steve for the work he has done since taking on the position last summer. His commitment to the job could not be questioned and I wish him the best for the future.'

While nobody had expected to McClaren to survive, the decision to dispense with him so quickly took most observers by surprise, not least because it came from an organization renowned for dithering and procrastination. Now they were already talking about a 'root and branch examination of the whole England senior set-up' and promising that everything would be done to recruit a new coach capable of delivering not just what the Football Association expected, but what the nation as a whole demanded.

Brian Barwick was in reflective mood. 'I spoke to Steve this morning – we get on very well with him. I've had many grown-up conversations and had another one with him this morning – and I can only wish him well. But in the end, not qualifying for Euro 2008 comes up short,' he said. Many 'grown-up conversations' as opposed, presumably, to juvenile ones.

Whatever Barwick meant, there was no disguising that England finishing third in their qualification group was the worst result imaginable for the country and the Football Association, as Geoff Thompson explained. 'Like every England fan, we are all bitterly disappointed that we have failed to qualify for Euro 2008, and I know Steve feels that disappointment more than anyone. The recruitment process for the new coach begins now and we will do everything to get the right man for the job.'

That afternoon, Steve McClaren emerged to hold a press conference of his own, this time at the same hotel in St Albans where Sven-Göran Eriksson had been unveiled as the new England coach in 2001. He looked tired and drained, his ruddy complexion exposed by the flashlights. McClaren reflected on his brief foray into international management, his sadness eased by a reported £2.5 million pay-out from his former employers.

> Eighteen months ago was the proudest day of my career and I was honoured to be the England head coach. I've enjoyed every minute. So it's sad to be leaving. But I can understand the FA's decision. I'm sad for the fans. There's regret that we've come to this situation. I'm not making any excuses. I take full responsibility. That's football … This is the down. But I'll bounce back. I'm a better manager now than I was eighteen months ago … It's been a rollercoaster. I've learned some lessons. I'll learn from this and move on.

Certainly, it had been a rollercoaster, only one that was incapable of going uphill. The truth was that McClaren was a man who seemed singularly ill-equipped for the position he found himself in. Not only was his the shortest tenure of any England coach in history, but his record of eighteen games, nine wins, five losses and four draws was one of the worst. That he had failed to qualify, especially with the so-called 'Golden Generation' of players at his disposal, was shocking. That he ever got the job in the first place was just inexcusable.

In the days that followed, Barwick began his quest to find a successor, conscious that England followers held him responsible for McClaren's appointment and that his organization itself stood accused of being out of touch with the demands of modern international football. Certainly, there were many questions that needed to be asked of the FA's structure, not least its board. Here, after all, was a committee that boasted not one ex-professional player or manager, a committee that had club chairmen and money-men at its heart, augmented by frankly inexplicable appointments from the amateur game. On one hand, there were big business heavyweights like the Manchester United chief executive David Gill and the Premier League chairman Sir Dave Richards, on the other was a clutch of anonymous names from the amateur game, such as the retired estate agent and Kent FA representative Barry Bright or the Gloucestershire FA's Roger Burden.

Across the country, the defeat to Croatia and the timid nature of England's capitulation had sparked debate about not just who should succeed McClaren as manager but what it was about the English psyche that prevented the national team from playing to their full potential. On television and radio, in the papers and on the internet, every facet of the national game would be explored and dissected. From schools football to coaching standards, from the influx of foreign players to the influence of money in the English game, at times it seemed as though we had not merely failed to qualify for the second most important international football tournament, but that the very fabric of English society was at risk. And why? Because of Steve McClaren.

The truth, of course, was much simpler, although no less easy to digest. England, as ever, simply weren't good enough.

EPILOGUE

I have a theory. It's an idea not based on hard science, admittedly, but I think there's something in it. You see, I believe that with the possible exception of Steve McClaren, it matters not a jot which manager or 'head coach' England has in situ, nor does it matter what personnel are employed to take to the field and play the game itself. No, my proposition is that the performance of any England football team competing in one of the two major tournaments in the post-1966 era is almost entirely reliant upon the quality of the official team song that sends them on their way.

Look at the facts, or at least look at these carefully selected 'facts'. At Italia 90, New Order's 'World In Motion', quite simply the greatest football song ever recorded, reaches number 1 in the charts, while England get to within a penalty or two of the World Cup final. And then there's Euro 96, here on home soil. Messrs Baddiel and Skinner, alongside Ian Brodie from the Lightning Seeds, joined forces to create 'Football's Coming's Home', an anthem that's still sung on the terraces to this day, a song so catchy and so maddeningly memorable that it came to define a golden summer and a tournament that, heartbreakingly, Germany prevented England from winning yet again.

And there lies the rub. England only ever do well (and by 'well' I mean reach the latter stages of a tournament) when they have a song that they and the nation can be justifiably proud of, that is to say, good song = successful tournament, Ant and Dec = premature and disappointing exit.

I mention Ant and Dec because, nice guys that they undoubtedly are, their song for England's 2002 World Cup campaign in Japan and Korea, the sickening 'We're On The Ball', was perhaps the nadir of the genre. Like so many songs before and since, it fell into the all too familiar trap of mentioning some of England's former glories, not that there are that many to reflect on, obviously. This time, though, the artists formerly known as PJ and Duncan evoked memories of England's 5–1 win over Germany in the qualifying games, an undeniably impressive result certainly, but also a sorry sign that if England's official World Cup song was milking a victory in a qualifying game it surely meant that success really had been thin on the ground for the team since the World Cup triumph of 1966.

Ever since New Order released 'World In Motion' for the 1990 World Cup in Italy and changed the face of football songs in four minutes and thirty seconds of finely crafted pop pleasure, every band worth their salt, and many more who patently weren't, have jumped on the football bandwagon whenever England qualify for the final stages of a major tournament, a trend which peaked in the track for the 1998 World Cup campaign.

'England United' was a not-so-supergroup featuring the inexplicable, incongruous and frankly indefensible union of the Spice Girls, Ian McCulloch of Echo and the Bunnymen, Johnny Marr of the Smiths, the Liverpudlian band Space and indie chancers Ocean Colour Scene. Interestingly, '(How Does It Feel To Be) On Top Of The World?' would be one of the few official songs where the players themselves were not asked to contribute their vocal talents. The reason? 'We just let them do what they're best at in the video,' shrugged McCulloch, before adding, 'missing penalties.'

Of course, the other issue with the England United effort was that it too was guilty of revisiting age-old themes, suggesting glory was not just possible, but imminent and inevitable. Moreover, posing the question '(How Does It Feel To Be) On Top Of The World?' is all well and good but when no football fan under the age of fifty could possibly know the answer it succeeded only in missing its target demographic by a country mile.

It was bad enough having one FA-approved song. Now, in these days of karaoke and computers, of YouTube and iTunes, there's a glut of unofficial ones also battling it out in the charts alongside the official number, invariably featuring some fading star of old or an ex-player or two willing to embarrass themselves so they can eke a few extra quid out of their retirement. Yes, Terry Venables, that means you.

Trouble is, things have got so bad with the England songs that one now pines for the days when the entire squad would be forced to shuffle on to the stage at Top of the Pops, *all awkward and embarrassed, and mime their way through some dirge of a song for three minutes as the crowd below them waved flags and pretended to care while they waited for Spandau Ballet to turn up.*

Like I said, it's not based in hard science ...

It's Sir Geoff Hurst I feel sorry for. What must it feel like to be him? Great, you'd doubtless respond. After all, as the first and only man in history to score a hat-trick in a World Cup final and a Knight of the Realm to boot, he must have it pretty well made. Well, yes and no. Imagine if every day of your life was spent just waiting for the same question. In every press interview, every after-dinner speech, there must come a moment when *that* question rears its ugly head. So Geoff, did it really cross the line?

Of course, Geoff will answer it, as he always does, with grace and humour while somehow endeavouring to make it sound like a completely different answer to the one he's given countless times already that day, but it's like Brian Epstein being asked about Ringo's drumming or Ricky Gervais being pressed to do *that* dance, only more predictable. Deep down, there must be a bit of Geoff that feels that maybe it would have been better if the Russian linesman hadn't given the goal. England would still have won, Hurst would still have been a hero and he could have woken up every morning without the fear. The answer, for Geoff's sake more than anything, is for England to make some new memories and to actually achieve something again. Maybe then we can talk about something else.

It was when I was speaking to the journalist Rob Shepherd that he mentioned in passing that maybe winning the World Cup in 1966 was the worst thing ever to happen to English football. I think he had a point. Ever since that sunny July afternoon, logic, reason and rational thought have all but vanished and perspective has taken a back seat to groundless optimism, culminating in inevitable, gut-wrenching heartache. England expects and it expects a lot. But why? For one, we have no record to speak of in modern-day international football. Look at the facts. Since England defeated West Germany at Wembley in 1966, they have just two semi-final appearances to show from their thirteen appearances at the European Championship or World Cup finals. In contrast, Germany has posted five victories and no fewer than six runners-up places. It's this warped tendency to celebrate mediocrity or the plight of the gallant loser that's got us into so much trouble. What other footballing nation with designs on elite, superpower status, for instance, would welcome their team home as heroes after a quarter-final exit?

Increasingly, English coaches have done anything they could to avoid defeat, rather than go all out to win games, such was the fear of failure and, perhaps, the headlines the following morning. That meant valuing industry over innovation and perspiration over inspiration, the net result being that the true talents of the English game, the real entertainers, have often been treated with suspicion, not gratitude or reverence.

Yes, for 'gifted' read lazy. For 'mercurial' read surplus to requirements. There's a glut of players who have fallen by the wayside over the years, all largely overlooked and labelled as 'luxury' players. Creative giants like Tony Currie, Peter Osgood or Alan Hudson or flying wingers like West Ham's Alan Devonshire or Aston Villa's Tony Morley. They may have got the odd B cap or a couple of starts for the full side, but their talent was never properly rewarded. Even some of the most prolific goalscorers of their era, like Clive Allen and Robbie Fowler, Andy Cole and Tony Cottee, were never given a real chance at international level despite their records in domestic football. And what of

Matt Le Tissier? He was the most gifted player of his generation and a man who scored a hat-trick in an England B game against Russia shortly before the World Cup finals of 1998 but was still overlooked by Glenn Hoddle when it came to the final squad for France.

Yes, it's a different game today to what it was in the 1970s or '80s. It is faster, more athletic and more demanding but it changes little. What England has always needed in charge was a real winner, a coach with a demonstrable track record at the highest level of the game and someone who couldn't and wouldn't stand for the circus that followed England around, or, like Sven-Göran Eriksson, inadvertently fuel it.

Enter Fabio Capello. Thick of hair, super-stylish and as fit as a butcher's dog, he's the man that every last man in England wants to be when they hit pensionable age. Here is a coach who commands respect, not simply because of his stellar CV, but because of his manner. He has a job to do – a £6 million job to do – and it's his way or the highway. Overnight, the mood in the England camp changed. Out went the mobile phones and the mateyness. War was declared on the WAG culture. It was bye-bye to bling.

And how the players have responded. Winning nine of their ten qualifying games, they reached the World Cup finals in South Africa with two games to spare while scoring a record number of goals in the process. Moreover, they have also beaten the team that did for Steve McClaren, Croatia, home and, more impressively, away, scoring nine goals and conceding just two against one of the best teams in the world. Capello has even got Frank Lampard and Steven Gerrard playing together. Mind you, that's the least you'd expect when you're paying the coach £6 million a year.

Though the playing personnel is largely the same, it seems like a different team. They are organized, industrious and, at times, ruthless. They now possess a cutting edge that was conspicuous by its absence in the dark ages of McClaren. There is a purpose, a cohesion and an energy. And there are options. David Beckham is no longer a starter but acts as a useful substitute (and box-office draw). Jermain Defoe has kept Wayne Rooney and Emile Heskey on their toes with some valuable goals from the bench and Glenn Johnson, first capped under Eriksson in November 2003, has matured into one of the most exciting full-backs in the game.

Now, there's a real belief that England have emerged (or perhaps escaped) from the tears and the trauma of the McClaren era and, finally, begun to establish themselves as genuine contenders for the World Cup. Strip away the millionaire lifestyles and the property portfolios, the commercial endorsements and the celebrity magazine spreads, there's now a team at work, not merely some congregation of rich young Premiership players.

Whisper it, but with a fair wind, some kindly officials and the absence of any penalty shoot-outs, England may have a real chance this summer …

ACKNOWLEDGEMENTS

Writing a book like this is, I presume, much like writing an autobiography in that the long, weary demise of the England team has largely seemed to coincide with my lifetime and I can place where I was and what I was doing usually just by looking at an England result or another exit from a major tournament. That said, it's also been fun to look at how, why and where England has gone so wrong over the years since Alf Ramsey vacated the manager's office (although, 'fun' isn't how I'd describe watching old videos of Hoddle and Waddle singing on *Top of the Pops*).

Over the months spent writing the book, there have been a great many people who have helped out and to all the people, players and managers who took the time to be interviewed for the book, and to those colleagues in journalism who offered a contact or a lead, can I just say thanks. All your contributions have been invaluable.

It would also be remiss of me not to mention a few people at Atlantic Books, so thanks to Toby Mundy and Sarah Norman for bearing with me. I'd also like to thank my agent John Pawsey for his continued graft.

On the friends front, I'd like to thank Alexis James for his keen and unwavering assistance, Iestyn George, Mark Brown, Mark Leigh and Neil Smith for their knowledge of the trivial/vital. If I've missed anyone out it's either because my memory is not what it is or perhaps I really don't have that many friends after all.

As ever, none of this would have been possible without the help and support of my gorgeous wife, Ann, and the endless entertainment offered by my three beautiful kids, Betsy, Frank and Cissy. I love you all. Now, for the last time, will you please get to bed.

Gavin Newsham
January 2010

Index